INDIAN REALISM

JADUNATH SINHA
M.A., Ph.D., Premchand Roychand Scholar,
Professor of Philosophy, Meerut College.

MOTILAL BANARSIDASS
DELHI : VARANASI : PATNA

Indological Publishers and Booksellers
Head Office : BUNGALOW ROAD, JAWAHARNAGAR, DELHI-7
Branches : 1. CHOWK, VARANASI (U.P.)
2. ASHOK RAJ PATH (OPP. PATNA COLLEGE), PATNA-4 (BIHAR)

By arrangement with M/s Routledge & Kegan Paul Ltd.
First Edition : London 1938
Reprinted : Delhi 1972
Price :

Printed in India
BY SHANTI LAL JAIN, AT SHRI JAINENDRA PRESS, BUNGALOW ROAD, JAWAHARNAGAR, DELHI-7, AND PUBLISHED BY SUNDARLAL JAIN FOR MOTILAL BANARSIDASS BUNGALOW ROAD JAWAHARNAGAR, DELHI-7

Dedicated
to
The Contemporary Western Realists
who may feel a sense of kinship with
the Realists of Ancient and Mediæval
India

CONTENTS

CHAPTER | PAGE

PREFACE xiii

I. THE YOGĀCĀRA VIJÑĀNAVĀDA I

Mādhavācārya's account—No permanent external object is possible—A momentary object cannot be perceived—It is neither perceived as a simple atom nor as a complex body—Cognition alone is real—It is self-luminous and apprehends itself—An external object cannot be related to a cognition and be apprehended by it—The identity of an object with its cognition is proved by the law of simultaneous perception (sahopalambhaniyama)—The distinction of subject and object is an illusory appearance due to subconscious impressions of difference (bhedavāsanā) rooted in avidyā—A similar argument in *Yogavāśiṣṭha*—The distinction of the real and the imaginary within cognitions—Comparison of the Yogācāra idealism with Berkeley's subjective idealism and Hume's sensationism—Śāntarakṣita and Kamalaśīla's exposition of the Yogācāra idealism—The Epistemological Arguments—A cognition is self-aware—Refutation of Kumārila's theory of imperceptibility of an act of cognition—Cognition is identical with the apprehension of an object-form which is illusory—No cognition of an external object—A formless (nirākāra) cognition cannot apprehend it—A cognition with a similar form (sākāra) cannot apprehend it—A cognition with a different form (anyākāra) cannot apprehend it—Vācaspati's summary of these arguments—The Yogācāra criticism of the Sautrāntika theory of correspondence (sārūpya)—The Law of Simultaneous Apprehension—No Evidence for the existence of an external object—It is neither perceptible nor inferrible—The Metaphysical Argument—The so-called external object can neither be a conglomeration of atoms nor a complex whole composed of atoms nor a gross body not made of atoms—The Yogācāra position.

II. The Sautrāntika Realism : The Representative Theory of Perception . . . 35

Comparison of the Sautrāntika Realism with Descartes and Locke's Representationism—The Sautrāntika criticism of the Yogācāra Subjectivism—Criticism of the law of simultaneous apprehension (sahopalambhaniyama)—An object is not identical with cognition—The object is physical (external) while cognition is psychical (internal)—Cognition is perceived as "I" while the object is perceived as "this" or not-self as distinguished from the self—Externality of the Object cannot be treated as an illusory appearance because it presupposes the real knowledge of externality—The circular argument of the Yogācāra—Common Sense bears testimony to the existence of the object—Different forms or contents of cognitions are caused by the variety of external objects—Ālayavijñāna and Pravṛttivijñāna—Criticism of the Yogācāra doctrine that the variety of perceptions is due to the variety of vāsanās.

III. The Yogācāra's Criticism of the Representative Theory of Perception 43

Jayanta's account of the Yogācāra's criticism of the Sautrāntika Realism—Cognitions with definite forms or contents can serve all practical needs of life—The existence of external objects is a needless assumption—Two forms of a cognition and an object are not perceived—The realist admits that a cognition is apprehended before it apprehends its object and that it has a definite form—Cognitions with definite forms apprehending themselves are the only reality—Objects cannot be inferred from forms of cognitions—They are due to vāsanās—Waking perceptions are without foundation in external objects like illusions, hallucinations, dreams and recollections—Pārthasārathi's account of the Yogācāra criticism of the Sautrāntika Realism—Objectivity (arthatva), Causality (hetutva), Similarity (sārūpya), Pragmatic use (vyavahāra), and Expressibility do not constitute the cognizability of an object—No cognition of an external object is possible—Śrīdhara's account—The Vaibhāṣika criticism of the Sautrāntika realism.

IV. THE JAINA REALISM 61

Mallisena's Exposition of the Yogācāra Idealism—The Metaphysical Argument—The Epistemological Argument—Comparison with Berkeley's argument—Mallisena's Criticism of the Yogācāra Idealism—An act of cognition must have an object—No cognitions are objectless—External objects as distinguished from imaginary ideas have practical efficiency—Both atoms and gross bodies are real—The metaphysical argument presents no difficulty to the Jaina who advocates pluralistic realism or relativism—The denial of an external object contradicts experience—Consciousness of the self implies consciousness of the not-self—The distinction of the self (subject) and the not-self (object) is real—Criticism of sahopalambhaniyama—Cognition by its very nature apprehends itself and its object—Perception of an object in a particular place cannot be explained by vāsanā—Criticism of vāsanā—The universal experience of mankind testifies to the existence of external objects—Objects cannot be identical with cognitions because they possess opposite qualities—The Jaina realism contrasted with the Sautrāntika realism—The fitness (yogyatā) of a cognition for apprehending an object (Jaina).

V. THE SĀṄKHYA-YOGA REALISM 77

The Sāṅkhya criticism of Vijñānavāda—The self and the not-self radically opposed to each other—The latter not reducible to the former—Criticism of vāsanā and the metaphysical argument (Aniruddha)—Bondage also reduced to an idea (Vijñānabhikṣu)—The Yoga exposition of Vijñānavāda—The Epistemological Arguments—No objects apart from cognitions but cognitions apart from objects—Identity the condition of knowability—It is proved by the law of simultaneous perception—The object, a construction of imagination—The Yoga criticism of Vijñānavāda—The existence of external objects proved by perception which cannot be invalidated by imagination (Vyāsa)—Valid waking perceptions different from invalid dreams caused by bodily and mental disorders (Vijñānabhikṣu)—Knowability of an object by a cognition presupposes difference between them—The law of simultaneous perception cannot prove identity because it is based on the method of agreement without the help of the method of difference which is not applicable here—Vācaspati's anticipation of the "ego-centric predicament"—A cognition cannot possess externality and extension (Vācaspati)—The object remaining the same, the ideas differ; so they are different from each other (Patañjali)—The explanation of the fact—External objects and cognitions cannot come into existence together—The past and the future are real—External objects are real and permanent.

VI. THE MĪMĀṂSAKA REALISM 98

Śavara's criticism of Vijñānavāda—Waking cognitions essentially different from dream-cognitions—A formless cognition apprehends an external object with a form—A cognition is apprehended by inference only after it has apprehended an external object—A cognition is produced by an external object—Kumārila's elaborate exposition and criticism of Vijñānavāda—The existence of external objects proved by perception which cannot be invalidated by inference—Dreams, illusions, and recollections have a foundation in external objects—Difference between waking perceptions and dreams—Technical flaws in the Yogācāra argument—Detailed criticism of vāsanā—The cognitive act is directed to an external object distinct from it—Cognition and object cannot be identical with each other—The subject-object-relation between them unique in nature—A formless cognition apprehends an object with a form—The diversity of cognitions due to the diversity of objects—Variation of appearances no proof of the unreality of an object which may be multiform—Explanation of the fact—Diversity of appearances due to psychical dispositions (vāsanā) or to comparison with other objects—The existence of external objects proved by perception and inference, and practical considerations of morality and religion—Pārthasārathimiśra's exposition and criticism of Vijñānavāda—Elaboration of Kumārila's arguments—Prabhākara's exposition and criticism of Vijñānavāda—Cognitions apprehend themselves and their objects—Prabhākara's criticism of the Sautrāntika Realism.

VII. THE NYĀYA-VAIŚEṢIKA REALISM . . . 170

The Nyāya critique of Vijñānavāda—Critical exposition of it by Gautama and Vātsyāyana—The Nyāya

ABBREVIATIONS

Bib. Ind.	Bibliotheca Indica, Calcutta.
B.S.	Brahma Sūtra of Bādarāyaṇa.
B.S.S.	Benares Sanskrit Series.
Ch. S.S.	Chowkhamba Sanskrit Series, Benares.
E.T.	English Translation.
G.O.S.	Gaekwad's Oriental Series, Baroda.
NBh.	Nyāya Bhāṣya of Vātsyāyana (fourth century A.D.), Jīvānanda's edition, Calcutta, 1919.
NK.	Nyāyakandalī of Śrīdhara, a commentary on Praśastapādabhāṣya (A.D. 990), V.S.S., 1895.
NM.	Nyāyamañjarī of Jayanta Bhaṭṭa (A.D. 880), V.S.S., 1895.
NR.	Nyāyaratnākara of Pārthasārathimiśra, a commentary on SV. (Ch. S.S.).
NS.	Nyāya Sūtra of Gautama (fourth century, B.C.), Jīvānanda's edition, Calcutta, 1919.
NV.	Nyāyavārtika of Udyotakara (about A.D. 500), Bib. Ind., 1887–1904.
NVTT.	Nyāyavārtikatātparyaṭīkā of Vācaspatimiśra (A.D. 840), V.S.S., 1898.
PKM.	Prameyakamalamārtaṇḍa of Prabhācandra (A.D. 825), Jāvāji's edition, Bombay, 1912.
PP.	Prakaraṇapañcikā of Śālikānātha (Ch. S.S.), 1903–4.
R.B.S.	Rāmānuja's Bhāṣya on Brahma Sūtra (eleventh century), Ananda Press, 1910.
S.B.H.	The Sacred Books of the Hindus, Allahabad.
S.B.S.	Śaṅkara's Bhāṣya on Brahma Sūtra (A.D. 788–820), (with Bhāmatī and Kalpataru), Jāvāji's edition, Bombay, 1917.
S.D.S.	Sarvadarśanasaṅgraha of Mādhavācārya (Ānandāśrama Sanskrit Series, Poona, 1906).
SD.	Śāstradīpikā of Pārthasārathimiśra (ninth century), Ch. S.S., No. 188.
SDP.	Śāstradīpikāprakāśa of Sudarśanācārya (Benares, samvat, 1964).
SPB.	Sāṅkhyapravacanabhāṣya (sixteenth century), Benares, 1909.
SS.	Sāṅkhyapravacanasūtra of Kapila (Bib. Ind., 1888).
SSV.	Sāṅkhyasūtravṛtti of Aniruddha (fifteenth century), Bib. Ind., 1888.
SV.	Ślokavārtika of Kumārila (seventh century), Ch. S.S., 1898–9.

Sadānanda Yati's elaboration of Śaṅkara's arguments—The empirical reality of the external world—Rāmānaja's exposition and criticism of Vijñānavāda—Distinction between the self and the not-self condition of consciousness—The law of simultaneous perception proves difference of cognitions and objects—Practical function of knowledge—Cognitions enable the Self to react to objects—Difference between waking cognitions and dreams both of which have a foundation in external objects—The Yogācāra subjectivism invalidates his own inference—Rāmānuja's criticism of the Sautrāntika realism—Nimbārka, Śrīnivāsa, Keśava Kāśmirin, Mādhva, Vallabha, Puruṣottamajī Mahārāja, and Baladeva Vidyā-Bhūṣaṇa's criticism of Vijñānavāda.

INDEX 275

PREFACE

This book is an attempt at a reconstruction of the Yogācāra *Vijñānavāda* (Subjective Idealism), and an exhaustive criticism of it by different schools of Indian realism. The exposition of the doctrine is based on the works of Śāntarakṣita and Kamalaśīla and the critics of *Vijñānavāda*. Generally I have given the exposition and criticism of the doctrine by every eminent thinker separately. Most of the critics give a fair and impartial account of *Vijñānavāda*, and contribute to the clarification of the idealistic position. I may mention the names of profound thinkers like Kumārila, Śaṅkara, Jayanta Bhaṭṭa, Vācaspatimiśra, and Śrīdhara among others. I have dealt with the criticism of *Vijñānavāda* by the Buddhist realists, the Jaina, the Sāṅkhya-Yoga, the Mīmāṃsakas, the Nyāya-Vaiśeṣika, and the different schools of the Vedānta. I have not traced the historical evolution of Indian subjectivism which is beyond the scope of this book. I have simply dealt with the controversy between subjective idealism and realism in Indian thought, and tried to give a fairly full account of the arguments by which Indian realists seek to establish the reality of the external world. I have not touched the metaphysical question as to the nature of the external world.

I have incidentally compared the Yogācāra subjectivism with the idealism of Berkeley and the sensationism of Hume, and briefly noted resemblances and differences between them. I venture to say, Berkeleyan idealism cannot claim the thoroughness and metaphysical acumen of the Buddhist idealism, which preceded it by at least one thousand years. I have not compared any type of Indian realism with an analogous type of Western realism. But I have quoted parallel arguments of many contemporary realists simply to indicate that the philosophical genius of a particular type is apt to move in the same groove, irrespective of the soil it thrives in. I have profusely quoted texts to corroborate my statements. The table of contents and the index may help the reader in following the arguments.

Realism is the dominant note of contemporary philosophy in the west. It is extremely critical and analytical. It presses into its service the achievements of modern logic and modern science. It has had its analogue in Indian philosophy with a glorious history for centuries. So *Indian Realism* may be of some interest not only to the students of Indian philosophy, but also to the students of contemporary western philosophy. If it evokes some interest in Indian realism, I shall consider my labours amply repaid.

I take the opportunity of expressing my gratitude to the authorities of the Agra University who permitted me to incorporate one of the Agra University Extension Lectures in this book, which I delivered at St. John's College, Agra, in December, 1934. I am also grateful to the authorities of the Meerut College who afforded me every facility to complete the book. I feel intense pleasure in expressing my thanks to my revered teacher, Dr. Hiralal Haldar, M.A., Ph.D., the renowned author of *Neo-Hegelianism*, who encouraged me to publish this book.

JADUNATH SINHA.

MEERUT COLLEGE,
MEERUT,
INDIA.
24th May, 1937.

ABBREVIATIONS

Bib. Ind.	Bibliotheca Indica, Calcutta.
B.S.	Brahma Sūtra of Bādarāyaṇa.
B.S.S.	Benares Sanskrit Series.
Ch. S.S.	Chowkhamba Sanskrit Series, Benares.
E.T.	English Translation.
G.O.S.	Gaekwad's Oriental Series, Baroda.
NBh.	Nyāya Bhāṣya of Vātsyāyana (fourth century A.D.), Jīvānanda's edition, Calcutta, 1919.
NK.	Nyāyakandalī of Śrīdhara, a commentary on Praśastapādabhāṣya (A.D. 990), V.S.S., 1895.
NM.	Nyāyamañjarī of Jayanta Bhaṭṭa (A.D. 880), V.S.S., 1895.
NR.	Nyāyaratnākara of Pārthasārathimiśra, a commentary on SV. (Ch. S.S.).
NS.	Nyāya Sūtra of Gautama (fourth century, B.C.), Jīvānanda's edition, Calcutta, 1919.
NV.	Nyāyavārtika of Udyotakara (about A.D. 500), Bib. Ind., 1887–1904.
NVTT.	Nyāyavārtikatātparyaṭīkā of Vācaspatimiśra (A.D. 840), V.S.S., 1898.
PKM.	Prameyakamalamārtaṇḍa of Prabhācandra (A.D. 825), Jāvāji's edition, Bombay, 1912.
PP.	Prakaraṇapañcikā of Śālikānātha (Ch. S.S.), 1903–4.
R.B.S.	Rāmānuja's Bhāṣya on Brahma Sūtra (eleventh century), Ananda Press, 1910.
S.B.H.	The Sacred Books of the Hindus, Allahabad.
S.B.S.	Śaṅkara's Bhāṣya on Brahma Sūtra (A.D. 788–820), (with Bhāmatī and Kalpataru), Jāvāji's edition, Bombay, 1917.
S.D.S.	Sarvadarśanasaṅgraha of Mādhavācārya (Ānandāśrama Sanskrit Series, Poona, 1906).
SD.	Śāstradīpikā of Pārthasārathimiśra (ninth century), Ch. S.S., No. 188.
SDP.	Śāstradīpikāprakāśa of Sudarśanācārya (Benares, samvat, 1964).
SPB.	Sāṅkhyapravacanabhāṣya (sixteenth century), Benares, 1909.
SS.	Sāṅkhyapravacanasūtra of Kapila (Bib. Ind., 1888).
SSV.	Sāṅkhyasūtravṛtti of Aniruddha (fifteenth century), Bib. Ind., 1888.
SV.	Ślokavārtika of Kumārila (seventh century), Ch. S.S., 1898–9.

S.V.M.	Syādvādamañjarī of Malliṣena (A.D. 1292), edited by A. B. Dhruva, Poona, 1933. (Bombay Sanskrit and Prakrit Series.)
TBh.	Tarkabhāṣā of Keśavamiśra (thirteenth century), Kulkrani's edition, Poona, 1924.
TS.	Tattvasaṃgraha of Śāntarakṣita (A.D. 705–762), G.O.S., No. 30.
TSP.	Tattvasaṃgrahapañjikā of Kamalaśīla (A.D. 713–763), G.O.S., No. 30.
T.V.	Tattvavaiśāradī on Yogabhāṣya (ninth century), Benares, 1911.
VK.	Vedāntakaustubha of Śrīnivāsa.
VKP.	Vedāntakaustubhaprabhā of Keśava Kāśmirin.
V.S.S.	Vizianagram Sanskrit Series, Benares.
Y.B.	Yogabhāṣya of Vyāsa (A.D. 400), Benares, 1911.
Y.S.	Yoga Sūtra of Patañjali, Benares, 1911.
YSP.	Yuktisnehaprapūraṇī of Rāmakṛṣṇa, a commentary on SD. (Ch. S.S.), No. 188.
Y.V.	Yogavārtika of Vijñānabhikṣu (sixteenth century), Benares. 1884.

Chapter I

THE YOGĀCĀRA VIJÑĀNAVĀDA

§ 1. *Mādhavācārya's Account of the Yogācāra's Subjective Idealism*

Mādhavācārya gives the following account of the Yogācāra idealism in *Sarvadarśanasamgraha*.

The Yogācāras are subjective idealists. They do not admit the existence of external objects. They admit the existence of series of momentary cognitions apprehending themselves, since the denial of their reality would lead to collapse of practical life. Dharmakīrti has said: " One who does not perceive cognitions cannot perceive their objects."[1] One who is not aware of cognitions cannot be aware of their objects. The Yogācāra admits that we are directly and immediately conscious of our own cognitions, and cannot, therefore, deny their reality. But he argues that these cognitions are self-luminous (svayaṃvedana): they apprehend themselves. They do not apprehend external objects which are non-existent.

Dharmakīrti's dictum seems to suggest representationism. Cognitions intervene between subject and object in perception. The subject does not stand face to face with the object. It cannot directly perceive the object. The perception of the object is mediated by the perception of its cognition. There is direct and immediate perception of a cognition. But there is no direct perception of the object. This is representationism. The Yogācāra argues that cognitions are directly aware of themselves (svasaṃvedana), but these cognitions are

[1] Apratyakṣopalambhasya nārthadṛṣṭiḥ prasidhyati. S.D.S., p. 12, cf. TS., vol. i, p. 579; NM., p. 538; SV. and NR., p. 276 (Ch. S.S.).

not copies or representations of external objects. Cognitions or ideas apprehend themselves. The new realist cuts off ideas intervening between the mind and the objects. "All things are known through being themselves brought directly into that relation in which they are said to be apprehended. . . . Things when consciousness is had of them become themselves contents of consciousness ; and the same things thus figure both in the so-called external world and in the manifold which introspection reveals." [1] But the Yogācāra, like Berkeley, cuts off the objects. He believes in the theory of immediacy of perception. We immediately perceive cognitions which apprehend themselves (svayamvedana). There are no external objects independent of cognitions. Similarly, Berkeley argues : "What are the forementioned (sensible) objects but the things we perceive by sense ? and what do we perceive besides our own ideas or sensations ? and is it not plainly repugnant that any one of *these*, or any combination of them, should exist unperceived ?" [2] G. A. Johnston states his doctrine thus : "Berkeley insists that if the thing is itself perceptible, there is no need of intermediate ideas to relate it to the percipient subject, for the thing itself is immediately presented to the percipient, and is accordingly, in Berkeley's terminology, itself an idea. In perception, then, we have only two factors, the percipient subject and the idea-thing perceived." [3] Thus the Yogācāra agrees with Berkeley in holding the presentative theory of perception in the same manner.

Mādhavācārya summarizes the arguments of the Yogācāra as follows :—

(1) An external object cannot exist. If it exists, it

[1] *The New Realism*, p. 35.

[2] Fraser, *Selections from Berkeley : The Principles of Human Knowledge*, 1910, p. 35.

[3] *The Development of Berkeley's Philosophy*, 1923, p. 150.

either arises from an entity or not. Both the alternatives are untenable. If the object were produced by an entity, it would have an origin and thus have no permanent existence of its own ; an object which owes its existence to another object cannot exist in itself and for itself. If the object were not produced by an entity, it would have no existence at all, for to exist is to come into being. The Buddhists hold that whatever exists must owe its existence to some prior existent ; what does not come into being does not exist ; being consists in becoming.[1]

(2) An external object cannot be the cause of its cognition, since it is momentary. It cannot exist for more than one moment. It does not exist when its cognition is produced. The object is the cause. The cognition is the effect. The cognition can come into being when its cause has ceased to be. Thus we are committed to the doctrine that a cognition apprehends a past object. But this is absurd. It contradicts the clear testimony of perception. We perceive a present object. An object is perceived not as existing in the past but at present. It is directly and immediately presented to consciousness. Therefore, it cannot be an external object ; it must be the cognition itself. Further, if past and non-existent objects could be perceived by present cognitions produced by them, the sense-organs also which are held to be imperceptible could be perceived by cognitions because they give rise to them.[1] This argument of the Yogācāra is based on the Buddhist doctrine of momentary existence and the causal theory of perception.

(3) If an external object exists, it must be either a simple atom or a complex body. It cannot be a complex body, for we do not know whether it is part or whole that is perceived. The whole is made up of parts. We cannot perceive the whole without perceiving the parts,

[1] S.D.S., p. 12.

and we cannot perceive the parts all at once. When we perceive one part, the other parts are past and future, and yet without perceiving all the parts at the same time we cannot perceive the whole.

Further, aggregates of atoms are either different or non-different from atoms. If they are different from atoms, they cannot be said to be composed of atoms. If they are non-different from atoms, they can never produce cognitions of gross bodies. The external object cannot be a simple atom, since it is supersensible and cannot be perceived. An atom cannot be said to be perceived when it combines with six other atoms and forms a three-dimensional object with six surfaces, for it is absolutely simple and devoid of parts. Further, an atom cannot combine with other atoms either partially or entirely. It cannot combine partially because it has no parts. Nor can it combine wholly because total interpenetration of atoms cannot increase the dimension of aggregates of atoms. Thus an external object can neither be a simple atom nor a complex body. Therefore it does not exist.

(4) There is, then, no external object of perception distinct from the percipient cognition. It perceives nothing other than itself: it is its own object of perception. It is self-subsistent. It is not produced by an object. It is self-luminous. It shines by its own light. It manifests and apprehends itself. So it is said: "There is no object of cognition (anubhāvya) other than the cognition (buddhi) itself. There is no act of cognition which is other than the cognition itself. The cognition apprehends itself. It is devoid of the distinction of subject (grāhaka) and object (grāhya). Cognition alone is real and shines by its own light."[1]

[1] Nānyo'nubhāvyo buddhyā'sti tasyā nānubhavo'paraḥ. Grāhyagrāhakavaidhuryāt svayaṃ saiva prakāśate. S.D.S., p. 13; cited from *Pramāṇaviniścaya* of Dharmakīrti; *Mediæval School of Indian Logic*, p. 107 n.; cf. S.V.M., p. 111; NM., p. 540.

The identity of the apprehending cognition with the apprehended object is inferred from the following syllogism:

That which is cognized by any cognition is not other than that cognition, as the cognition cognized by itself does not differ from itself. Hence all objects, blue and the like, are not other than the cognitions by which they are cognized.[1]

A cognition is not apprehended by another cognition as the Nyāya-Vaiśeṣika holds.[2] It is apprehended by itself.[3] The apprehending cognition and the apprehended cognition are the self-same psychical existent. Likewise the so-called objects of cognition, blue and the like, are no other than the cognitions which apprehend them. The cognition and its objects are identical with each other.

(5) If the cognized object were different from the apprehending cognition, the object would never enter into relationship with the cognition, and consequently would never be perceived. If the object and the cognition were essentially different from each other, they would never come into connection with each other ; the object would never be a mental content and be perceived by the cognition, and the cognition would never go over to the object and perceive it. An essential difference between the object and the cognition would make them self-contained, and make any connection between them impossible.[4] The possibility of such a connection, and

[1] Yad vedyate yena vedanena tat toto na bhidyate, yathā jñānena ātmā. Vedyante taiśca nīlādayaḥ. S.D.S., p. 13; cf. NK., p. 126; T.V., iv, 14, p. 293.

[2] J. N. Sinha, *Indian Psychology: Perception*, p. 214.

[3] Ibid., p. 220.

[4] Cf. TS., vol. i, 2003–4, p. 560. Similarly Berkeley argues: " Though we give the materialists their external bodies, they by their own confession are never the nearer knowing *how* our ideas are produced; since they own themselves unable to comprehend in what manner body can act upon spirit, or how it is possible it should imprint any idea in the mind." *Principles of Human Knowledge*, p. 46.

still more of a regular and uniform connection between them, can be explained by identity alone which is not admitted by the realist. Causality also cannot account for the uniform relation of the cognition to its object.[1]

(6) The identity of the object and its cognition is inferred from simultaneous perception of them. Whenever we perceive an object (e.g. blue), we perceive also the cognition of the object (e.g. cognition of blue) at the same time. Hence the object must be identical with its cognition.[2]

The apparent difference between them is an illusion like the appearance of the double moon. The cause of this illusion is a beginningless and uninterrupted series of subconscious impressions of difference (bhedavāsanā). Though there is no real distinction between subject and object in consciousness, it appears to be differentiated into subject and object owing to illusion ; the duality of subject and object is as illusory as the appearance of the double moon.[3]

We find a similar argument in *Yogavāśiṣṭha*. The subconscious impressions of difference (bhedavāsanā) due to nescience are imbedded in the mind. So different objects are presented to the mind like the illusion of the double moon owing to the revival of subconscious impressions of different objects perceived in the past, which have their root in nescience. The mind perceives a jar, a cloth, and the like under the influence of subconscious impressions of difference. The variety of cognitions is due to the variety of subconscious impressions which spring from nescience. It is not due to the variety of external objects.[4] The manifold world

[1] S.D.S., p. 13.

[2] Sahopalambhaniyamādabhedo nīlataddhiyoḥ, ibid., p. 13 ; cf. TS., vol. i, 2030, p. 567.

[3] S.D.S., p. 13.

[4] Sthitiprakaraṇa, 11th Canto, 24–5.

of objects is a mere construction of the mind ; and what is a mere construction of the mind is unreal and unsubstantial.[1] The being of the world is nothing but the being of the mind ; the being of the world is only mental.[2]

The Yogācāra believes in neither the permanent soul nor the external objects. He believes only in a self-subsistent series of momentary cognitions with no permanent spiritual substance behind them, and with no external objects as their causes. He is an uncompromising sensationist like Hume and J. S. Mill.

(7) The Yogācāra, however, does not abolish the distinction between the real and the imaginary. He does not identify a real object with an imaginary one, though both are ideas of the mind. According to him, the effect of an imaginary sweetmeat is not the same as that of a real sweetmeat.[3] There is no real distinction between objects and their cognitions or ideas. Yet, for practical purposes, a distinction may be drawn between objects and ideas, real things and imaginary things. Some ideas are common to all persons and coherent with other ideas. Others are peculiar to particular individuals and have no connection with other ideas. The former have a greater pragmatic value than the latter, and are treated as real objects as distinguished from mere ideas. All ideas are equally subjective. But some ideas are treated as objects when they are distinct and lively, and are governed by fixed and constant order of succession. Practical exigencies of life are responsible for the distinction between the real and the imaginary, though all alike are ideas of the mind. Merely subjective ideas of the mind appear to be diversified into diverse objects

[1] Ibid., 23 and 27.

[2] Citsattaiva jagatsattā jagatsattaiva cittakam, ibid., 17th Canto, 19.

[3] Na ca rasavīryavipākādi samānam āśāmodakopārjitamodakānāṃ syāt, S.D.S., p. 13; cf. NK., p. 130; S.V.M., p. 111.

and their cognitions which are illusorily superimposed on them by the efficacy of a beginningless series of subconscious impressions due to nescience.[1] Thus it is established that momentary cognitions appear in diverse forms owing to the influence of a beginningless series of subconscious impressions.[2]

Berkeley also does not abolish the distinction between the real and the imaginary, though he reduces external objects to ideas of the mind. He recognizes a distinction between the two within the contents of consciousness. Berkeley says : " It will be objected that there is a great difference betwixt real fire, for instance, and the idea of fire, betwixt dreaming or imagining oneself burnt, and actually being so. . . . To which the answer is that if real fire be very different from the idea of fire, so also is the real pain that it occasions very different from the idea of the same pain ; and yet nobody will pretend that real pain either is, or can possibly be, in an unperceiving thing, or without the mind, any more than its idea." [3]

Berkeley identifies real things with the ideas of sense or sensations and imaginary things with the ideas of imagination or images. He says : " The ideas imprinted on the senses by the Author of nature are called *real things* : and those excited in the imagination being less regular, vivid, and constant, are more properly termed *ideas*, or *images of things*, which they copy and represent. But then our sensations, be they never so vivid and distinct, are nevertheless ideas ; that is, they exist in the mind, or are perceived by it, as truly as the ideas of its own framing. The ideas of sense are allowed to have

[1] Ibid., pp. 13–14.

[2] Tasmād buddhirevānādivāsanāvaśādanekākārā'vabhāsate iti siddham, ibid., p. 14 ; cf. S.V.M., p. 111, lines 3–4 ; NM., p. 539 ; SV., śūnyavāda, 49–53, pp. 282–4 ; SD., p. 142.

[3] *Principles of Human Knowledge*, pp. 61–2.

more reality in them, that is, to be more strong, orderly, and coherent than the creatures of the mind ; but this is no argument that they exist without the mind." [1]

The realist believes that sensations are produced in the mind by physical objects. The Yogācāra and Berkeley both deny this. Berkeley holds that sensations are produced in the finite minds by God according to fixed laws. The Yogācāra does not believe in God.[2] He holds that sensations arise somehow from within the mind ; the variety of sensations is due to the variety of subconscious impressions imbedded in the mind. He does not recognize any extra-mental source of sensations. He is a thorough-going subjectivist. The Yogācāra differs with Berkeley on another point. He does not recognize even the reality of the soul. He regards the so-called soul as a series of momentary impressions, ideas, and feelings.[3] He agrees with Hume in his conception of the soul.

Thus the Yogācāra is compelled to recognize the distinction of the real and the imaginary within the contents of consciousness or cognitions (vijñāna). Those cognitions are treated as real things, which have practical efficiency and are common to many individuals or streams of consciousness (vyavahartṛparijñānānurodhena). Pragmatic utility and intersubjective intercourse demand a distinction of the real and the imaginary within the mental contents.[4]

Berkeley traces sensations or the ideas of sense to an

[1] Ibid., pp. 55–6.

[2] See TS., vol. i, 46–93, pp. 40–58.

[3] TS., vol. i, 171–335, pp. 79–125.

[4] S.D.S., p. 13. Aliotta says in explaining Mach's philosophy: "The difference between the illusory image and the perception of the real is one of a practical order only : the most fantastic dream is just as much a fact as any other, and if dream images were more coherent, more normal, and more stable, they would be of even greater practical importance to us." (*The Idealistic Reaction against Science*, p. 58.)

external source, viz. God.[1] My ideas of sense are not creatures of my will. There is therefore some *other* Will or Spirit (viz. God) that excites them in my mind. He does not excite sensations in our minds at random but according to set rules or established methods which are called the laws of nature.[2] The Yogācāra neither believes in the external world nor in God. So he cannot trace sensations to either. He must find their origin in the stream of consciousness itself, for he does not believe in the permanent self.[3] He finds the origin of sensations within the psychic continuum in subconscious impressions (vāsanā). The variety of sensations is due to the variety of subconscious impressions. The Yogācāra doctrine may be compared with Hume's sensationism. Hume also does not account for sensations by the hypothesis of God or external material objects. In fact, he does not seek to account for them. Discrete and unconnected sensations are the given element in our knowledge. Hume tries to connect them with one another by appealing to the subjective laws of association, the law of similarity, the law of contiguity, and the law of cause and effect. Thus Hume accounts for the connection among ideas by the laws of association, whereas the Yogācāra accounts for sensations by subconscious impressions. The Yogācāra is a more thorough-going subjectivist than Hume. Sensations are the causes of subconscious impressions. But how subconscious impressions can be the cause of sensations passes one's comprehension. The Yogācāra believes with Hume that sensations and ideas are discrete and unconnected. When *b* is in the field of consciousness *a* has gone out

[1] Hoernle: "If Berkeley denies the existence of matter, it is solely to make room for God." (*Idealism as a Philosophical Doctrine*, p. 60.)

[2] *Principles of Human Knowledge*, p. 54.

[3] See S. N. Das Gupta's *A History of Indian Philosophy*, vol. ii, pp. 178–181.

of it, and *c* has not yet come into it. Thus *a*, *b*, and *c* are discrete and momentary. There is no permanent self to connect them with one another. But the Yogācāra believes that *a* leaves behind a trace (vāsanā) *a'* before passing out of the field of consciousness, and this trace *a'* modifies the next sensation *b*, and similarly *b* leaves behind its trace *b'* which modifies the next sensation *c*, and so on. Thus the Yogācāra makes the hypothesis of subconscious impressions (vāsanā) and their transference to succeeding psychoses (vāsanāsamkrama) to account for the connection among discrete momentary sensations and ideas.[1]

§ 2. *Śāntarakṣita and Kamalaśīla's Exposition of the Yogācāra Vijñānavāda*

Mādhavācārya's account of the Yogācāra subjectivism may be taken as a safe guide. We shall attempt a reconstruction of the doctrine from the works of Śāntarakṣita and Kamalaśīla who are typical exponents of it. Their arguments against the existence of external objects have not been given in detail in any of the works dealing with the Yogācāra idealism.[2] The arguments may be mainly divided into two classes : epistemological and metaphysical. The epistemological argument consists in showing that cognitions are self-aware and cannot apprehend external objects distinct from them, and that the existence of external objects cannot be proved. Śāntarakṣita and Kamalaśīla have elaborately treated

[1] Vivaraṇaprameyasaṃgraha, p. 75 ; *Indian Psychology : Perception*, p. 158.

[2] See S. N. Das Gupta, *A History of Indian Philosophy*, vol. i, pp. 145–151 ; *Indian Idealism*, ch. v ; S. Radhakrishnan, *Indian Philosophy*, vol. i, pp. 624–643 ; A. B. Keith, *Buddhist Philosophy*, ch. xiv ; Th. Stcherbatsky, *Buddhist Logic*, vol. i, pp. 518–521 ; R. R. Sharma, *The Yogācāra Theory of the External World*, Proceedings, Fifth Indian Oriental Conference, Lahore, vol. ii, pp. 883–911, for treatment of the Yogācāra idealism.

this argument which we shall summarize here. The metaphysical argument consists in showing that the nature of an external object cannot be ascertained. It is neither a conglomeration of atoms, nor a complex whole composed of atoms, nor a gross object not made up of atoms. This argument also has been elaborately treated by Śāntarakṣita and Kamalaśīla. We shall briefly mention this argument here. We shall attempt a detailed treatment of this argument as given by the critics, Mallisena, Jayanta, Vācaspatimiśra and others later. It is beyond the scope of this book to attempt an exhaustive presentation of the Yogācāra idealism in its historical perspective from all the available sources.

I. THE EPISTEMOLOGICAL ARGUMENTS FOR SUBJECTIVE IDEALISM

(1) A Cognition is Self-aware (*svasaṃvedana*)

The Yogācāra holds that a cognition is self-luminous : it manifests itself : it is self-aware.[1] There is no real distinction of subject and object within it. It is not related to itself as subject and object. It is one and undivided. It is free from the distinction of subject and object. The Yogācāra differs from Berkeley on this point. The Yogācāra holds that a cognition apprehends itself : it is by its very nature self-aware. But Berkeley holds that the self, which is a permanent, active, spiritual principle, perceives an idea. The self is a thing entirely distinct from ideas, " wherein they exist, or, which is the same thing ,whereby they are perceived." [2] Berkeley recognizes the reality of spirits and ideas. The Yogācāra recognizes the reality of ideas alone. He regards the self as a stream of consciousness.

When a cognition comes into existence it is manifested as something different from matter. Matter is unconscious.

[1] Ātmasaṃvedanameva sadaiva jñānam, TSP., vol. i, 1999, p. 559.
[2] *Principles of Human Knowledge*, p. 33.

It does not manifest itself. But a cognition is non-material. Its essential nature consists in self-awareness (ātmasaṃvitti) or self-revelation. It reveals itself by its very nature. It does not require any cognitive act to reveal it. Self-revelation constitutes its very nature.[1]

Śāntarakṣita declares that a cognition, which is one and indivisible, cannot be broken up into the cognitive act (vedaka), the cognized object (vedya), and consciousness (vitti). It is of the nature of consciousness (bodha) which is self-luminous. Consciousness is self-awareness (svasaṃvedana).[2]

What is the meaning of self-awareness (svasaṃvedana)? Śāntarakṣita asserts that a cognition does not require any other cognitive act or cognizer (vedaka) to apprehend its own nature. The nature of self-awareness is self-evident. It is known to all.[3]

Śāntarakṣita's Refutation of Kumārila's View

Śāntarakṣita quotes Kumārila's verses (184–7) from Śūnyavāda, *Ślokavārtika*,[4] and criticizes them in *Tattavasaṃgraha*. We have elaborately dealt with Kumārila's doctrine of inferibility of an act of cognition (jñānakriyā) from cognizedness (jñātatā) in the object, and its detailed criticism by other schools elsewhere.[5]

Kumārila contends that a cognition does not apprehend itself when it apprehends an object. Though a cognition is of the nature of illumination, it depends upon some other cognition to manifest itself. It apprehends an external object. It cannot apprehend itself when it is engaged in the act of apprehending an object. When a cognition comes into existence it apprehends an object.

[1] TS. and TSP., vol. i, 2000, p. 559.
[2] TS., vol. i, 2001, p. 559.
[3] TS., vol. i, 2012, p. 562.
[4] SV., pp. 320–1; TS., vol. i, 2012–16, pp. 562–3.
[5] *Indian Psychology: Perception*, pp. 199–210.

At this moment it cannot apprehend itself. Then it is destroyed. Therefore it can never apprehend itself.[1] A cognition is of the nature of illumination (prakāśa) which consists in the apprehension of an object, but not in self-awareness. Just as the visual organ can manifest colour but cannot manifest itself, so a cognition can manifest an object but cannot manifest itself. It manifests an external object. This constitutes its illuminating character. It has no power of manifesting itself. Certain things have certain powers. Nobody can object to it.[2]

Śāntarakṣita urges that the apprehension of an object (arthasaṃvitti) is of the nature of a cognition (jñāna). They are non-distinct from each other. They are one and the same. A cognition by its very nature apprehends object-forms. It does not require any other cognitive act (vyāpāra) to reveal them. If the apprehension of an object is non-distinct from a cognition, no other cognitive act is needed for the cognition of the object.[3] " It is wrong to suppose that in knowing a thing there is any cognitive activity, for knowing simply means the illumination or revelation of a particular objective form ; that being so, what other activity can be imagined which would be necessary for the cognition of external objects ? "[4] The essential nature of an object is apprehension which is non-distinct from cognition. Its *esse* is *percipi*. Otherwise a cognition cannot function towards it. If the object is distinct from cognition it can never be apprehended.[5] If it is non-distinct from it, then a cognition apprehends itself. If the apprehension of an object is of the nature of a cognition, then a cognition also consists in the

[1] SV., śūnyavāda, 184, and NR., p. 320.

[2] Ibid., 185–7, pp. 320–1 ; TS., vol. i, 2013–2016, pp. 562–3.

[3] TS. and TSP., vol. i, 2017, p. 563.

[4] *Indian Idealism*, p. 136.

[5] Arthasyānubhavo'vaśyaṃ rūpaṃ svabhāvo'ṅgīkartavyaḥ. Anyathā kathaṃ tatra jñānaṃ vyāpriyeta. TSP., vol. i, 2018, p. 563; cf. Berkeley.

apprehension of an object. But Kumārila wrongly holds that an imperceptible cognitive act functions towards an external object and gives rise to its apprehension. Thus he distinguishes a cognition from the apprehension of an object. But if a cognition is distinct from the apprehension of an object, it can never give rise to it. If a cognition is non-distinct from it, then it apprehends itself. According to Kumārila, a cognition is formless, but the object apprehended by it has a form. But a formless cognition can never be related to an external object. If a cognition is by nature unconscious (jaḍa) and cannot, therefore, apprehend itself, as Kumārila thinks, then the cognition being imperceptible, the apprehension of the object also will become imperceptible. If the cognitive act itself is imperceptible, it cannot establish the existence of the apprehension of an object. If the cognition of an object requires another cognitive act to reveal itself, then the cognitive act also will require another cognitive act, and so on. Thus it will lead to infinite regress. We can avoid it only if we assume that all cognitions are self-luminous, and that they do not require any other cognitive act to manifest them. Therefore it is wrong to hold that an imperceptible cognitive act is necessary for the apprehension of objects.[1] " It is the self-revelation of an object-form cognition that is called the apprehension of the cognition."[2]

Kamalaśīla says : " A cognition apprehends itself, and does not apprehend anything other than itself. Though we speak of the cognition of blue, the cognition of yellow and the like, as if blue, yellow and the like were distinct from cognitions, yet they are not really distinct from them. It is the very nature of cognitions to manifest themselves as cognitions of blue, yellow, and the like, though there are no external objects independent of them. Cognitions are

[1] TS., vol. i, 2018–2025, pp. 563–5.
[2] *Indian Idealism*, p. 138.

by their very nature self-revealing." [1] "The external objects, such as blue and yellow, are really non-existent and knowledge cannot perceive them. Knowledge does not perceive any reality which is external and the so-called external reality cannot be the object of knowledge. The objects of perception such as blue, yellow, etc., do not really differ from the percepts of blue, yellow, etc. So he concludes that Vijñāna alone is the existent reality." [2]

(2) No Cognition of an External Object

A cognition is of the nature of consciousness. It is the opposite of unconscious matter. Matter does not manifest itself. But whenever a cognition is produced it manifests itself. It is non-material and self-manifest.[3] Therefore it can never apprehend an external object.[4] Consciousness constitutes the essence of a cognition which, therefore, apprehends itself. The so-called external object is supposed to be unconscious. How, then, can it be apprehended by a cognition ? [5] Whenever a cognition is produced it appears as consciousness and can, therefore, be cognized. But when an object is produced it does not appear as consciousness. Therefore it cannot be cognized.[6] A cognition is conscious whereas an object is unconscious. They are fundamentally different in nature. Therefore a cognition can never apprehend an object in the same manner as it apprehends itself.[7] Thus Śāntarakṣita concludes that a cognition can never apprehend an external object.

[1] TSP., vol. i, 2011, p. 562.

[2] Dr. Rakesh Ranjan Sharma, *The Yogācāra Theory of the External World*, Proceedings, Fifth Indian Oriental Conference, Lahore, vol. ii, p. 886.

[3] TS., vol. i, 2000, p. 559.

[4] Ibid., 1999, p. 559.

[5] Tadasya bodharūpatvādyuktaṃ tāvat svavedanam. Parasya tvartharūpasya tena saṃvedanaṃ katham. Ibid., 2002, p. 559.

[6] Ibid., 2004, p. 560.

[7] Ibid., 2003, p. 560.

It is self-contradictory to hold that an external object, which is unrelated to a cognition, is apprehended. If it is distinct from a cognition, and is unrelated to and independent of it, it can never be apprehended by it. There is no relation between an external object and an internal cognition. If there is any relation, it is either identity or the relation of cause and effect. The realist does not admit that there is identity between them. Nor is there any causal relation between them. A cognition cannot create an object. Nor can an object generate a cognition. A cognition is produced by the cognition which immediately precedes it.[1] Every cognition apprehends itself. It cannot apprehend anything other than itself. Therefore the cognition of blue also must be of the nature self-awareness (ātmasaṃvedana).[2] The existence of an external object is a needless assumption.

Śāntarakṣita seeks to establish that even if an external object exists, it cannot be apprehended by a cognition. If it is apprehended, it is apprehended either by a formless (nirākāra) cognition, or by a cognition invested with a similar form (sākāra), or by a cognition endowed with a different form (anyākāra). These are the only possible alternatives. A cognition cannot apprehend an object in any of these ways.[3]

(i) *A Formless Cognition cannot Apprehend an External Object.*

The first alternative cannot be maintained. A formless (nirākāra) cognition cannot come into connection with an external object. So it cannot apprehend it.[4] If such a

[1] Kṛṣṇamācārya's Introduction to TS., p. 17; also TSP., vol. i, pp. 569–570.
[2] TS., vol. i, 2033, p. 570.
[3] Ibid., 1999, p. 559.
[4] Ibid., 2020, p. 564.

cognition is supposed to apprehend an object, it cannot apprehend it as it really is because they are, in reality, different from each other. The cognition is devoid of the form of the object. Therefore it cannot apprehend its real nature, since it has no mode (prakāra) to represent it.[1]

The Nyāya-Vaiśeṣika, the Mīmāṃsaka, and the Jaina hold that a cognition apprehends an object without being invested with its form, even as a sword cuts an object without being invested with its form. A lamp illumines blue and other objects, but it does not assume their forms. So a cognition apprehends external objects, but it does not assume their forms.[2]

Śāntarakṣita shows that the argument is a false analogy. The blow of a sword is the cause of separation of the limbs of an elephant. A lamp makes an object fit for producing a cognition. But a cognition is not the cause of any change in the object. So it cannot apprehend it. On the other hand, an object produces a distinct cognition. Therefore a cognition which does not modify an object, can never apprehend it.[3]

Bhadanta Śubhagupta [4] argues that a formless cognition apprehends an object in the same manner as a cognition, which is in itself formless, is supposed by the Yogācāra to apprehend an unreal form. According to both, a cognition in itself is formless. But the Yogācāra holds that it apprehends an unreal form superimposed upon it. But Śubhagupta holds that it apprehends a real external object.[5]

[1] Ibid., 2005–6, p. 560.

[2] TS. and TSP., vol. i, 2007, p. 560; NK., p. 124.

[3] Ibid., 2008, p. 561.

[4] Binayatosha Bhattacarya: Foreword, TS., vol. i, pp. lxxxiv–lxxxv; S. C. Vidyābhuṣaṇa, *History of Indian Logic*, p. 346; MM. Phani Bhūṣaṇa Tarkavāgīśa calls Śubhagupta a Vaibhāṣika in *Nyāya-darśana* (Bengali), vol. iv, p. 165.

[5] TS. and TSP., vol. i, 2041, p. 572.

But Śāntarakṣita contends that cognitions cannot be said to have real knowledge (mukhyasaṃvedana) of external objects because they do not exist. They cannot be said to have even phenomenal knowledge (bhāktavedana) of external objects either because they arise from the same causal conditions, or because they are related to each other as cause and effect, or because they are similar to each other, since external objects do not exist and cannot have these qualities.[1] Cognitions apprehend unreal forms owing to an illusion. They cannot apprehend them as they really are inasmuch as they are devoid of reality. Cognitions are without any foundation in external objects (nirviṣaya).[2] But cognitions can apprehend themselves as they really are, since self-revelation constitutes their distinctive nature.[3] Kamalaśīla concludes that only illusory cognitions arise owing to avidyā (nescience), which reveal unreal forms, although there are no external objects corresponding to them.[4] Cognitions are not actually changed into the form of the objects. Nor are the objects modifications of some kind of "petrified consciousness" as some Vedāntists hold. "All the forms of cognition are ultimately to be regarded as illusory, for even one identical cognition may have many adiverse characters revealed in it, and if it be admitted that cognition has no parts, then it is impossible that one cognition should have such diverse characters. It is from this point of view that it has been said that the cognitions have no intrinsic nature of their own and therefore they have no definable nature."[5]

[1] TS. and TSP., vol. i., 2042–4, p. 572.
[2] Ibid., 2045–6, p. 573.
[3] Ibid., 2042, p. 572.
[4] Kevalamavidyāvaśādaviṣayamevābhūtākāropadarśakaṃ jñānaṃ bhrāntaṃ jāyate, TSP., vol. i, p. 572.
[5] *Indian Idealism*, p. 138.

(ii) *A Cognition with a Similar Form cannot Apprehend an Object.*

The second alternative also cannot be maintained. If a cognition invested with the form of an object (sākāra) is supposed to apprehend the object, then also it cannot apprehend its real nature. The object is apprehended by the cognition not directly but through its form which is reflected in the cognition. The cognition of the object is not direct and immediate, but indirect and mediate. Representative knowledge cannot claim to be real knowledge. It is secondary, derived, phenomenal (bhākta) knowledge.[1] Representationism is bound to lead to phenomenalism.

The modern new realist also offers a similar criticism of Descartes and Locke's representative theory of perception. According to this theory, " the mind never perceives anything external to itself. It can perceive only its own ideas or states. What we perceive is held to be only a picture of what really exists." [2] This leads to an absurd consequence. " The only external world is one that we can never experience, the only world that we can have any experience of is the internal world of ideas. When we attempt to justify the situation by appealing to inference as the guarantee of this unexperienceable externality, we are met by the difficulty that the world we infer can only be made of the matter of experience, that is, can only be made up of mental pictures in new combinations." [3] Thus representationism leads to phenomenalism.

Critical Realism also advocates indirect knowledge of an object. " Knowledge is not for Critical Realism a direct relation between mind and object. Knowledge, on the other hand, is a direct relation to the datum or essence, and this datum or essence is, both instinctively and reflectively, referred to the external world. Thus the datum is the means by which objects are known, or is, again, a ' vehicle ' of knowledge, but is not itself identical with the object. . . . The datum or essence indeed is what mediates

[1] Pratibimbasya tādrūpyād bhāktaṃ syādapi vedanam, TS., vol. i, 2005, p. 560.

[2] *The New Realism*, p. 4.

[3] Ibid., p. 5.

between the knower and the object, and this is possible just because the essence is the essence *of* the object. . . . Knowledge cannot in its very nature grasp the material objects in their existence. *What it does is to apprehend their form or pattern, and this form or pattern is referred to the object of which it is the pattern.*" [1]

C. E. M. Joad contends that we cannot have any *real* knowledge of the external world according to critical realism. "Its analysis of perception precludes the possibility of any real knowledge of reality. Perception is a three-termed process involving a knowing mind or mental state A, the datum or essence known B, and the physical object C with whose characteristics the data are in true perception identical. But if we always and in all circumstances know B and never in any circumstances know C, we cannot know anything about C. . . . If we are denied all *direct* knowledge of the qualities or *what* of C, we cannot know whether our data do in fact represent these qualities or not." [2]

Dr. J. E. Turner also criticizes critical realism in a similar manner. "'The physical thing and the psychical state . . . are unquestionably two and mutually independent. . . . The knower is confined to the datum, and can never literally inspect the existent. . . . We have no power of penetrating to the object itself and intuiting it immediately.' [3] On the other hand, we can 'immediately intuit' the sensation. 'You can turn your attention to the mere sensation of light or heat . . . you can consider them in themselves'; but if this immediate intuition is properly to be called knowledge, then it is plain that our consciousness of material existents, however it arises, is knowledge of a totally different order. . . . Critical realism posits an ontological dualism between sign and signate, while it further admits that the latter remains always beyond our immediate intuition; and this, in essence, is noumenalism." [4]

The Sautrāntika holds that a cognition with a similar form apprehends an external object. But Śāntarakṣita urges that even such a cognition cannot be connected with the object in its entirety, and so cannot apprehend it.[5] The form of the object is supposed to be imprinted on its

[1] L. A. Reid, *Knowledge and Truth*, pp. 125–6; the italics are mine.
[2] *Introduction to Modern Philosophy*, pp. 19–20.
[3] *Critical Realism*, pp. 240, 203, 225.
[4] *A Theory of Direct Realism*, p. 126.
[5] TS., vol. i, 2036, p. 571.

cognition. Therefore the cognition can be connected with the object in so far as it reflects its form. It cannot be wholly related to the object. So it cannot apprehend it. An illusory cognition with a particular form cannot rightly apprehend an object. It cannot be known whether the form of a cognition corresponds to that of its object or not. A cognition has no inherent real form through which it may apprehend a particular object.[1]

The Sautrāntika holds that there is a similarity (sārūpya) between the form of an object and that of its cognition. The similarity is either complete or partial. If there is complete similarity between a cognition and its object, a cognition will be as unconscious as its object. If there is partial similarity between them, the part of the cognition which is not similar to its object will apprehend it, and therefore every cognition will apprehend every object.[2]

The Sautrāntika's theory of correspondence leads to another absurd consequence. He admits that there are different minds or streams of consciousness. These minds with their attachment and aversion are apprehended by the cognition of the enlightened. If there is complete similarity between the apprehending cognition and the cognized minds, the former is affected by the attachment and aversion of the latter. But it is assumed to be pure and free from all emotions and passions which corrupt the mind. If there is partial similarity between them, then also the cognition of the enlightened is partly pure and partly affected with the impurities of other minds. But the same cognition cannot possess two contradictory characters.[3] Therefore the correspondence theory is unsound.

[1] TSP., vol. i, 2036, p. 571.
[2] TS., vol. i, 2039, p. 571; cf. NVTT., iv, 2, 33, p. 463.
[3] TS. and TSP., vol. i, 2048, p. 573; cf. NK., pp. 125–6, and *Indian Psychology: Perception*, pp. 366, 371–2.

Further, the Sautrāntika holds that the forms of external objects are reflected in the cognitions which apprehend them. The forms of cognitions are copies of those of external objects. They correspond to each other.[1]

Therefore if the object has one form its cognition also must have one form, and if the object has many forms its cognition also must have many forms. In the apprehension of a picture if the cognition has a single form the picture also must have a single form. Or if the picture has many forms the cognition also must have many forms. Otherwise the cognition and the object cannot be regarded as similar to each other.[2] But, as a matter of fact, it is found that a single uniform cognition apprehends a multiform object, e.g. a picture. This fact falsifies the theory of correspondence. If the correspondence theory is true, a cognition cannot apprehend an object. A cognition is unextended. It is devoid of parts. It is a simple psychosis. It is not a composite psychosis consisting of many elementary cognitions which may reflect the forms of a multiform object. At any rate, the forms of an unextended cognition can never represent the spatial characters of its

[1] Cf. "The content which we apprehend must have the property of reproducing something about the object, of conveying in its own medium the form of the object. The parts of a sensation have the same spatial arrangement as the parts of the object. (This is not admitted by the Sautrāntika.) Knowledge is the insight into the nature of the object that is made possible by the contents which reflect it in consciousness." (*Critical Realism*, pp. 218, 200; quoted in *A Theory of Direct Realism*, p. 131.)

[2] Cf. Joachim explains Leibnitz's theory of "reflection" thus: "It is not the same identical elements which appear both in the mirror and in the object. Yet the elements in the two factors, although not identical, are not barely other. For they are so related, that for each element on the one side there is a determinate element—one and only one—on the other. Correspondence, therefore, here means being related by a one-one relation. Two factors, each a one-of-many, 'correspond' when each constituent of the one stands in a one-one relation to a determinate constituent of the other." (*The Nature of Truth*, p. 9.)

object.[1] A cognition cannot, by its very nature, reflect the mutual externality of its parts.[2] Thus the correspondence theory pushed to its logical consequence seems to be absurd.

(iii) *A Cognition with a Different Form cannot Apprehend an External Object.*

If a cognition invested with one form apprehends an object with another form, then every cognition will apprehend every object and there will be nothing to restrict a cognition to a particular object. A cognition cannot be said to apprehend the object by which it is produced. In that case, the sense-organs would be apprehended by the cognition which is produced by them. Thus causality cannot regulate the relation of a cognition with one form to an object with another.[3]

Thus Śāntarakṣita concludes that cognitions never apprehend external objects either with or without their forms or with different forms.[4] They themselves rise one after another without reference to external objects. This is the nature of cognitions. They apprehend themselves. Just as the peculiarities of the so-called external objects cannot be explained, so the peculiarities of cognitions cannot be explained.[5] Therefore external objects do not exist. But there are different streams of consciousness in which cognitions apprehend themselves. There can be intercourse between one stream of consciousness (santāna) and another without an objective basis. So cognition alone (vijñaptimātratā) is the only reality. The Yogācāra idealism is subjectivism but not solipsism.[6]

[1] Contrast. "The parts of a sensation have the same spatial arrangement as the parts of the object." (*Critical Realism.*)

[2] TS. and TSP., vol. i, 2037–8, p. 571.

[3] Ibid., vol. i, 2040, p. 572.

[4] TS., vol. i, 1999, p. 559.

[5] TSP., vol. i, 2011, p. 562.

[6] Ibid., 1999, p. 559; see also Th. Stcherbatsky, *Buddhist Logic*, vol. i, pp. 521–4; *Indian Idealism*, pp. 133–4.

Vācaspati outlines the following arguments of the Yogācāra against the existence of external objects in *Nyāyavārtikatātparyaṭīkā*.

Supposing an external object exists, it is apprehended either by a formless cognition or by a cognition with a form. If it is apprehended by a formless cognition, it is apprehended either as merely existing, or as the cause of the cognition, or as depending upon the same causal conditions, or as being the substrate of manifestness produced by the cognition in it.

Firstly, an object cannot be apprehended by a cognition as merely existing. If it were true, every object would be apprehended by every cognition because existence is common to all objects, and there would be nothing to restrict a cognition to a particular object. Further, even non-existent objects are apprehended by cognitions. Therefore mere existence cannot be the determining condition of apprehension.

Secondly, an object cannot be apprehended by a cognition because it gives rise to it. The sense-organs also bring about a cognition. But they are not apprehended by the cognition. Besides, the object and the cognition are momentary. The object does not exist, when the cognition appears. Therefore, if it is apprehended at all, it should be apprehended as past. But, as a matter of fact, an object is apprehended as present in an act of perception. The causal theory of perception cannot account for the perception of an object as present. So the causal theory is unsound.

Thirdly, if the object is said to be apprehended by a cognition because they are brought into existence together by the same causal conditions, then the object can be apprehended as present. But this is not always possible. The past and the future, though non-existent, can be apprehended. They cannot possibly be brought into existence along with their cognitions by the same causal conditions.

Fourthly, the object cannot be said to be apprehended by a cognition because it is the substratum of manifestness produced in it by the cognition. Manifestness (prākaṭya) is a property of the object. It should, therefore, be accessible to all persons, like whiteness and other properties. But, in fact, it is found to be private (asādhāraṇa) to the observing person. The object is manifest to the person who apprehends it. Manifestness is produced by a cognition in the object, even as duality is produced by the discriminating intellect (apekṣābuddhi) of a person. Both are equally private to the apprehending person. Further, inference and verbal cognition apprehend past and future objects. But they cannot produce manifestness in them because they are non-existent. Therefore the assumption that a formless cognition apprehends an external object is groundless.

But it may be held that a cognition invested with a form apprehends an external object. The cognition with the form of blue apprehends the blue object. There is a similarity between the form of the cognition of blue and the form of the blue object. This is the doctrine of the Sautrāntika. The Yogācāra contends that the object may be apprehended by the cognition because of its complete similarity or partial similarity with the cognition. In the first place, the object is material and unconscious whereas the cognition is a mode of consciousness. Therefore there cannot be complete similarity between them. If there is, the cognition will be as unconscious as the object and thus lose its essential nature.[1] In the second place, if there is partial similarity between them, some part of the cognition, though not similar to the object, apprehends it, and therefore any cognition will apprehend every object, and similarity will cease to be the determining condition of apprehension of a particular

[1] Cf. Jaina criticism.

object. Therefore a cognition with a form also cannot apprehend an external object.

Further, two forms are not apprehended. Only one form is manifested to consciousness. It may be said that the form of the cognition itself is wrongly ascribed to an external object. The former is ascribed to the latter either when the latter is apprehended or not. The external object is not apprehended, since two forms are not manifested to consciousness. If the object is not apprehended, the form of the cognition cannot be ascribed to it. If a white and bright object is not perceived, the idea of silver cannot be ascribed to it. If the external object is not perceived, it cannot lead to a proper reaction. If an unperceived object can induce action, every unperceived object will lead to a reaction, which is absurd. There is no evidence to prove the existence of an external object because it is never perceived. Therefore the assumption that a cognition with a form apprehends an external object also is groundless.[1]

(3) The Law of Simultaneous Apprehension (*sahopalambhaniyama*)

This argument is generally stated thus : The cognized object (blue) and the apprehending cognition (cognition of blue) are invariably apprehended *together* (saha). Therefore they are identical with each other. But Śāntarakṣita puts the argument in a less objectionable form. He does not use the word *together* (saha) which implies difference. He asserts that the apprehension of the cognition of blue and the apprehension of blue are one and the same. This identical apprehension is called *sahopalambha*. It is the apprehension of a cognition that is always the apprehension of an object. There is no apprehension of an object distinct from the apprehension of a cognition. This is called the law of non-distinct

[1] NVTT., iv, 2, 33, pp. 462–4.

apprehension (sahopalambhaniyama). This proves that there is no difference between the cognized object and the apprehending cognition.

Śāntarakṣita says : "The cognition of an object is non-distinct from the cognition of the cognition. They are not different from each other. The cognition of blue is non-distinct from the cognition of the cognition of blue." [1] Kamalaśīla makes it more clear. He emphatically says : "There is one and the same cognition of the cognized object (jñeya) and of the apprehending cognition (jñāna). The cognition of a cognition is the very same as the cognition of the object. The cognition of the object also is the very same as the cognition of its cognition." [2] "The whole idea inherent in this logic is that the awareness and its object have the same revelation ; whatever is the apprehension of cognition is also the apprehension of the blue." [3]

The realist may argue that a cognition and an object are always related to each other as cognizer (viṣayin) and cognized (viṣaya), and therefore they are always apprehended together. It is the very nature of a cognition to apprehend an object. And it is the very nature of an object to be apprehended. They are always apprehended together because they depend upon the same causal conditions. The sense-organs are not apprehended by cognitions, though they may be produced together, because it is not their nature to be apprehended. The cognition of an object (blue) is produced by the intercourse of a sense-organ with the object. The cognition of the sense-organ is never produced. So blue and other objects are produced as objects apprehended by those cognitions.[4]

[1] TS., vol. i, 2030–1, p. 567.

[2] Ya eva hi jñānopalambhaḥ sa eva jñeyasya ya eva jñeyasya sa eva jñānasya, TSP., vol. i, p. 568.

[3] *Indian Idealism*, p. 137.

[4] TSP., vol. i, p. 569.

Śāntarakṣita contends that an external object which is different in nature from a cognition cannot be apprehended by it. A blue form is apprehended by a cognition. Therefore they are identical with each other.[1] If the object is distinct from the cognition, it cannot be apprehended because there is no invariable relation between them. If there is any, it is either identity or causality. The realist does not admit identity between a cognition and an object. They cannot be related as cause and effect because they are supposed to be produced together at the same time. Even if the cognition were the effect of the object, it could not apprehend it because, in that case, a sense-organ also would be apprehended by the cognition produced by it.

It may be argued that a cognition and an object are related to each other as cognizer and cognized because they are produced as such by their causes. This is wrong because the subject-object-relationship (viṣayiviṣayabhāva) is not established. It can be established if an invariable relation is established between them. There is no other invariable relation than identity and causality. Therefore the argument of the realist is unsubstantial. There cannot be invariably simultaneous apprehension of a cognition and an object unless they are identical with each other.[2]

(4) No Evidence for the Existence of an External Object

Śāntarakṣita argues that, if a cognition does not assume the form of an object it cannot be said to apprehend it, and if it does assume the form, there is no evidence for the existence of an external object.[3]

Kamalaśīla points out that if there is any evidence for its existence, it is either perception or inference. The Buddhist does not admit any other kind of evidence.

[1] TS., vol. i, 2032, p. 569.
[2] TSP., vol. i, 2032, pp. 569–570.
[3] TS., vol. i, 2051, p. 574.

If an external object is perceived, it is perceived either by a formless cognition or by a cognition with a form. It cannot be perceived by a formless cognition, since it cannot come into relation with the cognition. If a cognition does not take in the form of its object, it cannot apprehend it. An external object cannot be perceived by a cognition invested with the form of its object, since only the form of the cognition is perceived and that of the object is not perceived. Therefore the object may be inferred but cannot be perceived.[1]

Bhadanta Śubhagupta proves the existence of an external object by inference. The form of a cognition is the effect of an external object because of harmony (saṃvāda) between them. Śāntarakṣita urges that harmony means either the capacity for leading to the attainment of an external object or the capacity for producing cognitions of fruitful actions. A subjective idealist who denies the existence of an external object, cannot admit the possibility of harmony in the first sense. Harmony is possible in the second sense even if there is no external object. Mere cognitions can fulfil the practical needs of life. They are capable of producing cognitions of fruitful actions. Just as external objects are capable of producing fruitful actions according to the realist, so mere cognitions are capable of producing fruitful actions according to the idealist, since the so-called objects are non-distinct from cognitions. According to the Buddhist idealist, the validity of knowledge consists in the harmony of experience. Dr. B. N. Seal states it thus: "The ultimate criterion of truth is found, not in mere cognitive presentation, but in the correspondence between the cognitive and the practical activity of the self (stream of consciousness), which together are supposed to form the circuit of consciousness. That knowledge is valid which prompts an activity ending in fruition. Truth is *not*

[1] TSP., vol. i, 2051, p. 574.

self-evidence, *not* the agreement between ideas, *nor* the agreement of the idea with the reality beyond, if any, for this cannot be attained direct, but the harmony of experience (samvāda), which is implied when the volitional reaction, that is prompted by a cognition and that completes the circuit of consciousness, meets with fruition, i.e. realizes its immediate end." [1] Thus the existence of an external object cannot be inferred from harmony of experience (samvāda). Besides, a cognition which does not take in the form of an object cannot apprehend it. The cognition of colour cannot apprehend a sound. An inferential cognition does not assume the form of fire. It cannot, therefore, apprehend fire. Thus an external object can be neither perceived nor inferred. Therefore it does not exist.[2]

Udyotakara argues that an external object (e.g. blue) which is apprehended as existing out in space external to the cognition (deśavicchedabhāsi) is different from an internal cognition, because it is an object of valid knowledge, because it is not eternal, because it is of the nature of an effect, because it is of the nature of a cause, and because it has a reason for existence. This argument is fallacious because even internal cognitions possess all these characters which are the marks of inference. Therefore external objects cannot be inferred from internal cognitions.[3]

II. THE METAPHYSICAL ARGUMENT FOR SUBJECTIVE IDEALISM

The realist argues that if physical objects do not exist as distinct from cognitions, they cannot be perceived as such. But, as a matter of fact, they are distinctly perceived as external (vicchinna) to and independent of cognitions.

[1] *The Positive Sciences of the Ancient Hindus*, pp. 244–5.
[2] TS. and TSP., vol. i, 2052–6, pp. 574–5.
[3] Ibid., 2057–8, p. 576; cf. NV., iv, 2, 32–4, p. 529 (Bib. Ind.).

Therefore they do exist. If they are held to be non-existent, though they are distinctly perceived, cognitions also should be held to be non-existent, though they are distinctly perceived.[1]

Śāntarakṣita contends that the so-called physical object is perceived either as a conglomeration of atoms or as a complex whole composed of atoms, or as a gross object not made of atoms. The first alternative cannot be maintained. Atoms are supersensible. Only gross objects are perceived. Indivisible atoms are never perceived. They cannot impart their form of atomicity to cognitions. Or cognitions cannot reflect the atomicity of atoms. Atoms are indivisible, and cannot, therefore, be said to be corporeal. Even if many atoms are produced together, they cannot lose their indivisibility and bring about the cognition of a gross object.[2]

It may be argued that a conglomeration of similar atoms with spatial continuity generates the illusion of a gross object, even as an uninterrupted succession of similar moments appearing and disappearing generate the illusion of permanence. Śāntarakṣita urges that if the existence of atoms is already proved, then only the cognition of a gross object may be regarded as illusory. But the existence of atoms cannot be regarded as an established fact. Besides, the cognition of a gross object is not illusory because it is distinctly apprehended.[3]

The external object cannot be a complex whole composed of atoms with a distinct existence. We cannot establish a relation between the whole and its parts. Nor can the external object be a gross object not composed of atoms. Thus we cannot define the nature of the so-called external object. Therefore it does not exist.

[1] TS., vol. i, 1965–6.
[2] Ibid., 1967–1970.
[3] TS. and TSP., vol. i, pp. 552–3.

The so-called external object is an unreal appearance (sāṃvṛta satya). The only reality is a cognition (citta).[1] What is manifested as an external object is, in reality, a cognition. If the cognition also which apprehends the apparent object is regarded as an unreal appearance, it will lead to total collapse of practical life. So it must be taken as real. The cognition manifests itself. It is self-aware (svasaṃvedya). It is not manifested by any other cognition. In fact, it does not depend upon any other condition to reveal itself. It is momentary. It appears and disappears. It is preceded by other cognitions, and succeeded by others. Momentary cognitions are related to one another and form a stream of consciousness (santāna). Every individual, which is nothing but a stream of consciousness, differs from other individuals. They do not run into one another. They are an irreducible plurality. The psychic continuum of an adept is pure and free from mental constructs (kalpanā) whereas that of an ordinary individual is tainted with a mass of psychical dispositions (vāsanā) and interwoven with mental constructs (kalpanā) which are manifested as sense-data, e.g. blue, yellow, and the like. There are two parallel streams of cognitions in the psychic continuum of an ordinary individual. There is a core of persisting stream of self-cognitions characterized by ego-consciousness, which is called ālayavijñāna; and there is another series of object-cognitions or presentations variegated by blue, yellow, and the like, which is called pravṛttivijñāna. Both the series are, in reality, not different from the mind or cognition. They are nothing but cognitions. The two series are not unrelated to each other. The manifold series of object-cognitions (pravṛttivijñāna) spring from the series of self-cognitions (ālayavijñāna) owing to the maturescence of psychical dispositions (vāsanāparipāka), even as waves appear in the

[1] Vasubandhu says in *Viṃśatikārikā* that *citta*, *manas* (mind), *vijñāna* (cognition), and *vijñapti* (apprehension) are synonymous.

sea agitated by the wind. Presentations owe their origin to the mind, and not to external objects.

The ālayavijñāna is called the mind (citta). Manifold presentations (pravṛttivijñāna) are transformations of the ālayavijñāna. The internal mind or the stream of self-cognitions is transformed into manifold object-cognitions in contact with the forms of blue and the like. Thus subjective self-cognitions appear to be objective presentations of blue, yellow, and the like which serve the practical needs of life. Object-cognitions appear to be distinct from self cognitions, though, in reality, they are identical with them. When avidyā with psychical dispositions is destroyed there emerges a pure consciousness free from the distinction of subject and object and untainted by egoism. There is no other reality than cognition in the world. Cognition is the only ontological reality.[1]

[1] Kṛṣṇamācārya's Introduction to TS., pp. 13 ff. See *Vijñaptimātratāsiddhi* (Appendix to *The Journal of the Bihar and Orissa Research Society*, vol. xix, part iv, December, 1933), pp. 4, 6, 12–13, 25; *Laṅkāvatārasūtra*, Kyoto, 1923, pp. 9, 30, 41–4, 46, 54; *Mahāyānasūtrālaṅkāra*, pp. 58–9; TS. and TSP., pp. 581, 582. See TS. and TSP., vols. i-ii, for detailed Yogācāra criticism of other schools of Indian philosophy.

Chapter II

THE SAUTRĀNTIKA REALISM : THE REPRESENTATIVE THEORY OF PERCEPTION

The Sautrāntika is a realist. He recognizes the reality of external objects. But they are not objects of perception. They are inferred from their cognitions. Cognitions are effects of external objects which are their causes. Cognitions are directly perceived ; external objects are inferred from them as their causes. Thus the Sautrāntika, like Descartes and Locke, advocates the representationist theory of perception.

He holds that external objects give rise to cognitions and imprint their forms on them so that the forms of cognitions correspond to the forms of external objects. The correspondence between them or similarity of their forms (sārūpya) is the criterion of truth. The Sautrāntika is an advocate of realism, representationism, and the correspondence theory of truth.[1]

Descartes and Locke are advocates of representationism. Descartes affirms the independent existence of matter as distinguished from mind. But matter is not directly perceived ; it is only causally inferred. Adventitious ideas are modes of mind caused by matter. So the existence of matter is inferred from them. Locke holds that ideas are signs of things, and from ideas we infer things. We directly perceive ideas, and infer the existence of physical objects from them. Representationism is based on the causal notion of perception. " There is a substance, mind, on one side, and another substance, matter, on the other. The latter causes an effect in the former. This is the

[1] S.D.S., p. 15.

sensum ; and because it is an effect, it necessarily leads to the conclusion that its cause exists. Apprehension of an object is therefore an inference." [1]

The Criticism of the Yogācāra Idealism

Mādhavācāra outlines the arguments of the Sautrāntika against the Yogācāra doctrine of the non-existence of the external world.[2]

(1) The Yogācāra denies the existence of external objects on the ground that they cannot exist independently of the cognitions apprehending them. The objects perceived are identical with the percipient cognitions. The Yogācāra, like Berkeley, proves the identity of objects with cognitions from their invariably simultaneous perception (sahopalambhaniyama). The blue and the cognition of blue are invariably perceived together ; they are never perceived apart from each other. So they are identical with each other.

But the Sautrāntika urges that if two things are invariably perceived together, it does not necessarily follow that they are identical with each other because this rule is also found in dubious and contrary instances.[3] If A and B are invariably perceived together, it does not necessarily follow that A is identical with B. A sensation and its content are necessarily experienced together. The sensation is experience of the content. But this does not prove that sensation is identical with its content. This truth may be illustrated by an example from modern psychology. The intensity of a sensation is always perceived together with its quality. But they are not identical with each other.

(2) The object cannot be identical with the apprehending cognition (vijñāna). There is an obvious difference between them. The cognition is internal (antarmukha)

[1] S. Z. Hasan, *Realism*, p. 63. [2] S.D.S., pp. 14 ff.

[3] Ibid., p. 14.

while the object is external (vahirmukha). The cognition is a psychical event. It apprehends an external object. The object is perceived as-different from, and external to, the cognition. It is external to the cognition in the sense that it is independent of it. Further, the cognition and the object cannot be invariably referred to the same time and the same space. So they cannot be said to be perceived together either at the same time or in the same space. Hence they cannot be proved to be identical with each other.[1]

(3) If the object were a mere cognition, it would be apprehended as a mode of the subject. But, as a matter of fact, the object is never apprehended as a mode of the subject, but as something different from, and opposed to, the subject. For instance, a blue object is never presented to consciousness as " *I* am blue " but as " *this* is blue ".[2] This clearly shows that the object is not a mere mode of consciousness. It is " given ". It is of the nature of the not-self as opposed to the self. It is the other of the subject. To reduce the object to a mode of the subject is to miss its distinctive character.

(4) The Yogācāra argues that though the object is identical with its cognition and is nothing but a mode of consciousness, yet it is illusorily presented as distinct from, and external to, the cognition. The object which

[1] Jñānasya antarmukhatayā jñeyasya vahirmukhatayā ca bhedena pratibhāsamānatvādekadeśatvaikakālatvalakṣaṇasahatvaniyamāsambhavāt, S.D.S., p. 14. Cf. In criticizing Berkeley, Johnston observes: " He never attempted any exhaustive analysis of the actual process of perception. He draws no distinction between *sensations* and *sensible qualities*; and he even identifies *sensations* and *sensible things* or objects. For him the word *idea* means at one and the same time a *sensation* in the mind and a *thing* presented to the mind. . . . He does not distinguish between the actual process of perception, the particular experience in the psychical individual, and the thing or object perceived. His theory suffers seriously from absence of psychological analysis." (*The Development of Berkeley's Philosophy*, pp. 152–4; the italics are mine.)

[2] S.D.S., p. 14.

is a mere form of cognition (jñānasvarūpa) appears to us as if it were an external entity owing to an illusion. The duality of subject (grāhaka) and object (grāhya) is an illusory appearance. Cognition alone is real. What is really an internal cognition appears to be an external object.[1]

The Sautrāntika urges that if there are no external objects at all, we can never assert that internal cognitions appear to be external objects. The illusory appearance of externality presupposes the real knowledge of externality somewhere. If we were completely ignorant of the external world, we could never speak of the illusory appearance of externality. No sensible person would say : "Vasubandhu looks like the son of a barren mother.'[2] The sense of objectivity can never be derived from mere modes of consciousness.

(5) The Sautrāntika points out that the Yogācāra's argument involves a vicious circle. He argues :

(i) The cognized object is identical with the apprehending cognition because the appearance of their duality is illusory.

(ii) And the duality or distinction of the cognized object and the apprehending cognition is illusory because they are, in reality, identical with each other.

Thus the Yogācāra proves the identity of the object with its cognition by holding that the manifestation of their duality is illusory ; again, he proves the illusoriness of their duality by holding that they are really identical with each other. Thus there is mutual dependence (anyonyāśraya).[3]

(6) The Sautrāntika appeals to the verdict of common sense. We undoubtedly perceive blue and the like as *external* objects (bāhyameva) and react to them, and pass over internal cognitions in everyday life. This clearly

[1] Yadantarjñeyatattvaṃ tadbahirvad avabhāsate, ibid., p. 14.

[2] Ibid., p. 14.

[3] S.D.S., p. 14.

shows that cognitions do not apprehend themselves but external objects.[1] Here the Sautrāntika does not compromise his doctrine of representationism but simply states the common-sense view. Śaṅkara also gives a similar argument against the Yogācāra subjectivism.[2] Reid holds that we directly perceive external objects without the intervention of ideas.

(7) Further, if cognitions were merely subjective modes of consciousness, they would be all alike formless and indeterminate. But, in fact, cognitions are diversified by different objects which impose their forms upon them, and make them definite and determinate.[3] The different forms of cognitions are due to the different external objects. The internal forms of cognitions are copies or representations of the external forms of objects. We directly perceive our cognitions. We infer the existence of external objects from the forms of cognitions which are imprinted on them by the objects. The objects give rise to cognitions when they come in contact with the sense-organs, and impress their forms upon them.[4]

(8) The Sautrāntika advances the following formal argument to prove the existence of external objects. Those things which appear at times, while another thing is uniformly present, must depend upon something else. The series of self-cognitions (ālayavijñāna) is uniformly present. But object-cognitions (pravṛttivijñāna) appear occasionally. Therefore they must depend on something other than the series of self-cognitions. They are caused by external objects which are independent of all cognitions.

[1] Ibid., 14. [2] S.B.S., ii, 2, 28.

[3] Na hi vittisattaiva tadvedanā yuktā tasyāḥ sarvatrāviśeṣāt. Tāṃ tu sārūpyam āviśat sarūpayituṃ ghaṭayet. S.D.S., p. 15; cf. NK., p. 123; NM., pp. 538–9; SD., p. 150.

[4] S.D.S., p. 15. Berkeley states the representative theory of perception thus: "Though the ideas themselves do not exist without the mind, yet there may be things like them, whereof they are copies or resemblances, which things exist without the mind in an unthinking substance." (*Principles of Human Knowledge*, p. 38.)

The ālayavijñāna is a series of self-cognitions. The pravṛttivijñāna is a series of object-cognitions. The former is knowledge of the subject or ego (ahamāspada). The latter is knowledge of the object or non-ego, which manifests blue and the like. The object-cognitions are presented to the series of self-cognitions and induce activity. The ālayavijñāna is literally the home or abode of cognitions. But it is not the permanent self. The Buddhist is committed to the doctrine of impermanence. In the language of William James, the ālayavijñāna is a stream of passing thoughts which themselves are thinkers. " Each pulse of cognitive consciousness, each thought," he says, " dies away and is replaced by another. The other, among the things it knows, knows its own predecessor, and finding it 'warm' greets it, saying : 'Thou art *mine*, and part of the same self with me'. Each later Thought, knowing and including thus the thoughts which went before, is the final receptacle—and appropriating them is the final owner—of all that they contain and own. Each Thought is thus born an owner and dies owned, transmitting whatever it realized as its self to its own later proprietor. . . . It is this trick which the nascent thought has of immediately taking up the expiring thought and 'adopting' it, which is the foundation of the appropriation of most of the remoter constituents of the self." [1] This conception of James closely resembles the ālayavijñāna of the Buddhist. It is the core of the stream of consciousness. It is the centre of all reference.

The stream of self-cognitions (ālayavijñāna) is always there. The object-cognitions (pravṛttivijñāna) occasionally break in upon the stream of self-cognitions. They must, therefore, owe their existence to something other than the stream of self-cognitions. The object-cognitions are not evolved from within and do not depend upon the self-cognitions, but they are imposed upon them from

[1] *The Principles of Psychology*, 1890, vol. i, p. 339.

without by external objects. When sensations of speaking or walking are forced into my consciousness, though I do not speak or walk at the time, I am compelled to admit that the sensations are caused by other persons who speak or walk, since these are not caused by me.[1] Similarly, the object-cognitions which occasionally break in upon the stream of self-cognitions, which is uniformly present, are caused by external objects such as blue and the like. Thus we must admit the existence of external objects independent of the stream of self-cognitions (ālayavijñāna), which are the causes of object-cognitions (pravṛttivijñāna).[2]

(9) The Yogācāra holds that the occasional appearance of object-cognitions (pravṛttivijñāna) is not due to external objects, but to the maturation of subconscious impressions (vāsanāparipāka) within the stream of consciousness itself. The variety of object-cognitions or sensations is due to the variety of subconscious impressions (vāsanā) which appear and disappear in a beginningless series of nescience. Object-cognitions break in upon the field of consciousness owing to the revival of subconscious impressions in the same psychic continuum. They are not imposed from without but are evolved from within. Subconscious impressions are awakened by those antecedent mental states with which they were associated in the past, and are raised to the level of consciousness. The revival of subconscious impressions is responsible for the emergence of object-cognitions or sensations. They

[1] Th. Stcherbatsky, *Buddhist Logic*, vol. i, pp. 521–4; S. N. Das Gupta, *Indian Idealism*, pp. 134, 136; TS., vol. i, 2057, p. 576. Berkeley also holds that we have inferential knowledge of other finite spirits. He says: "I perceive several motions, changes, and combinations of ideas, that inform me there are certain peculiar agents, like myself, which accompany them and concur in their production." "We cannot know the existence of *other spirits* otherwise than by their operations, or the ideas by them excited in us." "Hence, the knowledge I have of other spirits is not immediate, as is the knowledge of my ideas." (*Principles of Human Knowledge*, pp. 108–9.)

[2] S.D.S., p. 15.

cannot be traced to external objects. Sensations are not " given ". They are creations of the mind. The Yogācāra advocates unadulterated subjectivism or mentalism.

But the Sautrāntika contends that if all subconscious impressions have a tendency to rise above the threshold of consciousness, why they should remain at all in the subconscious level as latent predispositions is unintelligible. Then, again, why a particular antecendent mental state awakens a subconscious impression and brings it to the level of consciousness is a mystery. It may be awakened by all the antecedent mental states in the same psychic continuum, because they all equally belong to the same continuum. If all the antecedent mental states cannot awaken a subconscious impression, a single antecedent mental state cannot awaken it either. Then, again, it is absurd to suppose that all previous mental states awaken a subconscious impression, and modify a particular psychosis. Thus subconscious impressions can never account for object-cognitions or sensations. Hence the Sautrāntika concludes that we must admit the reality of external objects capable of exciting the sensations of sound, touch, colour, taste, smell, and feelings of pleasure and pain occasionally.[1]

[1] S.D.S., p. 16.

Chapter III

THE YOGĀCĀRA'S CRITICISM OF THE REPRESENTATIVE THEORY OF PERCEPTION

§ 1. *Jayanta Bhaṭṭa's Account*

Jayanta Bhaṭṭa gives a lucid account of the subjective idealism of the Yogācāra in *Nyāyamañjarī*. He outlines the following arguments of the Yogācāra against the Sautrāntika doctrine of representationism.

(1) Firstly, it may be asked why we should admit the reality of ideas alone, since we do perceive external objects which are quite unlike our ideas. The Yogārāca replies that the existence of external objects cannot be proved. He asks : What do we perceive in the perception of the so-called external object? It is either the form of the internal cognition, or the form of the external object, or both. If we perceive both the forms—the form of the cognition representing the form of the object—realism is established. If we perceive only the form of the cognition which does not represent the form of the object, subjective idealism is established. The Yogācāra holds that only one form is manifested to consciousness in the perception of an object, and it is the form of a cognition. It cannot be the form of an object, since the object is material and unconscious, and cannot manifest itself. It can be manifested to consciousness only through a cognition. It cannot be apprehended except through the form of a cognition. Thus the forms of cognitions must be admitted. What, then, is the use of admitting the reality of external objects ? The forms of cognitions serve our purpose. The hypothesis of external objects is gratuitous. The parsimony of hypotheses demands that

we should recognize the reality of cognitions alone with their various forms and determinations.

If the realist contends that the cognized object itself is the apprehending cognition, and appears as consciousness, there is only a verbal difference between the realist and the subjective idealist.[1] The realist holds that the object breaks up into subject and object while the Yogācāra holds that the consciousness breaks up into subject and object. Both of them identify the subject (cognition) with the object and abolish all distinction between them. The realist may argue that there is a difference between the percipient cognition and the perceptible object inasmuch as the former is internal and the latter is external.[2] But this is wrong. The externality of the object means its externality to the cognition, and not its externality to the body. The object is external in the sense that it is extra-mental, and not in the sense that it is extra-organic. But if the realist admits that the percipient cognition is not other than the perceptible object, the object cannot be regarded as external to the cognition. It cannot be extra-mental because it is nothing but the cognition itself.[3] Thus there is no real difference between realism and subjective idealism.

Hence the Yogācāra concludes that there is no external world. There is no dispute as to the existence of cognitions. But the existence of external objects is open to controversy. Besides, external objects require cognitions to manifest or apprehend them. So, for the sake of parsimony of hypotheses, we must admit the existence of cognitions only, but not of external objects. The forms of cognitions are not due to the forms of

[1] Athārtha eva grāhyātmā yaḥ sa eva grāhaka iti kathyate sa tarhi prakāśa eveti sajñāyām eṣa vivādaḥ syāt, NM., p. 537. This passage anticipates new realism.

[2] Bāhyāntarakṛto viśeṣaḥ, ibid., p. 537.

[3] Grāhyāt arthāt avyatirikta eva grāhakaḥ, ibid., p. 537.

external objects ; they are determinations of consciousness itself.[1]

(2) Secondly, the realist admits that a cognition manifests an unconscious object which cannot manifest itself.[2] So he must admit that a cognition cannot apprehend an object until the cognition itself is first apprehended, even as a luminous lamp cannot manifest other objects, without itself being first perceived. As soon as a cognition is produced by an object it must be apprehended, for nothing stands in the way of apprehension of the cognition. It does not depend upon any other manifestation, since cognition itself is self-luminous like a lamp.[3] Hence as soon as a cognition is produced it must apprehend itself. If a cognition is not apprehended at the time of its production, it can never be apprehended at some other time because it will remain the same and not acquire any new character by virtue of which it will be apprehended at some other time. If the cognition is said to be apprehended at some other time by another cognition, that cognition, again, will require another cognition to apprehend it and so on, and thus will lead to infinite regress. If the cognition of an object be not apprehended, the object which is manifested by the cognition can never be apprehended. Hence the realist must admit that there is apprehension of a cognition before there can be apprehension of an object.[4] So it is said that an object cannot be perceived unless its cognition is apprehended.[5]

[1] Ibid., p. 537.

[2] Jñānaṃ hi prakāśakam aprakāśasya arthasya bhavadbhirabhyupagamyate, ibid., p. 537.

[3] This is a favourite analogy of Indian philosophers. Hamilton also compares consciousness " to an internal light, by means of which, and which alone, what passes in the mind is rendered visible ". (*Metaphysics*, vol. i, p. 183.)

[4] Ibid., pp. 537–8.

[5] Apratyakṣopalambhasya nārthadṛṣṭiḥ prasidhyati, ibid., p. 538.

It is a fact of experience that sometimes we apprehend an object and then reflect upon this apprehension. We have a reflective consciousness of the cognition of an object such as " this object is known by me ". This is a secondary cognition of the simple apprehension of an object. A qualified object cannot be known unless its qualifying adjuncts are known. The apprehension that " this object is known by me " presupposes apprehension of the cognition. This clearly shows that a cognition must be apprehended before an object can be apprehended.[1]

(3) Thirdly, the cognition which is apprehended before its object is apprehended, must have a definite form, since a formless cognition can never be apprehended. And if cognitions were devoid of forms, they would never lead to different reactions. Even if we admit the existence of external objects, we cannot but admit the existence of definite forms of cognitions. Otherwise we can never explain how different cognitions should apprehend different objects.[2] Cognitions, in their essence, are all alike ; they are of the nature of consciousness. They differ from one another only in their forms or modes. If cognitions were formless and indeterminate, every cognition would be able to apprehend all objects without any distinction. But, as a matter of fact, different cognitions apprehend different objects. For example, the cognition of blue apprehends the blue object. Why should it apprehend only the blue object to the exclusion of all other objects, though it is produced in the presence of many other objects ? The reason is obvious. It is endowed with a definite form by virtue of which it can apprehend only a blue object. If it were not so, it would not always be followed by the same reaction. It cannot be argued that the cognition of blue apprehends the blue object because it is produced by it. In that case, the

[1] Ibid., p. 538. [2] Ibid., p. 538.

cognition of blue should apprehend the imperceptible sense-organs also which produce it. But this is not the case. Hence we must admit that there is a definite form of the cognition of blue by virtue of which it apprehends only a blue object and leads to the same reaction. The Yogācāra goes further and holds that there is no external object other than the apprehending cognition with a definite form. The form is inherent in the cognition itself, and not in an external object.[1]

(4) Fourthly, the Yogācāra criticizes the Sautrāntika doctrine that external objects are inferred from our cognitions which are impressed with the forms of the objects. Consciousness, which is formless and indeterminate in itself, is modified in different ways by external objects, even as a crystal, which is transparent by nature, is coloured by its contact with lac. The different forms of consciousness are produced by the different external objects which are inferred from them.[2]

The Yogācāra urges that this argument is wrong. Even if we suppose that cognitions have definite forms in the presence of their objects, we never perceive formless and indeterminate cognitions in the absence of objects. The method of difference cannot be applied here. The method of agreement cannot yield a certain conclusion unless it is supplemented by the method of difference. The Sautrāntika cannot, therefore, legitimately conclude that the forms of cognitions are produced by the forms of external objects.[3]

Further, the analogy of crystal and lac is not appropriate. The crystal, which is by nature transparent, assumes a red colour when it comes in contact with lac. But we never perceive an indeterminate cognition which assumes a definite form in contact with an object. We perceive the natural transparence of crystal, the red colour of lac, and the colour of the crystal as modified by its red colour.

[1] Ibid., p. 538. [2] NM., pp. 538–9. [3] Ibid., p. 539.

But we never perceive a formless and indeterminate cognition before it assumes the form of an object, nor the form of the object as distinct from the form of the cognition.[1]

There cannot be two forms, the form of cognition as well as the form of the object, since we are not conscious of them. The assumption of two forms will lead to infinite regress. If both the form of the object and the form of its cognition produced by it are perceived, the former will be perceived by a determinate cognition with a definite form. And this determinate cognition, again, being the object of apprehension, will be perceived by another determinate cognition, and so on. If the form of the object is said to be apprehended by a determinate cognition which is self-luminous and apprehends itself without depending upon any other determinate cognition, it is needless to assume the existence of the form of the object as distinct from the self-luminous determinate cognition because it is never manifested to consciousness. If the determinate cognition itself is said to be an object, there is only a verbal difference between realism and idealism. In fact, cognitions themselves should be regarded as endowed with the forms of blue and the like. The hypothesis of external objects is needless and unwarranted.[2]

(5) Fifthly, if it be argued that consciousness in itself is formless and indeterminate, and consequently its determinations and modifications must be due to some other cause, the Yogācāra replies that the determinations of consciousness are caused by subconscious impressions due to avidyā (nescience). The variety in the modes or determinations of consciousness is due to the variety of subconscious impressions originating in a beginningless series of avidyā.[3] Cognitions (jñāna) and subconscious

[1] Ibid., p. 539. [2] NM., p. 539.

[3] Svataḥ svacchamapi jñānam anadyavidyāvāsanāvibhavena tattadanekākārakaluṣyarūṣitavapuriva prakāśate, ibid., p. 539.

impressions (vāsanā) are connected with each other as causes and effects, like seeds and sprouts, forming an unending series. Hence it is needless to assume the existence of inferrible external objects to account for the variety of determinate cognitions, since it can be easily explained by the variety of subconscious impressions within the stream of consciousness itself. The so-called external objects are nothing but the forms or determinations of consciousness itself.[1]

(6) Sixthly, we distinctly apprehend cognitions without external objects in dreams, illusions, hallucinations, recollections, and the like. These are subjective forms of cognitions without any external objects corresponding to them.[2] Hence it is established that the forms or determinations of consciousness are inherent in the cognitions themselves, and not due to the forms of external objects. It cannot be said that the form (ākāra) is neither inherent in the object, nor in the cognition, but arises out of the relationship of the cognition with the object. If we first perceived a formless object separately, then a formless cognition separately, and at last the form of the cognition and the form of the object coming into relationship with each other, then only we would be able to say that the form of the cognition arises out of the relationship of the cognition with its object. But this is not the usual order of our experience. So the form of a cognition cannot be said to be due to the relationship of the cognition with its object. It is admitted by all that dreams and similar states are determinate cognitions independent of external objects. Our waking perceptions are on the same footing with dreams and the like. They also are determinate cognitions independent of external objects.

[1] Anādivāsanāvaicitryaracitajñānavaicitryopapatteḥ kṛtamanumeyenāpi bāhyenārtheneti jñānasyāyamevākara iti siddham, NM., p. 539

[2] Cf. Y.B., iv, 14.

§ 2. *Pārthasārathimiśra's Account*

Pārthasārathimiśra sets forth the following arguments of the Yogācāra against the Sautrāntika realism in *Śāstradīpikā*.

The Yogācāra holds that a cognition apprehends itself. It does not apprehend an external object. If an external object distinct from the apprehending cognition is apprehended by it, we cannot account for the cognitive relation and define the nature of cognizability (vedyatva) of the object.

(1) Objectivity (arthatva) cannot constitute cognizability (vedyatva). An object is not apprehended by a cognition because it is an object. If an object by its very nature is apprehended, every object will be apprehended by every cognition, and there will be nothing to restrict a particular cognition to a particular object. So an object cannot be said to be apprehended because it is a mere object.

Causality (hetutva) may be said to account for the relation of a particular cognition to a particular object. It may be regarded as the restricting condition. An object may be said to be apprehended by that cognition which is produced by it. But the sense-organs also produce a cognition, and should be apprehended by it. But they are regarded as imperceptible. So causality cannot be regarded as the restrictive condition.

Causality together with similarity (sādṛśya) may be said to account for the cognitive relation. The sense-organs produce a cognition, but they are not similar to it. That is the reason why they are not apprehended. But a blue object is the cause of the cognition of " blue ", and is similar to it. So it is apprehended by the cognition. But if causality and similarity be regarded as the grounds of the cognitive relation, the immediately preceding cognition (samanantarapratyaya) will be apprehended by the succeeding cognition, since it gives rise to it and is similar to it. But the immediately preceding cognition is not apprehended by the succeeding cognition.[1]

(2) The Sautrāntika holds that consciousness is common to all cognitions, but the blue form is the special mark of the cognition of " blue " which is similar to a blue object. An object is apprehended by that cognition which is similar to it in its specific form. But the Yogācāra contends that in a serial cognition of " blue " (dhārāvāhikajñāna) the preceding cognition resembles the succeeding cognition in form, and yet the former is not apprehended by the latter. So similarity in form cannot account for the cognitive relation.[2]

(3) The Sautrāntika urges that mere similarity in form does not account for cognizability of an object. He holds that an object is apprehended by a cognition, which imparts its special form to the cognition. A cognition, in itself, is formless ; but when it is related to its object, it assumes its form. But the immediately preceding cognition does not impart any such form as blue or the like to the succeeding cognition. So the former is not apprehended by the latter. If the preceding cognition did impart its form to the succeeding cognition, the cognition of " blue " would always be followed by the cognition of " blue ", and there would be no variety of cognitions such as those of " blue ", " yellow ", and the like in the same stream of consciousness, since similar causes cannot produce dissimilar effects. Hence the Sautrāntika concludes that the variety of cognitions is due to the variety of external objects such as blue, yellow, and the like which are presented to them ; the external objects are objects of cognition.[3] If there were no external objects, there would be a uniform series of similar cognitions. The variety of cognitions cannot be produced by the immediately preceding cognitions. The cognition

[1] SD., p. 148. [2] Ibid., p. 148. [3] SD., pp. 148–9.

of " blue " can give rise to a series of similar cognitions. It cannot give rise to a variety of cognitions. So a variety of objects is inferred from a variety of cognitions.[1]

The Yogācāra urges that an object is not apprehended by a cognition because it produces the cognition and imparts its form to it. There is nothing to prove that an object produces a cognition and imparts its form to it. The variety of cognitions is not due to the variety of external objects, but to the variety of immediately preceding cognitions. Everybody admits that the variety of dream-cognitions is produced by the variety of immediately preceding cognitions or subconscious impressions in the absence of external objects. Similarly, the variety of waking cognitions also is produced by the variety of immediately preceding cognitions or subconscious impressions, and it is needless to assume the existence of external objects.[2] Hence an object cannot be said to be apprehended by a cognition because it produces the cognition and imparts its form to it.

Berkeley also similarly argues : " What reason can induce us to believe the existence of bodies without the mind, from what we perceive, since the very patrons of Matter themselves do not pretend there is any *necessary* connection betwixt them and our ideas ? I say it is granted on all hands—and what happens in dreams, frenzies, and the like, puts it beyond dispute—that it is possible we might be affected with all the ideas we have now, though there were no bodies existing without resembling them. Hence, it is evident the supposition of external bodies is not necessary for the producing our ideas ; since it is granted they are produced sometimes, and might possibly be produced always in the same order we see them in at present, without their concurrence." [3]

[1] Ibid., p. 149. [2] SD., pp. 150–1.
[3] *The Principles of Human Knowledge*, p. 45.

(4) Further, the Yogācāra urges that an object cannot be said to be apprehended if it is accepted or rejected. The cognizability of an object cannot depend upon its pragmatic use. If it were true, the atoms of a blue object and its tastes and other qualities would be apprehended by the cognition of "blue", since these also are accepted when the blue object is accepted. But, in fact, only the blue object is apprehended by the cognition of "blue". If it is urged that only a substance is accepted, and not its qualities such as tastes and the like, then blue colour cannot be apprehended because it cannot be accepted. Further, all actions are the means to the attainment of pleasure; but pleasure, which is a mental state, is incapable of being accepted, and cannot therefore be apprehended. But, as a matter of fact, pleasure is perceived, though it is not accepted. Pleasure is the effect of the acceptance of an agreeable object. When pleasure has already been felt, there is no scope for further acceptance. Hence the cognizability of an object does not depend upon its use in the form of acceptance.

It may be urged that the use of an object is not confined to its acceptance. The use of a name also is included in it. The cognizability of an object depends upon its being denoted by a name. The blue is cognized because it is denoted by the word "blue", which depends upon the cognition of blue. This accounts for the cognition of pleasure. Pleasure is apprehended because it is denoted by the word "pleasure"; and the use of the word "pleasure" depends upon the cognition of pleasure.

The Yogācāra contends that if the use of an object depends upon its being expressed by a name, acceptance also should be regarded as a kind of use, since it is expressed by a name; and a substance being accepted and thus apprehended, its constituent atoms also would be apprehended—which is not the case. Further, the cognizability of an object does not depend upon the use of a name ; on the other hand, the use of a name depends upon the cognition of an object. There can be no use of a mere name independent of the cognition of an object. A name and its object are related to each other as the denoter and the denoted. A name is the sign of the object which is signified by it. It denotes that object the cognition of which is produced by it. Hence the ascertainment of the denotation of a name depends upon the ascertainment of the object of the cognition. If the latter is held to depend upon the former, there will be mutual dependence or arguing in a circle. Thus an object can be expressed by a name only when the object of the corresponding cognition has already been ascertained. Therefore, the cognizability of an object does not depend upon its being expressed by a name or being accepted. An external object can never be apprehended. Hence the Yogacara concludes that the cognizability of an object consists in its identity with the apprehending cognition. An object of cognition must be of the nature of cognition ; it cannot be anything distinct from cognition.[1]

(5) Further, the Yogācāra urges that even if an external object exists, it cannot be apprehended by a cognition. Both the object and its cognition are momentary. The object is the cause. The cognition is the effect. When the cognition has appeared, the object has vanished. Therefore the cognition cannot apprehend the object.

The Sautrāntika replies that coexistence at the same time is not the necessary condition of the relation between the cognition and its object. The cognition and the object need not necessarily coexist at the same time in order that the former may apprehend the latter. An object is apprehended by a cognition to which it imparts its form.

The Yogācāra contends that in the cognition of "blue" the blue form is manifested to consciousness as a present form which cannot be the form of the object which has

[1] SD., pp. 151–2 ; cf. Berkeley : *Esse is percipi.*

disappeared. So the form manifested in the cognition must be the form of the cognition itself which is present. The form of an external ob ect cannot be manifested in an internal cognition. Hence a cognition can never apprehend an external object.[1]

(6) The Sautrāntika holds that an external object is inferred from the cognition produced by it. The cognition is directly perceived. But the object is inferred from the cognition. The Yogācāra asks how an inferrible object can be said to be perceived. The Sautrāntika replies that an object, which directly imparts its form to a cognition without the help of another cognition, is said to be perceived, while an object, which imparts its form to a cognition through the medium of some other cognition, is said to be inferred. Fire is said to be inferred because it produces the cognition of fire through the medium of the cognition of smoke. Perception and inference are the two means of valid knowledge because the object is different from its cognition. If the object were identical with its cognition, perception would be the only means of valid knowledge, since all cognitions are directly perceived. But if the object is not identical with its cognition, its existence can be ascertained from its cognition as its cause. When the object directly imparts its form to the cognition produced by it, it is said to be perceived by the cognition. When the object indirectly imparts its form to its cognition with the help of other cognitions, it is said to be inferred. Hence the validity of a cognition consists in its similarity with its object, which proves the existence of the object.[2] The cognition of silver in a shell is illusory because it is not similar to the shell which produces it. If the similarity of a cognition with its object were not the test of its validity, any cognition would apprehend any object, and prove its reality.

The Yogācāra repeats that there is no necessary

[1] SD., p. 149. [2] SD., pp. 149–150.

connection between an object and a cognition. There is no evidence to show that an object produces a cognition and imprints its form on it. The form manifested to consciousness is the form of the cognition itself. The cognition is directly perceived. It is the only object of perception. The so-called external object is not inferred from its cognition. The variety of cognitions is due to the variety of subconscious impressions. The hypothesis of external objects is gratuitous.

§ 3. *Śrīdhara's Account*

Śrīdhara outlines the following arguments of the Yogācāra against the Sautrāntika realism in *Nyāyakandalī*.

The question is asked what is apprehended by a cognition with a definite form (sākāra jñāna). It is either the form of the object, or that of the cognition itself, or both. Both the forms cannot be apprehended by the cognition, since only one form is always manifested to consciousness such as " this is blue ". Then the cognition apprehends either the form of the object or its own form. The cognition cannot apprehend the form of the object, since at the time when the object exists in itself the cognition does not come into being, and when the cognition comes into being the object disappears. Hence a cognition cannot apprehend a past object as existing at present. The cognition cannot be said to apprehend the moment existing along with the cognition as present, since the moment of time is never held to be the object of apprehension.

Further, if a cognition apprehends the form of its object, why should a particular cognition apprehend a particular object? There is no identity (tādātmya) between the cognition and the object, which may restrict the cognition to the object. If the cognition is produced by the object, then also it cannot be restricted to the object. The sense-organs produce a cognition, but they are never apprehended by the cognition. It may be held that a cognition apprehends that object which imparts its form to the cognition. If similarity of form (tadākāratā) be held to be the restrictive agent, then one moment of blue should apprehend another moment of blue because they possess the same form, which is not the case. It may be argued that a cognition alone can, by its very nature, apprehend an object, and an object can never apprehend another object. In that case, a single cognition of blue would apprehend all moments of blue, since it possesses the blue form in common with all moments of blue.

The Sautrāntika argues that a cognition apprehends that object only which gives rise to the cognition and imparts its form to it. In that case, the sense-organs and the immediately preceding cognition too would be apprehended by the cognition, since the cognition is produced by them also and bears resemblance to them. The cognition apprehends that object which is the appropriate object of a sense-organ, and is thus similar to the sense-organ. And the cognition is of the nature of consciousness, and is thus similar to the preceding cognition. This is not right. These resemblances of the cognition to the sense-organs and the preceding cognition are common to all cognitions. The peculiar property of a cognition is its similarity with the object (viṣayasārupya). The form of blue can exist only in the cognition of blue produced by a blue object. It is the specific property of a cognition that restricts it to a particular object. It is on account of this similarity with the object that it apprehends a particular object. The sense-organs and the preceding cognition which produce the cognition cannot restrict it to a particular object.

This argument is unsubstantial. If a cognition is held to apprehend an object because of its similarity with the object, then in a serial cognition (dhārāvāhikavijñāna) the succeeding cognition will apprehend the preceding cognition which apprehends the same object. The Sautrāntika asserts that it is the blue object which imparts the blue form to the cognition, and this is the reason why the blue object is apprehended by the cognition of blue. But in a serial cognition the blue form of the cognition is not produced by the blue form of the preceding cognition, but by the blue form of the object. This is proved by the method of agreement and the method of difference. The cognition of the blue form exists only when the blue object exists. It does not exist, when the blue object does not exist. On the other hand, a cognition has only the power of bringing about a form of consciousness. It can never produce the form of an object in a cognition.

The Yogācāra contends that no reason is given why only that object is apprehended by a cognition, which imparts its form to it. If the blue object is held to be cognizable by the cognition of blue by its very nature, it is the Law of Nature (svabhāvaniyama) that governs the relation between a cognition and an object, and it is needless to assume that the object imprints its form on the cognition. The act of cognition apprehends the object by its very nature without being invested with the form of the object, even as the act of cutting is related to a tree by its very nature without being invested with the form of the tree. The nature of the cognition and that of the object are such that the cognition apprehends the object, and the object is apprehended by the cognition. The relation of a cognition to an object is due to the nature of the cognition itself, and not to the form of the object.[1] The Yogācāra refutes the Sautrāntika doctrine here with the Nyāya-Vaiśeṣika argument. Therefore it is needless to assume that the form of an external object is indirectly known through the form of its cognition. In fact, the Yogācāra does not recognize the reality of external objects.

[1] NK., pp. 123–4.

He believes in the presentative theory of perception by cutting off external objects. Perception is direct and immediate. It directly apprehends cognitions. It does not apprehend external objects because they do not exist. Thus the Yogācāra's theory of immediate perception is similar to Berkeley's theory.[1] According to both, cognitions or ideas alone are directly perceived.

§ 4. *The Vaibhāṣika Criticism of the Sautrāntika Realism*

It will not be out of place to contrast the Yogācāra theory with the Vaibhāṣika theory of immediate perception. The Yogācāra is a subjectivist. The Vaibhāṣika is a realist. He holds that momentary external objects are real and are directly perceived.

Mādhavācārya gives the Vaibhāṣika criticism of the Sautrāntika doctrine in *Sarvadarśanasaṃgraha*. The Vaibhāṣika contends that it is self-contradictory to assert that sensible objects are inferrible. The Sautrāntika holds that external objects are inferred, and never perceived. But inference is based on an observation of invariable concomitance (vyāpti) between the mark of inference and the inferred property. This invariable concomitance is the ground of inference, and cannot, therefore, be derived from inference. Hence it must be derived from perception. Thus perception is the ultimate ground of inference. But the Sautrāntika denies perception of all objects. If there is no perception of an external object, it can never be an object of inference.[2]

[1] *Principles of Human Knowledge*, p. 38.

[2] "We could never know whether our ideas did copy reality unless we already had a direct apprehension of reality." (*Idealism*, p. 29.) "Indirect or representative knowledge implies direct acquaintance at some point." (*A Study in Realism*, p. 11.) "It is manifest that representation cannot be the whole of knowledge, for no one can know that anything represents anything else without apprehending the representative non-representatively, and without apprehending the connection between representative and original non-representatively." (Ibid., p. 209.)

Besides, the Sautrāntika doctrine contradicts the experience of all mankind. Everybody directly perceives external objects.[1] Therefore the representative theory of perception is wrong. The Vaibhāṣika recognizes the existence of external objects which are directly perceived. He holds to the doctrine of direct realism. He believes in the presentative theory of perception. But he does not recognize the permanence of external objects. They are momentary but directly perceivable.

[1] S.D.S., p. 43.

CHAPTER IV

THE JAINA REALISM

§ 1. *Mallisena's Exposition of the Yogācāra Idealism*

Mallisena, a Jaina philosopher, elaborates some of the arguments of the Yogācāra and criticizes them in *Syādvādamañjarī*. The Yogācāra holds that mere cognition free from the distinction of subject and object is the only reality. An external object does not exist, since its existence cannot be proved. The non-existence of an external object may be proved by a series of dilemmas.

(1) If the external object exists, it is either an aggregate of simple atoms or a complex body with an existence over and above that of the constituent atoms. It cannot be an aggregate of simple atoms, since their existence cannot be proved either by perception or by inference. We never perceive atoms. We perceive only gross objects like jars, posts, and the like. The yogins are said to perceive atoms. But the perception of the yogins being far removed from that of ordinary men like us, it can be accepted on faith only. The existence of atoms cannot be established by inference. Inference depends upon an observation of invariable concomitance of the middle term and the major term. Atoms are to be inferred : they constitute the major term. They are imperceptible. So their invariable concomitance with the middle term or the ground of inference can never be perceived. Thus the existence of atoms can be neither perceived nor inferred.

Then, again, atoms are either eternal or non-eternal. If they are eternal, they produce their effects gradually or all at once. They cannot produce their effects gradually, for, in that case, they slowly change in their nature and are non-eternal, which is contrary to our hypothesis. Nor can they produce their effects all at once, for, in that case, all their causal efficiency being exhausted in one moment, they cease to exist in the next moment inasmuch as existence consists in causal efficiency. If the atoms are non-eternal, they are either momentary or last for a short space of time. If they are momentary, they are either caused or uncaused. If they are uncaused, they exist always or never at all, since they do not depend on any cause. If they are caused, they are caused either by gross matter or by atoms. They are not caused by gross matter, since there is no gross matter at all. The external object is an aggregate of atoms by hypothesis. If momentary atoms are caused by other atoms, these atoms produce their effects while they are existing, or non-existing, or both existing and non-existing. If they produce their effects while they are existing, they do it either at the moment when they come into being or at a subsequent moment. They cannot produce their effects at the first moment, since they are engaged in coming into existence at the time. If they produce their effects while they come into being, then being, acting, and causality are all one. If the mere existence of atoms be the cause of production of their effects, the atoms of colour will be the cause of the atoms of taste, since they do not differ from each other so far as their existence is concerned, and there will be nothing to regulate the production of the atoms of colour from the atoms of colour only, and not from the atoms of taste. If the atoms produce their effects while they are non-existent, they will be perpetually producing their effects except in the moments of their existence, since they will be non-existent all the time except at the time of their existence. The atoms cannot produce their effects while they are both existent and non-existent, since this alternative involves the difficulties of both the alternatives. Therefore the atoms are not momentary.

The atoms cannot exist for more than one moment and last for a short space of time. This alternative involves all the difficulties of the other alternative, viz. the momentariness of atoms. Moreover, these atoms lasting for some time either produce effects or not. If they do not produce any effects, they are non-existent since existence consists in producing effects. If they produce effects, their effects are either existing, or non-existing, or both existing and non-existing. If the effects produced by the atoms are non-existent, the atoms have produced nothing. If the effects are existing, the atoms have produced something that is already existing which leads to infinite regress. If the effects are both existing and non-existing, this position will involve the difficulties of both the alternatives. So the external object cannot be of the nature of atoms.

The external object cannot be a complex body which has an existence over and above that of the constituent atoms. If a single atom cannot be established, a complex body also which is made up of many atoms cannot be established. Without atoms the gross body, which is a mere aggregate of atoms, is a mere name. If the gross body is made up of many atoms, the constituent atoms are in conflict with one another or not. If they are in conflict with one another, they are endowed with contradictory qualities and neutralize one another, and cannot, therefore, constitute a complex body. If they are not in conflict with one another, they contradict our experience. We do find in a single gross object that some parts are at rest while others are in motion, some parts are red while others are not-red, some parts are covered while others are uncovered. Thus the parts of a gross body with contradictory qualities are in conflict with one another.

Further, there are difficulties as to the existence of the whole in its parts. Does the whole exist in the atoms wholly or partially? If the whole exists in each atom wholly, it is exhausted in a single atom and cannot exist in other atoms. Again, if the whole body exists in a single atom entirely, there will be as many bodies as there are atoms. If the whole body exists partially in each atom, the atom will cease to be indivisible. If an atom is made of parts, they are either different or non-different from the atom. If they are different from the atom, they exist in their parts either wholly or partially. If they are non-different from the atom, it cannot be said to have parts. Therefore there is no external object.[1]

(2) Cognition alone is real. It assumes the forms of blue and the like. The so-called external objects are mere forms of cognitions. The cognitions of jars, cloths, and the like are not produced by external objects. They are objectless (nirālambana). They are excited by beginningless, false subconscious impressions (vāsanā). They have no objects like illusions and dreams. There is no object of perception distinct from the percipient cognition. Mere cognition free from the distinction of subject and object is manifested to consciousness. An external object does not exist. A subconscious impression (vāsanā) produces the appearance of an external object.[2] The so-called external object is material, and cannot, therefore, be manifested to consciousness. It has been well said : "If blue is perceived, it cannot to be external. If it is not perceived, it cannot be said to be external."[3] If blue is perceived, it is not independent of perception. If it is not perceived, we have no authority to assert that it is external. Thus whatever is perceived is reduced to a cognition.

Berkeley similarly argues : "I ask whether those supposed originals or external things, of which our ideas are the pictures or representations, be themselves perceivable or no ? If they are, then they are ideas and we

[1] S.V.M., pp. 108–110.

[2] Vāsanāluṭhitaṃ cittamarthābhāsaṃ pravartate, ibid., p. 111.

[3] Yadi saṃvedyate nilaṃ kathaṃ bāhyaṃ taducyate. Nacet saṃvedyate nilaṃ kathaṃ bāhyaṃ taducyate. Ibid., p. 110 (cf. Berkeley); cf. SD., p. 147.

have gained our point; but if you say they are not, I appeal to any one whether it be sense to assert a colour is like something which is invisible; hard or soft, like something which is intangible; and so of the rest."[1]

§ 2. *Mallisena's Criticism of the Yogācāra Idealism*

(1) Cognition is an act (kriyā). It is an act of knowing an object. It must have an object. The act of cognition is directed to an object. It is an act by which an object is known. An objectless cognition is impossible.[2] An illusion is not absolutely objectless. The illusory perception of hairs in the sky presupposes perception of real hairs at some other time and place. Dreams also are recollections of objects actually perceived in the past. Neither illusions nor dreams are absolutely objectless.[3] The object which is apprehended by a cognition is external. The cognition of externality cannot be said to be illusory, since an illusion consists in the apprehension of an object actually perceived in the past and attributed to another object perceived at present owing to defects of the sense-organs and the like. An illusion presupposes perception of an external object at some other time and place. It is not without a substratum in external objects. Therefore it cannot disprove the existence of external objects.[4]

(2) An external object has practical efficiency; it produces effects and fulfils our needs. So the cognition of an external object cannot be said to be illusory. If it is supposed to be illusory in spite of its practical efficiency, the distinction between valid perception and illusory perception will be abolished, and the satisfaction of a person eating real sweetmeat will be the same as that of

[1] *Principles of Human Knowledge*, p. 38.
[2] Nirviṣayāyā jñapteraghaṭanāt, S.V.M., p. 111; cf. Rāmānuja.
[3] Cf. NB., iv, 2, 34; NK., p. 185, and SV., Nirālambanavāda, pp. 107–9, and NR.
[4] S.V.M., p. 111.

a person who dreams of eating sweetmeat.[1] But real sweetmeat is never the same as imaginary sweetmeat. There is a distinction between real things and imaginary things. Real things serve our practical purposes. But imaginary things have absolutely no practical use. Therefore the existence of external objects is proved by their pragmatic value.

(3) The Jaina admits the existence of both a complex body and the atoms which compose it. The existence of atoms is proved by perception and inference. The atoms are perceived, in a way, when their effects, jars and the like, are perceived. And they are directly perceived by yogins. We cannot perceive them owing to their subtlety. The existence of atoms is proved by inference also as causes of complex bodies. Without atoms we cannot explain gross bodies. A gross body is not always made of atoms. It is sometimes made of gross parts. For instance, a cloth is made of threads. The ātman (self) and the ākāśa (ether) are not made of matter at all. Where, however, a gross body is made of atoms, the atoms are somehow combined by such forces as time and other conditions, and produce a gross body. Thus there is real production of a gross body by atoms.

The Jaina admits that a body is one and yet manifold so that in the same body some parts are at rest while others are in motion, and so on. Whether the parts of a body are in conflict with one another or in harmony with one another presents no difficulty to the Jaina who is an advocate of pluralistic realism or relativism (anekāntavāda). The Jaina is not perplexed by the question whether the gross body exists in the constituent atoms wholly or partially. He holds that the complex whole exists in its parts inseparably.[2]

[1] Ibid., p. 111; cf. S.D.S., p. 14; cf. Kant. If the idea of an object proves its existence, the idea of a hundred dollars in my pocket will prove their actual existence in it.

[2] S.V.M., pp. 111–12.

(4) If there is no external object at all, we cannot have a definite perception of blue in the absence of a blue object. The Yogācāra holds that the blue object which we perceive is the form of a cognition. But this contradicts our experience. The object is perceived as external. If the blue object which is perceived were a mere form of cognition, it would be perceived as " *I* am blue " and not as " *this* is blue ".[1]

The Yogācāra may say that there are many forms of cognition, some of which are cognitions of " I ", while others are cognitions of " this ". Both the self and the not-self are really forms of cognition. The Jaina urges that the self and the not-self are not of the same nature. The self is not the same for all. But the not-self or object is the same for all. My self is known as " I " by me. But it is known as " you " by another person. But the object is fixed ; it is perceived as the same by all. It may be said that a blue object is perceived as yellow by a jaundiced person ; so the object is not the same for all. But this is a case of illusion and should not be taken into account. The object is the same for all normal persons.[2] But there is an irreducible plurality of selves.

(5) The Yogācāra may argue that when a person perceives his own self he always perceives it as " I " ; the self is the same for him. So there is no distinction between the self and the not-self or object. There is as much fixity or sameness in the self as in the object. Both of them are forms of cognitions. But Mallisena urges that the consciousness of the self implies the consciousness of something other than the self or not-self. Consciousness of the self implies consciousness of the not-self. The self is a relative term ; it always implies the not-self. The self knows itself as it distinguishes itself from the not-self. Hence the not-self is as much real as the self.[3]

[1] Ibid., p. 112 ; cf. NM., p. 541.
[2] S.V.M., p. 112.
[3] Ibid., p. 112 ; cf. Rāmānuja and Hegel.

(6) The Yogācāra may contend that the distinction of the self and the not-self is within consciousness itself. Cognitions only are real, which are free from all such distinction. The perception of the distinction is illusory. Mallisena urges that this is contrary to our experience. The distinction between the self and the not-self is distinctly perceived. It must, therefore, be real.[1]

The Yogācāra argues that the perception of the distinction is illusory because cognition and its object are not different from each other. Their identity (abheda) is inferred from their invariably simultaneous perception (sahopalambhaniyama). That which is invariably perceived along with some other thing does not differ from it.[2] If A is invariably perceived along with B, A is not different from B. An object is invariably perceived along with its cognition. So the object is not different from its cognition. On the other hand, if an object is not invariably perceived along with some other thing, they differ from each other. Blue and yellow are not invariably perceived together. So they are different from each other.

Mallisena shows that this argument is wrong. Cognition apprehends itself and its object.[3] This is the very nature of cognition. But this does not prove that the object is identical with its cognition. They are distinct entities and have distinct natures. The object is perceived as external; the cognition is perceived as internal. The object is external to the self; it is already there. It is perceived by the self afterwards. The existence of the object is not affected by its cognition by the self. The cognition of the object, on the other hand, is a state of the self; it is within the self and is perceived as

[1] Pratyakṣeṇa pratīto bhedaḥ kathaṃ na vāstavaḥ, ibid., p. 112.

[2] Yadyena saha niyamenopalabhyate tattato na bhidyate, ibid., p. 113.

[3] Jñānaṃ hi svaparasaṃvedanam, ibid., p. 113; *Indian Psychology: Perception*, p. 209.

such.[1] Thus the object cannot be identified with its cognition.

A cognition has always an object. There is no objectless cognition.[2] That is why an object is perceived whenever its cognition is perceived. They are perceived together. But they are not identical with each other. The cognition is perceived as belonging to the self. The object is perceived as other than the self or the not-self. Besides, an object and its cognition are not invariably perceived together. The cognition of the object is not perceived at the time when the object is perceived. The object and its cognition are not perceived at the same moment. Reflective consciousness of the cognition of the object succeeds the perception of the object. So the object cannot be said to be identical with its cognition. Moreover, the difference between the object and its cognition is distinctly perceived. Perception proves their difference. Inference cannot disprove it. The evidence of inference is of no value against the evidence of perception. Perception decides the issue when there is a conflict between perception and inference.[3]

(7) If there is no external object, we cannot have perception of a particular object in a particular place. We perceive one thing in one place, another thing in another place, and so on. We assign different places to different things perceived. This shows that our perceptions are produced by different external objects in different places. The Yogācāra may explain it by the hypothesis of subconscious impressions (vāsanā). We assign a particular place to a particular object not because it exists in that place, but because our subconscious impression determines that it should be assigned to that place and no other. This is no explanation. It is putting the cart before the horse. If an external object exists in a

[1] S.V.M., p. 113. [2] Nirviṣayāyā jñapteraghaṭanāt, ibid., p. 111.
[3] Ibid., p. 113.

particular place we perceive it as such. Our perception refers it to a particular place because it really exists in that place. Localization and projection involved in perception presuppose the existence of an object in a particular place. Vāsanā is the subconscious impression or residuum left in the self by a previous perception. If an external object exists in a particular place, its perception refers it to that place, and subsequently the vāsanā produced by the perception refers it to that place. Thus vāsanās cannot determine the places of objects unless they have already been perceived by cognitions.[1] "There *is* the external world in which things have their definite places ; our anubhava (perception) obeys external facts, and our vāsanās (subconscious impressions) are determined by the anubhava (perception). Thus, the final determining agent in our pramā (valid knowledge) is the external world."[2]

(8) The Yogācāra argues that the variety of perceptions is not due to the variety of external objects but to the variety of vāsanās. Mallisena asks whether vāsanā is the same as cognition or different from it. If vāsanā is identical with cognition, it cannot have variety since cognition has no variety. If vāsanā is different from cognition, it is as good as an external object which is different from cognition. If the Yogācāra insists that vāsanā is different from cognition and yet not identical with an external object, he betrays only his inveterate prejudice against the existence of the object ! Vāsanā is said to produce perception. It is said to be also different from perception. An external object also produces perception, and is distinct from it. So vāsanā differs from an external object only in name. Everybody perceives an external object. The universal experience of mankind bears testimony

[1] Sati hyarthasadbhāve yaddeśo'rthastaddeśo'nubhavastaddeśā ca tatpūrvikā vāsanā. Bāhyārthābhāve tu tasyāḥ kiṃkṛto deśaniyamaḥ. S.V.M., p. 113.

[2] Ibid., A. B. Dhruva's notes, p. 199.

to its existence. To deny the reality of external objects is to fly in the face of it.[1]

(9) A cognition and its object are two distinct realities. They are distinct from each other because they possess opposite qualities. Firstly, cognition is internal while its object is external. Secondly, cognition is posterior to its object while the object is prior to its cognition. The object exists before its cognition is produced by it. It is independent of its cognition. Its existence is not affected by its cognition. Thirdly, cognition springs from the self; the object springs from its own causes in the external world. Fourthly, cognition is luminous while the object is non-luminous. Cognition manifests itself and its object. The object is unconsciousness and is manifested by a cognition.[2] Hence an object can never be regarded as identical with its cognition.[3] The Jaina recognizes the existence of enduring external objects which are manifold in nature.

§ 3. *The Jaina Realism Contrasted with the Sautrāntika Realism*

The Sautrāntika recognizes the reality of external objects independent of their cognitions. The objects are real but momentary. They are reflected in their cognitions with their qualities so that the forms of cognitions correspond to those of external objects. The Jaina, on the other hand, believes not only in the reality of external objects but also in their permanence.

[1] Ibid., pp. 113–14; cf. Reid; Berkeley challenges even "the universal concurrent assent of mankind" to the existence of matter. (*Principles of Human Knowledge*, pp. 71–2.)

[2] S.V.M., p. 114.

[3] Ibid., pp. 108–114; A. B. Dhruva's notes, pp. 193–200; see also Jainatarkavārtika (with Vṛtti), Benares, 1917, pp. 101–126; Pramāṇaparikṣā, Benares, 1914, pp. 57–61; Āptamīmāṃsā, Benares, 1914, pp. 37 ff.; Ratnākarāvatārikā on Pramāṇanayatattvālokālaṅkāra, pp. 27–34 (Benares, Veera Era, 2437).

He recognizes the permanence of the soul and the permanence of external objects. But the Sautrāntika denies both. He admits the reality of momentary cognitions and momentary objects. He is an advocate of the representative theory of perception. But the Jaina advocates the presentative theory of perception. The Sautrāntika is an exponent of indirect realism, while the Jaina is an exponent of direct realism. Thus the Jaina realism is substantially different from the Sautrāntika realism.

§ 4. *The Jaina Criticism of the Sautrāntika Realism*

Mādhavācārya gives the following Jaina criticism of the Sautrāntika realism in *Sarvadarśanasaṃgraha* :—

(1) If both the cognition and the object are momentary, they cannot be related to each other as the percipient (grāhaka) and the perceived (grāhya), since they do not coexist at the same time. The object exists at the first moment while the cognition exists at the second moment. The object does not exist when the cognition exists, and the cognition does not exist when the object exists. Hence there can be no perception of the object by the cognition, which will lead to collapse of all our practical life.[1]

(2) The cognition and the object cannot be said to be synchronous, because in that case they cannot be related to each other as cause and effect inasmuch as causality always involves succession, and consequently the object cannot be regarded as a cause of perception.[2] The two horns of a cow springing up together at the same time are not related to each other as cause and effect. But the Sautrāntika holds that perception is due to four causes: (1) objective data (ālambanapratyaya) ; (2) subconscious impression or suggestion (samanantarapratyaya) ; (3) medium (sahakāripratyaya) ; and (4) the dominant cause or sense-organ (adhipatipratyaya).

[1] Cf. S.V.M., p. 106.
[2] Cf. ibid., p. 106.

(3) It may be argued that the object exists at the first moment and the cognition exists at the second moment ; but though they exist at different moments, the object imprints its form on the cognition and can thus be perceived by it. This argument is wrong. Firstly, the momentary cognition cannot be impressed with the form of the momentary object. The object which exists at the first moment cannot imprint its form on the cognition which exists at the second moment. The momentary object cannot leave its form behind, which may be imprinted on the cognition that has not yet come into being. The form of the object cannot leave the object and pass over to the cognition. Secondly, there can be no variety of determinate cognitions which are due to different objects, because objects cannot imprint their forms upon cognitions. Thirdly, if cognitions are held to assume the forms of objects though the objects do not exist at the time, then formless cognitions also may be held to perceive different objects owing to their different capacities. Thus the assumption of forms of cognitions is groundless.[1]

Mādhavācārya borrows the other arguments from *Prameyakamalamārtaṇḍa*. The Jaina holds that cognitions devoid of the forms of objects perceive external objects with a definite reference to each self. Cognitions are not copies or reflections of external objects. The self is not merely the passive recipient of reflections of objects like a mirror ; it reacts upon external objects, refers the cognitions produced by them to the unity of apperception, and converts them into self-conscious experience.[2]

(4) If the cognition were a mere reflection of the object, it would reflect its spatial qualities also such as proximity

[1] S.D.S., p. 51.

[2] Pratyakṣeṇa viṣayākārarahitameva jñānaṃ pratipuruṣam ahamikayā ghaṭādigrāhakam anubhūyate. Na punardarpaṇādivat pratibimbākrāntam. PKM., p. 26 ; cf. S.D.S., p. 52 ; cf. Kant.

and remoteness. But just as remoteness of a distant object is not reflected in a mirror, so its remoteness cannot be reflected in its cognition which is supposed to be its reflection. And because proximity and remoteness are not reflected in the cognition which is the means of knowing the existence of the object, we cannot speak of external objects as far and near. But we do speak of mountains as farther or nearer. Such perceptions are not contradicted. So they cannot be treated as illusory. It cannot be said that it is the object, which imprints its form on the cognition, that really possesses the qualities of farther and nearer, and they are attributed to the cognition by a fashion of speech though they do not really belong to it, because we never perceive it in the case of a mirror. The reflection of a remote object is not a remote reflection.

(5) Again, if the cognition produced by a blue object assumes its blue form, it must assume its insentience also, and thus itself become insentient. And if it becomes insentient, it loses its self-luminous character. Thus the assumption of the cognition assuming the form of its object will lead to an absurd conclusion.[1]

(6) In order to avoid this difficulty, if it is urged that the cognition does not assume insentience of the object, we can never perceive that the object is insentient. Thus if the cognition is held to reproduce insentience of the object, it will itself become insentient ; and if it is held not to represent insentience of its object, we can never perceive that the object is insentient.[2]

(7) If it is held that insentience of the object is not

[1] S.D.S., p. 52 ; PKM., p. 26.

[2] S.D.S., p. 53 ; PKM., p. 26. Cf. Berkeley : "It may be objected that if extension and figure exist only in the mind, it follows that the mind is extended and figured. . . . I answer, those qualities are *in the mind* only as they are perceived by it—that is, not by way of *mode* or *attribute*, but only by way of *idea*." (*Principles of Human Knowledge*, p. 67.)

perceived, then its blue form also cannot be perceived. If its blue form only is held to be perceived while its insentience is not perceived, the two may be quite distinct from each other, and may not coexist in the same object. It is inexplicable how insentience of the object is not perceived, though its blue form is perceived, for in that case there can be no conformity between them so that both of them together may constitute the character of the object. If an unperceived quality is held to constitute the character of the object, we may as well maintain that when we perceive a post the unperceived universe enters into it and constitutes its character.[1]

(8) The Sautrāntika argues that a particular cognition apprehends a particular object because it is produced by the object, and is impressed with its form. If it were not produced by the object, and were not impressed with its form, it would be equally related to all objects, and would apprehend anything and everything in the universe.

Mallisena contends that a cognition apprehends an object not because it is produced by the object, but because it possesses the capacity (yogyatā) to destroy the veil of ignorance in regard to the particular object and thus reveal it. Even if it is held that a cognition is produced by a particular object, the capacity of the object to produce a particular cognition cannot be denied. And if the Sautrāntika admits a special capacity in the object to produce a cognition, he may as well maintain that a cognition has a special capacity to reveal an object. Then, again, he cannot explain why a particular cognition should be produced by a particular object in the presence of many objects. If it is held that a particular object imparts its form to the cognition produced by it, then the cognition will be invested with a form, and the object will become formless inasmuch as the form will pass over from the object to the cognition. Further, the object is corporeal

[1] S.D.S., p. 53; PKM., pp. 26–7.

while the cognition is incorporeal ; therefore there cannot be any likeness between them. Hence the Jaina concludes that a particular formless cognition apprehends a particular object because it possesses a special capacity or fitness (yogyatā) to reveal the object[1]; and the so-called form of the cognition which is said to be imprinted upon it by the object is nothing but a modification of the cognition of a particular object (arthaviśeṣagrahaṇapariṇāma).[2]

[1] Tanna Yogyatāmantareṇānyadgrahaṇakāraṇaṃ paśyāma iti, S.V.M., p. 108.

[2] S.V.M., pp. 107–8 ; for detailed criticism see PKM., pp. 26–31.

Chapter V

THE SĀṄKHYA-YOGA REALISM

§ 1. *The Sāṅkhya Criticism of Yogācāra Idealism*

The Yogācāra holds that there is no external reality; the world is made up of ideas (vijñāna). But the Sāṅkhya believes in the reality of the external world. Kapila says, " The world is not of the nature of mere ideas because external objects are perceived." [1]

Aniruddha sets forth the following arguments against subjective idealism :—

Firstly, the world is not made up of mere ideas because, if it were so, an external object, e.g. a jar, would be perceived as " *I* am a jar ", and not as " *this* is a jar ". But, as a matter of fact, an external object is always perceived as " this " and not as " I ". It is perceived as of the nature of not-self as distinguished from the self.[2] The self and the not-self are diametrically opposed to each other.

Secondly, the difference in the perceptions of objects cannot be due to the distinctive peculiarities of the subconscious impressions (vāsanāviśeṣa); for if there is no external reality at all, there can be no subconscious impressions of jars and the like, and so there can be no such distinctive peculiarities in subconscious impressions.[3]

Then, again, we may ask what is the cause of the so-called subconscious impression (vāsanā). It is either another subconscious impression or an impression left by a previous perception of something external (bāhyavāsanā). If the former, there will be no determining

[1] Na vijñānamātraṃ bāhyapratīteḥ, SS., i, 42.

[2] Cf. The Jaina.

[3] Cf. Jayanta's criticism.

condition of the perception of different objects, and there will be perception of everything at all times. If the latter, there does exist something other than cognitions, and this very object is an external reality.

Thirdly, the Yogācāra argues that the external reality cannot verily exist, because the whole which is distinct from its parts does not exist. In other words, the parts and the whole are one because they are perceived as one. The whole is a mere aggregate of parts; it has no existence over and above that of the parts ; the whole is identical with its parts.

Aniruddha refutes this argument. He points out that the whole is distinct from its parts. Sometimes the whole moves when a part moves ; but sometimes the whole does not move when a small part moves. For example, when a branch is shaken by a storm, the whole tree moves ; but when it is touched by a mild wind, the whole tree does not move. Since the whole does not move while its parts move, opposite properties are attributed to the whole and its parts. Therefore the whole is not identical with its parts. In like manner, we find that a part is red but the whole is not-red ; a part is covered but the whole is not-covered ; a part is confined to a place but the whole is not confined to that place, and so forth. From these it is quite clear that the whole is distinct from the parts and has an existence over and above that of the parts.

Fourthly, even if we grant that the whole does not exist as distinct from its parts and endued with properties contradictory to those of its parts, still the existence of external objects cannot be denied, because it is an aggregate of atoms, that is apprehended as extensive.

But the Yogācāra urges that the whole is the effect, and the parts are the cause. The existence of atoms is inferred from that of the whole which is their effect. If the whole does not exist, we cannot infer the existence of atoms. Since atoms are subtile and supersensible, and cannot give any additional property (atiśaya) to their aggregate, the perception of the aggregate as extensive is erroneous. Hence the world is nothing but a system of ideas.

Aniruddha declares that this argument is wrong because the whole is different from its parts.[1] And because the two are different from each other, the whole does not move while the parts move. But the whole certainly moves where a large number of parts move. We can reconcile the other contradictory attributes of the whole and the parts, such as red and not-red, etc., in the same way. Thus the existence of the external reality is proved.[2]

Vijñānabhikṣu puts the case of the Yogācāra idealist thus: There is no existence of any being other than ideas. Therefore, bondage also is a mere idea like an object apprehended in a dream. But Vijñānabhikṣu asserts that not only ideas are real but also external objects are real inasmuch as they are proved by perception.[3]

§ 2. *The Yoga Exposition of Yogācāra Idealism—The Epistemological Arguments for Subjective Idealism*

Vyāsa explains the position of the Yogācāra and criticizes it in his commentary on Yogasūtras. The Yogācāra argues : There is no object existing apart from its cognition. But there are cognitions existing apart from their corresponding objects, such as those that are imagined in dreams and similar states.[4] The so-called external objects are mere imagination of the mind. They are mental constructs like objects of dreams with no existence in reality.[5]

[1] Cf. Nyāya-Vaiśeṣika.

[2] SSV., i, 42. See Richard Garbe and Nanda Lal Sinha's E.T. of Sāṅkhyavṛtti.

[3] SPB., i, 41–2.

[4] Nāstyartho vijñānavisahacaro'sti tu jñānamarthavisahacaraṃ svapnādau kalpitam, Y.B. on Y.S., iv, 14, p. 293.

[5] Jñānaparikalpanāmātraṃ vastu svapnaviṣayopamaṃ na paramārthato'asti, Y.B. on Y.S., iv, 14, p. 294.

Vācaspati elaborates this argument of the subjective idealist. An unconscious object cannot manifest itself; it is not self-luminous like a cognition; it always requires a cognition to manifest it. Thus an object does not exist which is not coexistent with a cognition. Coexistence means relation. The absence of coexistence means the absence of relation. There is no object which is not coexistent with a cognition. The object which is not related to a cognition deserves to be treated as non-existent. If an object does not come into relationship with a cognition, it is as good as non-existent.[1] Not to be perceived is not to exist. This is the same as the dictum of Berkeley: The *esse* is *percipi*—to exist is to be perceived.

The cognition, however, exists without being coexistent with the object, since it is self-luminous and apprehends itself, and does not depend upon the unconscious object for its being used in practical life. A cognition is self-luminous; it apprehends itself. But an object is not self-luminous; it does not apprehend itself but requires a cognition to apprehend it. A cognition does not stand in need of an unconscious object. But an object cannot be used unless it is apprehended by a cognition; an unknown object is of no use in practice. Thus a cognition can exist without the corresponding object, but an object can never exist without the corresponding cognition.

This argument of the Yogācāra clearly anticipates the main argument of Berkeley. He also argues that to exist is to be perceived, and what is perceived is an idea of the mind. He says: "The absolute existence of unthinking things without any relation to their being perceived, is perfectly unintelligible. Their *esse* is *percipi*; nor is it possible they should have any existence out of the

[1] Vijñānasambandhī nāstitivyavahārayogyaḥ, T.V. on Y.S., iv, 14, p. 293.

minds or thinking things which perceive them."[1] "Can there be a nicer strain of abstraction than to distinguish the *existence* of sensible objects from their *being perceived*, so as to conceive them existing unperceived? Light and colours, heat and cold, extension and figures—in a word the things we see and feel—what are they but so many sensations, notions, ideas, or impressions on the sense?"[2] So "all the choir of heaven and furniture of the earth, in a word all those bodies which compose the mighty frame of the world, have not any subsistence without a mind—that their *being* is *to be perceived or known*".[3]

Vācaspati points out that the above argument of the Yogācāra implies the rules of knowability (vedyatva) and invariably simultaneous perception (sahopalambha).

(1) The rule of knowability means this. That which is known by a cognition does not differ from it in the same way as cognition does not differ from cognition of itself. The object is known by an act of cognition. So it does not differ from it. The known object is identical with the act of knowledge, even as a cognition is identical with its own cognition.[4]

The physical elements and their phenomena are known by an act of knowledge. But they do not seem to be ideas of the mind. So they seem to contradict the above rule that whatever is known by an act of knowledge does not differ from it. But the Yogācāra argues that the physical elements which are known are no exception to the rule. They also do not differ from the cognitions by which they are apprehended.

The object which is known by an act of knowledge must be identical with it. It is pervaded by identity which contradicts the difference to be denied. It brings to consciousness the identity between itself and the cognition, which pervades it, and thus disproves their difference

[1] *Principles of Human Knowledge*, p. 34. [2] Ibid., pp. 35–6.
[3] Ibid., p. 36. [4] T.V. on Y.S., iv, 14, p. 293.

which contradicts it. The object can never be known by a cognition if it differs from it. Identity (abheda) is the condition of knowability.[1]

Berkeley also resorts to a similar argument in refuting Descartes and Locke's representative theory of perception according to which ideas are copies of external objects. Berkeley does not admit the reality of external objects. He argues that if ideas are like the so-called external objects, the latter also must be ideas. The objects must be identical in nature with ideas. He says : "But, say you, though the ideas themselves do not exist without the mind, yet there may be things like them, whereof they are copies or resemblances, which things exist without the mind in an unthinking substance. I answer, an idea can be nothing but an idea ; a colour or figure can be like nothing but another colour or figure. If we look but never so little into our own thoughts, we shall find it impossible for us to conceive a likeness except only between our ideas."[2] Again he says, "An idea can be like nothing but another idea · and consequently neither they nor their arthetypes can exist in an unperceiving substance."[3] Thus there is an identity of nature between cognitions and the objects apprehended by them.

(2) The Yogācāra explains the rule of invariably simultaneous perception thus : That which is always perceived with something else invariably, does not differ from it, just as one moon does not differ from another moon in the illusory perception of the double moon. And an object is invariably perceived together with the act of knowledge. So it does not differ from it. The objects which are different from each other are not invariably perceived along with each other. The two stars called Aśvinī are not invariably perceived together. When one is hidden by a cloud the other is perceived.

[1] T.V. on Y.S., iv, 14, p. 293.

[2] *Principles of Human Knowledge*, p. 38.

[3] Ibid., p. 39.

So they are not identical with each other. But an object is never perceived apart from the act of perception. So the perceptible object is identical with the perception of it : the object and its cognition are identical with each other.[1]

Berkeley also similarly argues : " As it is impossible for me to see or feel anything without an actual sensation of that thing, so is it impossible for me to conceive in my thoughts any sensible thing or object distinct from the sensation or perception of it. In truth, the object and the sensation are the same thing and cannot therefore be abstracted from each other." [2]

(3) But if the object is not different from its cognition how is it that it looks as if it were different from it ? The Yogācāra answers that the apparently external object is a construction of imagination ; it is a fabrication of the mind.[3] The known object is a creation of the act of knowing. Knowledge is creation. It is not discovery.

§ 3. *The Yoga Criticism of the Yogācāra Idealism—Refutation of the Epistemological Arguments*

The subjective idealism of the Yogācāra has been severely criticized by Vyāsa, Vācaspatimiśra and Vijñānabhikṣu.

(1) Vyāsa appeals to experience which bears a clear testimony to the reality of the external world. The external reality is presented to consciousness as " this " by its own presentative power. It is the given. It is an object of perception which is valid. The Yogācāras deny the

[1] Yad yena niyatasahopalambhaṃ tat tato na bhidyate. . . . Niyatasahopalambhascārtho jñānena. T.V. on Y.S. iv, 14, p. 293 ; cf. Berkeley also.

[2] *Principles of Human Knowledge*, p. 36.

[3] T.V., iv, 14. But the modern realist gives an ontological status even to images. Images must have the same status as percepts have. If the latter are objects the former are too. " Images have the same status as perceived or remembered things. They are apprehended things confronting the mind, and not varieties of mental operations. They are given to the mind, like anything else that it discovers." (*A Study in Realism*, p. 64.)

reality of the external world on the strength of imagination which is invalid. Imagination cannot override the authority of perception.[1] The external object is real and independent of cognition ; it is presented to the cognition by its own power.[2] The Yogācāras first suppose that external objects are presented to consciousness because they are mere construction of imagination ; then they deny the reality of the external world on the strength of such an imaginary hypothesis. So they cannot be trusted.[3]

Vijñānabhikṣu explains Vyāsa's criticism thus: All perceptible objects are presented to consciousness through their intercourse with the sense-organs by their own power. They are perceived by their own power of perceptibility. They are objects of direct perception. They cannot be likened to objects of dream-cognitions which owe their existence to some disorders of the body or the mind. The objects of perception are not contradicted like those of dream-cognitions. So the existence of external objects apprehended by valid perception can never be denied on the strength of invalid dream-cognitions. The Yogācāras who deny the reality of the external world cannot be trusted, since, on their own hypothesis, their ideas have no counterparts in reality, and their words are not expressions of true ideas and do not denote real objects. Thus by denying the reality of the external world the Yogācāras deny the truth of their own statements.[4]

Vācaspati explains Vyāsa's criticism thus : The object is the cause of its cognition. If the object does not exist, its cognition cannot arise. The object presents itself to its own cognition. Whatever is manifested to consciousness as "this" is real and existent, and is presented to

[1] Na ca pratyakṣamāhātmyaṃ vikalpamātreṇa apodyate, T.V., iv, 14, p. 295. Cf. Laird : "When I perceive, let us say, a coloured patch, I am directly and immediately acquainted with this patch, and no process of argument can overthrow this palpable certainty." (*A Study in Realism*, p. 17.) [2] Pratyupasthitam idaṃ svamāhātmyena vastu, Y.B., iv, 14, p. 294.
[3] Y.B., iv, 14, p. 294. [4] Yogavārtika, iv, 14.

consciousness by its own power. The object which is present and apprehended by a cognition can never be regarded as mere fabrication of imagination. The external object produces its cognition by its own power of perceptibility [1]; and this is the reason why the cognition apprehends it. Such a real object which exists in itself and is the cause of its presentation to consciousness can never be done away with by the unauthoritative force of imagination which is absolutely invalid.[2]

May Sinclair states the position of the realist thus : " No act of mere knowing, even if it were absolute—and knowing is purely relative to the known and the knower—no act of knowing could confer reality upon its object. Things are not there because we know them ; we know them because they are there." [3] " In no sense are things there because we perceive them ; we perceive them because they are there and they owe nothing to our perceiving." [4] Thus an object is known by an act of cognition, not because it is identical with the cognition, but is different from it.

(2) Vācaspati argues that knowability (vedyatva) of an object by an act of cognition is not pervaded by identity between the object and the cognition, and therefore it cannot negate the difference between them. An object is not known by a cognition because it is identical with the cognition. Therefore its knowability cannot disprove its difference from the cognition. In fact, knowledge of an object by a cognition presupposes a difference between them.[5]

May Sinclair states the realist's position thus : " If a thing is known, *ipso facto* it is something more than the act, or state of knowing. Idealism assumes that this act

[1] Arthena svakīyayā grāhyaśaktyā vijñānam ajani, T.V., iv, 14, p. 294.
[2] Ibid., p. 294.
[3] *The New Idealism*, p. 17.
[4] Ibid., p. 19.
[5] Vedyatvasya abhedavyāpyatvābhāvāt kuto bhedapratipakṣatvam, T.V., iv, 14, p. 295.

or state is simpler than it really is. Knowing involves at least two terms and a relation, whether you take the subject and object as your terms and consciousness as your relation, or consciousness and the object of consciousness, when your relation will be an unknown *x*. In either case the object will stand on its own feet as a separate and independent entity, which is all that realism wants." [1] "According to realists, the process of knowledge always implies that the mind is confronted with an object, and always implies that we are never under any conceivable circumstances identical with that object. Even when we apprehend our own experiences, the process of apprehension cannot be identical with the experience which is apprehended." [2] Therefore the cognitive relation is not the same as identity.

Vācaspati points out that the reasons advanced by the Yogācāra for the denial of external reality, viz. knowability (vedyatva) and invariably simultaneous perception (sahopalambha) are not conclusive, since the application of the method of difference here is doubtful, or rather impossible.[3]

(3) The rule of invariably simultaneous perception (sahopalambhaniyama) also cannot prove the identity of the object and its cognition. The Yogācāra applies the method of agreement here. The cognition of an object and the knowledge of the cognition always go together. So the object is identical with its cognition. Or wherever there is presentation of an object there is also presentation of its cognition ; every case of the presentation of an object is a case of the presentation of its cognition. Hence the object is identical with its cognition. This conclusion is arrived at by the method of agreement.

Dr. Das Gupta puts it thus : "Wherever there is

[1] *The New Idealism*, p. 16. [2] *A Study in Realism*, p. 11.

[3] Sahopalambhaniyamaśca vedyatvaṃ ca hetū sandigdhavyatirekatayā anaikāntikau, T.V., iv, 14, p. 294.

knowledge there is external reality, or rather every case of knowledge agrees with or is the same as every case of the presence of external reality, so knowledge is the cause of the presence of the external reality, i.e. the external world depends for its reality on our knowledge or ideas and owes its origin or appearance as such to them. But Vācaspati says that this application of the method of agreement is not certain, for it cannot be corroborated by the method of difference. For the statement that every case of absence of knowledge is also a case of absence of external reality cannot be proved, i.e. we cannot prove that the external reality does not exist when we have no knowledge of it." [1]

The self can never overstep the bounds of knowledge and know the reality which exists unknown by it. It can know the reality as it is known by it, or as it is related to its knowledge. It can never know the reality as it is unknown by it, or as it is unrelated to its knowledge. Therefore the method of difference cannot be applied here to corroborate the conclusion reached by the method of agreement.[2]

[1] *Yoga as Philosophy and Religion*, pp. 33–4.

[2] Vedyatvasya abhedavyāpyatvābhāvāt kuto bhedapratipakṣatvam, T.V., iv, 14, p. 295. This argument of Vācaspati anticipates the ego-centric predicament discovered by the new realist. " The ' ego-centric predicament ' consists in the impossibility of finding anything that is not known. . . . It is impossible to eliminate the knower without interrupting observation ; hence the peculiar difficulty of discovering what characters, if any, things possess when not known. When this situation is formulated as a proposition concerning things, the result is either the redundant inference that all known things are known, or the false inference that all things are known. . . . The falsity of the inference, in the case of the latter proposition, lies in its being a use of the method of agreement unsupported by the method of difference. It is impossible to argue from the fact that everything one finds is known, to the conclusion that knowing is a universal condition of being, because it is impossible to find non-things which are not known. The use of the method of agreement without negative cases is a fallacy." (*The New Realism*, pp. 11–12; f. Perry, *Present Philosophical Tendencies*, pp. 129–132.)

Hence the invariably simultaneous perception of the object and its cognition (sahopalambhaniyama) is no proof of their identity. It is wrong to argue that the object and its cognition are identical with each other because they are invariably presented together. For the method of agreement cannot by itself conclusively prove identity without the help of the method of difference which is not applicable here. The object of knowledge and the act of knowledge may be co-ordinate existents ; they may be both real and existing along with each other ; and they may be invariably perceived together on account of their very nature (svabhāva), or owing to obstruction from some cause. The knowable object and the act of knowledge are related to each other as cause and effect, and consequently they are invariably presented together. They are always perceived along with each other not because they are identical with each other.[1]

Thus both the arguments of the Yogācāra are fallacious. Neither knowability of the object (vedyatva) nor invariably simultaneous perception of the object and the act of knowledge (sahopalambha) can prove the identity of the object with its cognition.

(4) Further, the power of perception cannot be done away with by mere imagination. The certainty of perception which gives us a direct and immediate knowledge of external objects can never be rejected on the strength of imagination or logical abstraction.[2]

(5) Further, externality (bāhyatva) and extension (sthūlatva), the attributes of the material objects and phenomena which are apprehended by cognitions, can never exist in them. Extension means pervading many

[1] Sahopalambhaniyamaśca vijñānasthaulyayoḥ satorapi svabhāvādvā kutaścit pratibandhādvā upapatsyete, T.V., iv, 14, p. 295.

[2] Na ca pratyakṣamāhātmyaṃ vikalpamātreṇa apodyate. T.V., iv, 14, p. 295. Cf. Laird : " Realists maintain that perception is the discovery of a world independent of the perceiver. Now, whatever is discovered is given or found." (*A Study in Realism*, p. 30.)

portions of space. Externality means being related to separate space. It means mutual exclusiveness in space or coexistence in space. Now, a single cognition can never possess extension and externality, since it cannot extend into many portions of space, and yet coexist separately in different points of space. A cognition cannot coexist with other cognitions in space and extend into many points of space at one and the same time. The two contradictory qualities of being confined to a particular point of space and not being confined to that point of space cannot exist in one and the same cognition. If it were possible the whole universe would be one existing in a single cognition. Thus a single cognition cannot possess extension and externality. Nor can a plurality of cognitions possess these qualities, since they are very subtle, and unconscious of the existence of each other, but are conscious of their own sphere of operation. The Yogācāra holds that cognitions are discrete and momentary ; they cannot coexist with each other ; they are self-luminous, but they are not aware of the existence of other cognitions. They cannot, therefore, possess the qualities of extension and externality.[1] These are qualities of physical objects existing independently of cognitions.

It cannot be said that imagination creates and apprehends external objects possessing the qualities of extension and externality, since imagination does not come in contact with external objects and apprehend them. Moreover, the external objects presented to consciousness through perception are clear, distinct, and vivid ; they can never be creations of imagination which are vague and indistinct. Imagination can never construct the given element in knowledge. It can never negate the existence of the external reality which is actually perceived.[2]

[1] T.V., iv, 14, pp. 294–5.

[2] Na ca vikalpagocarābhilāpaḥ saṃsargābhāvāt viśadapratibhāsatvāt ca, T.V., iv, 14, p. 295.

It cannot be said that, because extension and externality cannot exist either in external objects or in our cognitions, therefore they should be considered to be false. For the false is not inseparable from its cognition. If it were inseparable from its cognition, the cognition would become as false as the false itself.[1] If the notions of extension and externality are considered to be false, all ideas of external objects would be equally false.

(6) Further, Patañjali says: "Though the object remains the same, the ideas about it may be different. So their ways of being are different."[2]

Vyāsa explains the above argument thus: One and the same object is common to many minds. It is not the "private property" of any individual mind. It is the "public property" of all minds. It is the common object of observation of all minds; it is equally accessible to them all. So it cannot be regarded as creation of imagination. It is neither imagined by one mind nor imagined by many minds. But it exists in itself and for itself *independently* of all minds. The object has extra-mental existence. It is not the subjective creation of fancy.[3] Even though the object remains the same it excites different feelings in different persons. It excites the feeling of pleasure on account of merit (dharma). It excites the feeling of pain on account of demerit (adharma). It excites the feeling of delusion on account of nescience (avidyā). It excites

[1] Ibid., p. 295.

[2] Vastusāmye cittabhedāt tayoḥ vibhaktaḥ panthāḥ, Y.S., iv, 15.

[3] Bahucittālambanībhūtaṃ ekaṃ vastu sādhāraṇaṃ, tat khalu naikacittaparikalpitaṃ, nāpyanekacittaparikalpitaṃ, kintu svapratiṣṭham, Y.B., iv, 15, p. 297; cf. Perry. Vijñānabhikṣu says that the object is neither the mental construct of one mind nor the mental construct of many minds; but it exists in itself and for itself independently of all minds. The object cannot be the creation of a single mind, for in that case the same object would not be able to excite different feelings in different minds. Nor can it be the creation of many minds for the imagination of one mind cannot excite similar imagination in other minds. Y.V., iv, 15, p. 279.

the feeling of indifference on account of right knowledge (samyak darśana). Since one and the same object excites different feelings in different persons, it cannot be regarded as creation of anybody's imagination because one's imaginary ideas cannot produce similar ideas in other minds. Thus the object exists in itself independent of all minds.[1]

The object and its cognition are different from each other; the object is apprehended (grāhya) and the cognition is the apprehending mental mode (grahaṇa); both of them are real and existent and can never be confused with each other.[2] Similarly Vijñānabhikṣu says that both the object and the mind are said to be self-existent (svatantra), since they are independent of each other.[3]

Vācaspati argues that of two things, if one remains the same and the other differs, they must be absolutely different from each other. The same object is perceived by Caitra, Devadatta, Viṣṇumitra and Maitra. Here though the object remains the same, the ideas of different persons differ from one another. So the object must be different from ideas.[4] The identity of the object is ascertained by different persons perceiving it by comparing notes, though their ideas of the same object differ from each other. If the same woman is loved, hated, ignored, and treated with indifference by different persons, they

[1] Cf. A. C. Ewing: "I do not see how any idealism can possibly stand which identifies the spatial coloured objects we usually regard as physical with feelings. They are not in the least like feelings (or acts of mind of any sort). Whatever they are, these objects are not emotions, pleasures or pains, or anything remotely resembling these, and our feelings and acts of mind are not coloured or round." (*Idealism*, p. 392.)

[2] Tasmāt vastujñānayorgrāhyagrahaṇabhedabhinnayorvibhaktaḥ panthāḥ. Nānayoḥ saṅkaragandhao'pi asti. Y.B., iv, 15, p. 297.

[3] Y.V., iv, 16, p. 281.

[4] Yannānātve yasyaikatvaṃ tat tato' tyantyaṃ bhidyate. . . . Jñānanānātve' pi cārtho na bhidyate iti bhavati vijñānebhyo'nyaḥ. T.V., iv, 15, p. 297.

can always compare notes and recognize the identity of the object of their different feelings. A lovely woman excites the feeling of pleasure in the beloved person, the feeling of pain in the co-wives, and the feeling of delusion in the disappointed person. If the object were the product of an individual's imagination, all persons would have the idea of blue when one person had the idea of blue.[1]

The Yogācāra may ask how one and the same object becomes the cause of different feelings of pleasure, pain, delusion, and indifference. It is not proper that the cause remaining the same, the effects should be different. How can the same cause produce diversity of effects? The Sāṅkhya can easily account for it. He regards an external object as made up of three ultimate reals, sattva (essence), rajas (energy), and tamas (inertia) which are ever changing in their nature. But the same three-fold object does not produce the three-fold feeling of pleasure, pain, and delusion in all persons. The object comes into relationship with the mind with the co-operation of the exciting causes, viz. merit, demerit, etc., and produces different feelings in different minds. Sattva (essence) in co-operation with rajas (energy) produces the feeling of pleasure when there is merit in the knower. Sattva free from rajas produces the feeling of indifference when there is right knowledge in the person. These exciting causes, merit, demerit, nescience, and right knowledge do not exist, all of them, in all persons everywhere. It is only one of them that exists in a person somewhere at some time. This is the reason why the same object excites different feelings in different persons.[2] Feelings are partly due to subjective conditions and partly to objective conditions.

Bhojadeva argues that the object cannot be a creation of the mind, since the same object excites different feelings

[1] T.V., iv, 15, p. 297.
[2] T.V., iv, 15, pp. 297–8.

in different minds.[1] If the object were the creation of an individual mind, it would appear to consciousness as uniform, and it would cease to exist when that mind would attend to some other object, and it would never be perceived by any other mind. But, as a matter of fact, an object is observed by many minds, and so it cannot be regarded as the product of an individual mind.[2] If it were created by many minds at the same time, it would differ from the creation of an individual mind. If the diversity of effects were not produced by the diversity of causes, the universe would be uniform or causeless. If the same effect followed from different causes, the whole universe resulting from many causes would be uniform, or it would be independent of causes, and thus would be uncaused. Why does not the mind, then, made up of sattva (purity), rajas (energy), and tamas (inertia) produce in the same person the feelings of pleasure, pain, and delusion at the same time ? The Sāṅkhya replies that both the object and the mind (citta) are made up of three ultimate reals, viz. sattva, rajas, and tamas ; and in the perception of objects by the mind, merit and demerit are accessory causes, and owing to their manifestation and suppression the mind perceives the same object in different ways. Thus in the presence of a beautiful woman the mind of an amorous person feels pleasure owing to merit in co-operation with sattva ; the mind of a co-wife feels pain owing to demerit in co-operation with rajas ; and the mind of an angry co-wife feels delusion owing to intense demerit in co-operation with tamas. Hence the cognizable object is independent of its cognition, and consequently the cognizable object and the cognition, being contradictory in their nature, cannot be related to each other as cause and effect. Thus it is possible that though the cause is the same, the effects may be different ;

[1] Bhojavṛtti on Y.S., iv, 15, p. 72 (Calcutta, 1903).
[2] Cf. Y.S., iv, 16, and Y.B., p. 299.

though the object remains the same, the feelings produced by it may differ. Hence it is established that the object is independent of cognitions and feelings excited by them.[1] Kumārila and Jayanta explain the fact by appealing to vāsanā.

Dr. Rajendra Lal Mitra observes : " The question discussed in the preceding aphorism [2] raises a doubt as to whether perception is due to objects or to the cognitive power (citta). It cannot be said that objects produce perception, for in that case a given object would always and everywhere produce the same sensation, as a given cause cannot produce dissimilar effects. A handsome woman should be a handsome woman to all beholders, without a distinction. In the world this is, however, not the case. A woman produces dissimilar feelings in different beholders, and she, as the object, cannot therefore be said to be the cause of perception. On the other hand, the thinking principle (citta) cannot be the cause, for if you accept it to be one in all persons, it, as a cause, cannot produce different effects ; and if you accept it to be different in different individuals, dissimilar causes would lead to one uniform result, which is impossible. The solution offered is that thinking principle and object are different, but inasmuch as both are governed by the three qualities (guṇa), the prevalence of a particular quality at a particular time in the thinking principle produces a difference in the perception of an object. The ' diversity of the thinking principle ' (cittabheda) in the text implies a diversity in its condition as regards the state of the qualities working within it." [3]

§ 4. *The Yoga Criticism of a Type of Buddhist Realism*

Some Buddhists hold that the objects are real and external to minds, but they come into existence along with

[1] Bhojavṛtti on Y.S., iv, 15, pp. 71–2. [2] Y.S., iv, 15.
[3] *The Yoga Aphorisms of Patanjali* (Bib. Ind.), Calcutta. 1883, p. 184.

our cognitions, since they are experienced like pleasure and pain.[1] They are not subjective idealists. The external objects, according to them, have no existence either in the past or in the future, but have only a momentary existence in the present moment. They come into existence when we perceive them, and they cease to exist when we cease to perceive them. Dr. Das Gupta puts it thus : "The moment I have an idea of a thing, the thing rises into existence and may be said to exist only for that moment and as soon as the idea disappears the object also vanishes, for when it cannot be presented to me in the form of ideas it can be said to exist in no sense."[2]

Vācaspati explains the above Buddhist position thus : Let the object be different from its cognition. Still the object being unintelligent cannot be apprehended without a cognition. It is manifested by a cognition. So it cannot be said to exist at a time when it is not the object of immediate knowledge.[3]

Vyāsa urges that this conception of an object coming into existence with a cognition contradicts the fact that the object is common to all persons, and thus denies the existence of the object in the past and in the future.[4]

Vācaspati says that an object is certainly common to all minds. It continues to be apprehended by persons for a succession of many moments though it is changing in its nature.[5] This clearly shows that it does not come into being along with its apprehending cognition. If the object comes into being with a cognition, its appearance and disappearance must depend upon cognitions.

[1] Jñānasahabhūrevārtho bhogyatvāt sukhādivat, Y.B., iv, 16, p. 298.

[2] *Yoga as Philosophy and Religion*, 1924, p. 36.

[3] T.V., iv, 16, p. 298 ; see also Y.V., p. 280.

[4] Y.B., iv, 15, p. 298.

[5] Vastu khalu sarvacittasādhāraṇam anekakṣaṇaparamparohyamānaṃ pariṇāmātmakam anubhūyate laukikaparīkṣakaiḥ, T.V., iv, 16, p. 298.

But this is not the case. Further, if an object owed its existence to a cognition, it would never be presented to consciousness as "this" (idam). But, as a matter of fact, an object is always perceived as "this"; and it cannot, therefore, owe its existence to a cognition.[1]

Patañjali says: "An object does not depend on a particular mind; for what will happen to it when it is not apprehended by that mind?"[2] Vyāsa explains the aphorism thus: If the object depends on a particular mind, what will be the fate of the object when that mind will attend to some other object, or restrain all its functions, since at that time it will neither be apprehended by that mind nor by any other mind. So it will cease to exist at that time. And if it thus ceases to exist, how can it again come into existence when the attention of the individual is again directed towards it?[3] Further, all parts of an object are not apprehended by the mind at the same time. So those parts which are not apprehended would not exist. Thus when the front side of an object is apprehended, its back side which is not apprehended at the time cannot be said to exist. And if the back side does not exist, the front side also may as well be said not to exist because they are held to be coexistent with each other. Thus the whole object would be regarded as non-existent. Hence Vyāsa concludes that the external reality is independent of all minds, and is the common object of observation of all persons[4]; there are different minds in different persons; and all the experiences of the self arise from the relation of the mind with the external world.[5]

[1] Ibid., pp. 298–9.

[2] Na caikacittatantraṃ vastu tadapramāṇakaṃ tadā kiṃ syāt, Y.S., iv, 16, p. 299.

[3] Cf. Bhojavṛtti, p. 72.

[4] Svatantraḥ arthaḥ sarvapuruṣasādhāraṇaḥ, Y.B., iv, 16, p. 300.

[5] Y.B., iv, 16, pp. 299–300; Y.V., iv, 16, pp. 280–1.

The Reality of the Past and the Future

Vyāsa criticizes another doctrine of the Buddhist that neither the past nor the future exists but only the momentary present. He says : " The future is the manifestation which is to be. The past is the manifestation which has been experienced. The present is that which is in active operation. It is this three-fold substance which is the object of knowledge. If it did not exist in reality, there would not exist the knowledge of it. How could there be knowledge in the absence of anything that might be known ? For this reason the past and the future exist in reality." [1]

Vācaspati argues that knowledge manifests an object to consciousness. It cannot exist in the absence of the object. The yogin has knowledge of the past, the present, and the future at a single glance of intuition. Men, like ourselves also, have knowledge of the past in recollection, of the present in perception, and of the future in expectation and inference. But neither our knowledge nor that of the yogin can be produced in the absence of the corresponding object. But such knowledge is produced. For this reason, the knowledge of a person who feels that the past and the future exist along with the present in a general way, is said to be a reason for the existence of the object itself.[2] Thus the past and the future exist as much as the present. The present is patent. The past is latent. And the future is sublatent. The past and the future exist in the present.[3]

[1] Y.B., iv, 12, p. 289; Rama Prasada's E.T. (S.B.H.), p. 275; Das Gupta, *Yoga as Philosophy and Religion*, p. 31.

[2] T.V., iv, 12, p. 289.

[3] B. N. Seal, *The Positive Sciences of the Ancient Hindus*, p. 17.

Chapter VI

THE MĪMĀṂSAKA REALISM

§ 1. *Śavara's Criticism of Vijñānavāda*

(1) The Yogācāra argues that all waking cognitions are without a real substratum in the external world, like dream-cognitions, because they are cognitions. Cognitions have no substratum in external objects in the dream-state. Waking cognitions of a pillar, a wall, and the like are cognitions ; hence waking cognitions also must be without a substratum in external objects. Waking cognitions are on a par with dreams. Even as there are no external objects corresponding to dream-cognitions, so there are no external objects corresponding to waking cognitions. If it be argued that waking cognitions of the pillar, the wall, etc., are definite and determinate and consequently cannot be wrong and objectless, it may equally be argued that dream-cognitions also are definite and determinate during the dream-state, and there is no difference between dream-cognitions and waking cognitions in their character. The subjective idealist starts from ideation and reduces perception to ideation. Ideas and images are mental ; percepts are continuous with images. Hence percepts also are mental.[1]

Śavara urges that waking cognitions are essentially different from dream-cognitions. Dream-cognitions are

[1] The modern realist goes to the opposite extreme. He regards not only percepts but also images as objective and independent of consciousness. According to Alexander, "in fancy, dreams, and constructive imagination, it is not that we are creating something which does not exist. All the elements of these constructions exist in the real physical world, in the ideational mode." Hasan, *Realism*, p. 141.

contradicted by waking cognitions. But waking cognitions are not so contradicted. If waking cognitions were similar to dream-cognitions in nature, they would be contradicted by other cognitions. Dream-cognitions are not false because they are cognitions. If they were false because they are cognitions, then waking cognitions also would be false because they are cognitions. But dream-cognitions are false because they are produced by the mind perverted by drowsiness. Therefore waking cognitions are not false and without a real substratum in external objects. The Yogācāra argues that cognitions are false, because they are devoid of real external objects corresponding to them. But Śavara urges that cognitions are false, because they are brought about by some defects in the instruments of perception.

(2) The Yogācāra argues that there is no real external object corresponding to a cognition, because we do not perceive any difference between the form of the object and the form of its cognition. What we perceive is a cognition with a determinate form. We do not perceive the form of an object distinct from the cognition itself.

Śavara urges that a cognition has no form, but the external object which it apprehends has a form and is actually perceived as existing in external space. The Nyāya-Vaiśeṣika also holds this view. The cognition is not apprehended as having a form distinct from that of the object, simply because it is formless. Further, the external object is the object (karma) of the act of cognition (kriyā), not another cognition, for the simple reason that a cognition, which is momentary, cannot endure till another cognition comes into being and apprehends it as its object.[1] Momentary cognitions appearing in succession cannot be related to each other as the percipient and the perceived. Cognition is an act

[1] Arthaviṣayā hi pratyakṣā buddhiḥ, na buddhiviṣayā, kṣaṇikā hi sā. Śavarabhāṣya (with Bṛhatī), Madras, 1934, pp. 80–1.

of knowing. It apprehends an external object. The object is non-mental. It is the object of knowing.

(3) The Yogācāra argues that even the Mīmāṃsaka cannot deny that a cognition apprehends itself before it apprehends its object, even as a lamp is perceived before an object is perceived through the light of the lamp. A cognition is apprehended before its object is apprehended by it. The Yogācāra holds that reflective consciousness is prior to simple apprehension.

Śavara urges that a cognition is never apprehended before an object is apprehended by it. It is only after the object has been apprehended by a cognition, that the existence of the cognition comes to be known. Simple apprehension of an object always precedes reflective consciousness. The act of cognition is inferred from the fact of the object being apprehended ; if there were no cognition of the object, the object would never be apprehended. Thus the cognition is not cognized before its object is cognized by it. Nor is the cognition cognized simultaneously with its object. The cognition is cognized after its object is cognized by it. The Mīmāṃsaka does not recognize the perceptibility of cognition. He holds that it is inferred from the object being cognized.[1]

(4) The Yogācāra argues that a cognition must come into existence first, and be apprehended before it can apprehend its object. An object cannot be apprehended until its cognition has already appeared and been apprehended. Therefore the cognition cannot be apprehended after the object has been apprehended. The Yogācāra here confounds consciousness with self-consciousness He holds that consciousness can apprehend an object only when it is self-conscious. Then he turns round and says that self-consciousness creates its object.

Firstly, Śavara urges that it is true that the cognition first comes into existence before its object can be cognized

[1] *Indian Psychology : Perception*, pp. 199–201.

by it.[1] But it is not true that the cognition is apprehended first before it apprehends its object. First the object is apprehended by a cognition. Then there is awareness of the cognition. It sometimes happens that even a cognized object is spoken of as not cognized. Kumārila gives an example of it. Sometimes a person says, " I do not remember that I ever knew this thing," even though it was actually known to him in the past. Śavara is faithful to facts of experience.

Secondly, the form of the cognition is never perceived except in terms of the object. It would not be possible if both the cognition and the object were apprehended by sense-perception. The cognition cannot be spoken of as the object of sense-perception. Therefore it cannot be the object (karma) of the act of sense-perception. Cognition is an act. It is directed outward to an object. Moore also insists that experience has two factors, (1) the act of experiencing and (2) the object experienced, both of which exist and are distinct from each other.

Thirdly, even if the cognition and the object were identical in form, we would have to deny the cognition a separate existence, and not the object which is actually perceived.[2] As a matter of fact, however, the cognition and the object are not identical in form ; the cognition which is inferred from the object being cognized has no form ; it is inferred simply as cognition without a form and not as cognition of a particular thing. But when an object is directly perceived, it is perceived with a form. Thus a formless cognition apprehends an external object

[1] Satyaṃ purvaṃ buddhirutpadyate, na tu pūrvaṃ jñāyate. Śavarabhāṣya, p. 86.

[2] Reid does not admit ideas intervening between the mind and the object. " He denied the theory of representative perception and stoutly maintained that what is perceived is not an idea but a thing. In perception the mind is face to face with an objective fact. Between the perceived object and the perceiving mind no idea intervenes." H. Haldar. *Neo-Hegelianism*, p. 404.

with a form. Hence a cognition has a foundation in an external object.[1]

Fourthly, the cognition of " cloth " appears only when the yarns are there ; it is not produced when the yarns are not there. This conclusively proves that the cognition of cloth is produced by the yarns compòsing the cloth. If there were no causal connection between the cloth constituted by the yarns and the cognition of the cloth, then a person with perfectly healthy sense-organs might have the cognition of a jar in the presence of yarns. But this never happens. Hence it follows that a cognition has a real substratum in an external object by which it is produced.[2] Thus Śavara recognizes the existence of non-mental objects which produce cognitions. He advocates the causal theory of knowledge.[3]

§ 2. *Kumārila's Exposition of the Yogācāra Idealism*

Kumārila discusses the doctrine of the non-existence of external objects in *Ślokavārtika* in two sections, *Nirālambanavāda* and *Śūnyavāda*. Among the Buddhists the Yogācāra believes in the reality of cognitions only but not in the existence of external objects ; and the Mādhyamika denies the reality of cognitions also after proving the non-existence of objects. The denial of the existence of external objects is common to both the schools.

[1] Nirākārāmeva hi buddhim anumimīmahe, sākāraṃ cārthaṃ pratyakṣam avagacchāmaḥ. Tasmādarthālambanaḥ pratyayaḥ. Śavarabhāṣya, p. 88.

[2] C. D. Broad holds that the laws of the real causes of our perceptions are most probably " those which science finds it necessary to assume in order to account for what is perceived. Now these laws are not in the least like those which perceptions obey among themselves, although they are of course connected with the latter. They are in fact laws about the kind of changes that we can observe in the object of a single continuous perception ; and the only common characteristics of the objects of our perceptions and the perceptions themselves is that both have temporal relations and can enter into causal laws." (*Perception, Physics and Reality*, p. 185.)

[3] Śavarabhāṣya, i, 1, 5, pp. 68–90.

The Mādhyamika's denial of the reality of cognitions is based on his denial of the reality of external objects. Hence Śavara examines the reality or unreality of external objects in his *Bhāṣya*, and Kumārila follows him in discussing this doctrine.[1] Kumārila states the following principal arguments of the Yogācāra for the denial of the external reality.

(1) The Yogācāra argues : " The cognitions of posts and the like are false ; because whatever is a cognition has always been found to be false, for instance, the cognitions in a dream."[2] All cognitions are without corresponding realities in the external world, for instance, dream-cognitions ; waking cognitions are cognitions ; therefore, waking cognitions also are without corresponding realities in the external world.[3] Waking cognitions are on the same footing with dream-cognitions and illusions.[4] They are without any foundation in external reality (nirālambana). They are not produced by external objects.[5]

[1] SV., i, Nirālambanavāda, 14–16.

[2] Ibid., 23.

[3] Ganganatha Jha's E.T. of SV., p. 122, n.

[4] SD., pp. 142–3. " Illusions and hallucinations, dreams and fancies and error, are the strongholds of subjectivism." (*Realism*, p. 176.)

[5] *Yogavāśiṣṭha* also practically abolishes the distinction between dream-cognitions and waking cognitions. It does not recognize any fundamental difference between them. The only difference between them lies in the fact that waking cognitions are stable (sthirapratyaya) while dream-cognitions are unstable (asthirapratyaya). Dream-cognitions are felt as waking cognitions, if they are distinct and stable, and endure for a long time ; waking cognitions are felt as dream-cognitions, if they are indistinct, unstable, and momentary. Dream-cognitions are of the nature of waking cognitions ; waking cognitions are of the nature of dream-cognitions ; they are homogeneous in nature ; their contents are the same always and everywhere. They do not differ from each other in their intrinsic nature. They differ only in that waking cognitions are distinct, steady, and stable, while dream-cognitions are indistinct, unsteady, and unstable. (*Sthitiprakaraṇa*, 9–14.)

Berkeley similarly recognizes only the difference of degree between sensations and images : The former are more intense, steady, and coherent

(2) Recollections, dreams, and the like are not produced by the contact of objects with cognitions. They are cognitions of objects which do not exist at the time. So there is no possibility of any contact of objects with cognitions here. The forms of cognitions in recollections and dreams are due to subconscious impressions (vāsanā) only. They are not due to external objects.[1] In illusions also the forms of cognitions do not depend upon external objects.[2] Similarly the variety of waking cognitions also is due to mere subconscious impressions.[3] Thus the forms apprehended belong to cognitions, and not to external objects. We can prove it by the method of agreement and the method of difference. We perceive forms of cognitions independently of external objects as in dreams and recollections. But we never perceive forms of external objects independently of cognitions.[4] Hence forms of cognitions are not caused by external objects. They are brought about by the contact[5] of formless cognitions with subconscious impressions.[6]

than the latter. David Hume also, like Berkeley, recognized only the difference of degree or intensity between sensations and images. Images, according to him, are merely faint copies of impressions or sensations. *Yogavāśiṣṭha* likens waking cognitions to dream-cognitions, and the waking world to the dream-world. The waking experience is apprehension of an unreal world; the dream experience is apprehension of an unreal town or the like (iii, 57, 50). The objects of both are unreal. Illusions, dreams, wrong cognitions with their objects like imaginary cities (gandharvanagara) are creations of the power of the mind. Likewise the body is a construction of the mind and the whole world is nothing but mind and its construction. Sthitiprakaraṇa (11th Canto, 21–3).

[1] SV., 5, śūnyavāda, 51–2; SD., p. 143.

[2] Ibid., 57.

[3] Ibid., 52; SD., p. 142.

[4] Ākāro na hi bāhyasya jñānāpeto nidarśyate, ibid., 53. Cf. Berkeley, "Light and colours, heat and cold, extension and figures—in a word the things we see and feel—what are they but so many sensations, notions, ideas, or impressions on the sense? and is it possible to separate, even in thought, any of these from perception? For my part, I might as easily divide a thing from itself." (*Principles of Human Knowledge*, pp. 35–6.)

[5] Causal agency.

[6] Ibid., 52–4.

(3) Is a cognition able to function, only when objects exist in the external world? Or does the cognition apprehend itself, and not an external object? If a cognition apprehends an external object realism is established. If it apprehends itself, subjective idealism is established. The realist argues that it is a well-established fact that all apprehend objects in the forms of blue, yellow, long, short, etc., which are therefore objects of cognition (grāhya); here both cognition and its object are manifested to consciousness, and therefore the existence of both should be admitted.[1]

The Yogācāra urges that we do not distinctly apprehend the cognition and its object with different forms; only one form is manifested to consciousness. We apprehend a single object in the form of blue or the like. The form that is apprehended may be regarded as the form of the cognition or the object, if it is distinctly apprehended as such. But we do not distinctly apprehend the form as belonging either to the cognition or to the object.[2]

It may be argued that both cognition and its object are real though the form of one is apprehended and that of the other is not apprehended. But this is wrong. Only that which is apprehended can be said to have an existence; and that which is not apprehended can be said to have no existence because there is no proof for its existence. Therefore we must admit that an object does exist with a form inasmuch as it is apprehended.[3] If we perceive the form to belong to the cognition, the validity of perception will depend on the cognition itself, and there

[1] SV., 5, Śūnyavāda, 3–5. Similarly Dr. G. E. Moore says: "I am as directly aware of the existence of *material things* in space as of my own sensations; and *what* I am aware of with regard to each is exactly the same—namely that in one case the *material thing*, and in the other case my *sensation* does really exist." (*Philosophical Studies*, p. 30, the italics are mine.)

[2] Na cāpyākārabhedena jñānajñeyāvadhāraṇā. Na cānyataradharmatvaṃ vispaṣṭaṃ tatra gṛhyate. Ibid., 6, and NR.

[3] Ibid., 7.

will be no ground for postulating the existence of an external object. If, however, we perceive the form to belong to the external object, we must admit that the object exists because we actually perceive it ; and we must also admit the existence of its cognition in order to establish the existence of the object.[1] A cognition is self-luminous and manifests itself ; it does not depend on any extraneous condition for its manifestation. Therefore its existence is established without the help of an external object. But an external object is manifested as endowed with a form because it is apprehended as such. It is unconscious and non-luminous. It does not manifest itself. It depends upon cognition for its manifestation. Therefore we must admit the existence of cognition in order to establish the manifestation of its object.[2]

Is, then, the form that is apprehended the form of the cognition ? Or is it the form of the object ? We apprehend a single form such as blue, and it is the form of the cognition that is apprehended.[3] The Naiyāyika also admits that we apprehend a single form, but it is the form of the object.[4] The Yogācāra argues that it cannot be the form of the object. If an external object is assumed to have the form, we must postulate something else to apprehend it ; otherwise the form of the object would never be apprehended. We must admit the existence of a cognition in order to establish the form of an external unconscious object.[5] Thus over and above the well-established external object endowed with a form, we would be postulating a formless cognition to apprehend it, which is altogether foreign to the object though there is no ground for its existence.[6] If the external object itself is supposed to be its cognizer, there is no real difference between realism and subjective idealism, since, according

[1] Ibid., 8–9.
[2] NR., on ibid., 8–9.
[3] Ibid, 10.
[4] NM., p. 541.
[5] SV., 5, Śūnyavāda, 11, and NR.
[6] Ibid, 12.

to both, one and the same thing is both subject and object. The realist holds that an external object is both subject and object, while the subjective idealist holds that a cognition is both subject and object.[1] The Yogācāra argues that a single form is apprehended, and that is the form of a cognition which is both subject and object. The cognized object is identical with the apprehending cognition.[2] The former cannot be said to be external and the latter cannot be said to be internal. The distinction of "external" and "internal" is purely imaginary and false. Externality and internality imply duality of existence. But cognition, which is the only reality, is non-dual; it does not admit of any distinction within it.[3] The Yogācāra admits the reality of cognition only which appears to be polarized into subject and object. There is nothing other than cognition; so the object external to the cognition is not real. Cognition in itself is free from all distinction; the distinction of subject and object within it is an illusory appearance.[4]

The Yogācāra holds that cognition alone constitutes the reality. In itself it is pure and transparent (svaccha).[5] But in this beginningless cycle of existence there are manifold psychical dispositions (vāsanā) produced by past cognitions. These manifold dispositions, in their turn, produce manifold cognitions. The pure and formless cognition appears to be diversified by these dispositions into apprehending cognitions (grāhaka) and apprehended objects (grāhya) which appear to be quite distinct from

[1] Ibid., 13, and NR.; cf. NM., p. 541.
[2] Grāhyagrāhakayoraikyaṃ sarvathā pratipādyate, ibid., 14.
[3] Ibid., 14. [4] NR., pp. 271–2.
[5] "If consciousness is an empty transparency that makes no difference to its objects, its objects, presumably, must make a difference to it. But it is hard to see how anything can make a difference to an empty transparency. Either objects are the content of consciousness or they are not. If they are they cannot be said to be either outside or independent of consciousness. If they are not, consciousness remains an empty, meaningless transparency." (*The New Idealism*, p. 42.)

the cognition itself. Though the cognition in itself is one and undivided, it appears to be divided into subject and object, and is modalized into various modes without depending upon external objects.[1] It may be argued that the variety of dispositions depends upon the variety of cognitions ; and the variety of cognitions, in its turn, depends upon the variety of dispositions. Thus there is mutual dependence (itaretarāśraya). The Yogācāra tries to avoid it thus : A particular disposition produces a particular cognition. This cognition produces another disposition which is different from the disposition from which it sprung. And this disposition, again, produces another cognition which is different from the former cognition. Thus in the beginningless cycle of causes and effects there is no mutual dependence though there is reciprocal causality of dispositions and cognitions.[2]

Disposition (vāsanā) is simply the latent power of cognition.[3] The assumption of a diversity in dispositions is better than that of a diversity in external objects. Even the realist who admits the existence of external objects must admit the existence of dispositions in the form of latent powers of cognitions. The Yogācāra does not believe in anything other than cognitions. They are not produced by external objects. They are produced by immediately preceding cognitions. There is a beginningless stream of cognitions flowing as causes and effects without depending on external objects. Even the realist has to admit distinct forms of cognitions in order to establish the existence of different objects. Thus the assumption of forms of cognitions which are admitted by the realist as well as by the subjective idealist is better than the assumption of external objects. The assumption of one is better than the assumption of many.[4]

[1] Ibid., 15–17. [2] NR., pp. 272–3.
[3] Jñānasyaiva śaktimātraṃ vāsanā, NR. on ibid., p. 273.
[4] Ibid., 18–19, and NR.

If the realist denies the reality of forms of cognitions, he cannot account for the apprehension of different objects. If there were no distinct forms of cognitions, mere formless cognitions would not be able to apprehend distinct objects such as blue and the like. If there were no forms of cognitions, they would be identical with one another, all of them being of the nature of consciousness, and would fail to apprehend different objects. If there are no distinctions among cognitions there can be no apprehension of different objects. Different objects cannot be apprehended by cognitions, if they are not in themselves different from one another. A formless cognition cannot apprehend a blue object as a mere existent, since existence is common to blue, yellow, and the like. A specific cognition only can apprehend a specific object. Hence we must admit specific forms of cognitions. If cognitions differ from one another in themselves without the help of distinct forms, the difference among them cannot be apprehended unless they are tinged with distinct forms such as blue and the like. Cognitions can be said to correspond to their objects if they are endowed with distinct forms. These forms which are manifested to consciousness cannot belong to external objects. If they belong to external objects, they cannot be apprehended by cognitions on account of their remoteness and difference from each other.[1]

There is no such difficulty in the subjective idealism of the Yogācāra. He identifies objects with cognitions so that the objects can be apprehended by cognitions. The cognized object is identical with the apprehending cognition so that it is in close proximity to the cognition, is connected with it, and apprehended by it. The relationship of the object and its cognition is explained by their identity (tādātmya).[2] The blue object is related to the

[1] NR. on ibid., 20, pp. 273–4.
[2] Ibid., 20, and NR., pp. 273–4.

cognition of blue because it is identical with the cognition; and because it is related to the cognition it is apprehended by it. This is the nature of a cognizable object that it must be identical with its cognition.[1] The object which is supposed to be independent of its cognition is not identical with it; it is distinct from the cognition. It cannot, therefore, be related to the cognition, and be apprehended by it. There is no other relation between the object and the cognition, which can bring them into relationship with each other, and enable the cognition to apprehend the object.[2] If a cognition could apprehend an object without being related to it, every cognition would apprehend all objects. If an object is said to be apprehended by a cognition because it is the cause of the cognition, then the visual organ, which is imperceptible, will be apprehended by the cognition, because it brings about the cognition.

The Sautrāntika argues that the cause of a cognition is that object which imparts its form to the cognition. But there is no proof for the existence of such an object.

[1] Berkeley also holds that the object perceived is identical with perception. Gentile is of opinion that Berkeley is right in holding this view. "Reality is conceivable only in so far as the reality conceived is in relation to the activity which conceives it, and in that relation it is not only a possible object of knowledge, it is a present and actual one. To conceive a reality is to conceive, at the same time and as one with it, the mind in which the reality is represented; and therefore the concept of a material reality is absurd." (*Theory of Mind as Pure Act*, p. 1.)

[2] Croce holds that mind is the only reality, and there is no reality which is not mind. Mind is essentially activity and mental activity is all reality. He says, "When being is conceived as external to the human mind, and knowledge as separable from its object, so that the object could be without being known, it is evident that the existence of the object becomes a datum, something, as it were, placed before the mind, something given to the mind, extraneous to it. . . . And yet . . . there is nothing outside mind, and there are therefore no data confronting it. The very conceptions we form of this something, which is external . . . show themselves to be not conceptions of data which already are external but data furnished to mind by itself." (*Logica*, p. 120, quoted in Wildon Carr's *The Philosophy of Benedetto Croce*, p. 12.)

A blue object cannot impart its form to the cognition. The variety of cognitions is not due to the variety of objects. All cognitions are brought about by immediately preceding cognitions. The Sautrāntika holds that an object is apprehended by its cognition because of its similarity (sārūpya) with it. In that case, a blue object would be apprehended by the cognition of blue, though it was remote in time and space. What does similarity mean? Is it partial similarity or absolute similarity? Objects cannot be apprehended by cognitions because of their partial similarity with them, since all cognitions are partially similar to all objects inasmuch as they are all momentary, and therefore every cognition would apprehend all objects—which is absurd. Objects cannot be apprehended by cognitions because of their absolute similarity with them, for in that case cognitions would be similar to objects in all respects and thus would be as inert and unconscious as objects are. If that is said to be apprehended by a cognition, which is similar to it and is the cause of it, then in a serial cognition the preceding cognition will be apprehended by the succeeding one because the former is similar to the latter and is its cause. Hence all cognitions apprehend themselves and not any external objects distinct from them; cognitions are not apprehended by other cognitions; they are apprehended by themselves. There are no objects other than cognitions. Thus cognitions only must be supposed to have forms, and not external objects.[1]

(4) Cognitions must be held to have forms for another reason. Cognitions manifest objects. Even the realist admits that external objects are non-luminous, and are manifested by cognitions. An object, which depends for its manifestation on a cognition, cannot be apprehended by a cognition unless the cognition itself is

[1] NR., pp. 274–5, cf. SD., p. 148.

apprehended even as a jar is illumined by the light of a lamp when the light is perceived.[1]

There is a difference between objects and cognitions. Objects are not apprehended as soon as they are produced, either because they are not illumined by consciousness, or because something stands in the way of their apphrehension. Cognitions, on the other hand, are apprehended as soon as they are produced, because they are not non-luminous like objects, and nothing stands in the way of their apprehension.[2] Hence cognitions must be apprehended as soon as they are produced.

Even the realist admits that a cognition is produced before it apprehends an object ; it cannot possibly apprehend an object before it comes into being. And it must be apprehended no sooner than it is produced because it is self-luminous and there is no impediment to its apprehension. If it is not apprehended at the time of its production, it cannot be apprehended even after the apprehension of the object. It does not acquire any new power after apprehending the object by virtue of which it can be apprehended only after its apprehension of the object. The cognition is self-luminous and apprehends itself ; it does not depend upon any other cognition for its apprehension. If it required another cognition to apprehend it, this cognition also would require another cognition to apprehend it and so on *ad infinitum*.[3]

We have recollections in the absence of external objects. Recollections are reproductions of past cognitions such as " the jar was known by me ". We could not have these recollections, if the cognitions did not embrace

[1] SV., 5, Śūnyavāda, 21–2 ; cf. NM., pp. 537–8 and S.D.S.

[2] Ibid., 23–4. Alexander holds that awareness is, as such, awareness of awareness. Consciousness is, in itself, consciousness of consciousness, self-consciousness. " My awareness and my being aware of it are identical." (*Space, Time, and Deity*, vol. i, p. 12.)

[3] Ibid., 25–7, and NR.

the forms of objects, and if these cognitions were no apprehended in the past before they apprehended their objects. Thus recollections presuppose past cognitions with definite forms, which were apprehended. Even the cognitions of objects existing here and now cannot apprehend them unless they embrace their forms, and are apprehended before they apprehend their objects.[1] Hence cognitions can apprehend their objects only when they themselves are already apprehended ; and cognitions cannot be apprehended if they are devoid of definite forms. Therefore we must admit that cognitions have distinct forms.[2]

(5) Even granted that cognitions are apprehended and have definite forms, we may admit the existence of external objects with distinct forms. The Yogācāra argues that we cannot discriminate between the forms of cognitions and the forms of objects, and we apprehend only distinct forms ; hence these forms must belong to cognitions.[3] We cannot assume that at first formless cognitions are apprehended, and then objects are apprehended as endowed with forms. This would be possible if we recognized the distinction between formless cognitions and cognitions endowed with definite forms. But formless cognitions are never apprehended, and objects cannot be apprehended unless cognitions have already been apprehended. If cognitions could apprehend their objects without themselves being apprehended, we could conclude that cognitions are formless while external objects are endowed with forms. But this is not possible.[4]

The Sautrāntika holds that the forms of objects are

[1] Ibid., 28–30.

[2] Tasmāt pūrvagṛhītāsu buddhiṣvarthopalambhanam. Na copalabdhirastīha nirākārāsu buddhiṣu. Ibid., 31.

[3] Vivekabuddhyabhāvācca sākārasya ca darśanāt. Ākāravattayā bodho jñānasyaiva prasajyate. Ibid., 32 ; cf. SD., p. 148.

[4] Ibid., 33–4, and NR.

apprehended when they are impressed upon their cognitions. But the Yogācāra argues that the forms of objects are external, and cannot enter into connection with internal cognitions. Besides, if the objects imprinted their forms on the cognitions which apprehend them, the forms would pass over from the objects to the cognitions, and the objects would vanish since they cannot exist denuded of their forms.[1] There is no proof for the existence of the forms of objects. So they cannot be said to be reflected in their cognitions. The moon is reflected in the water. We see the surface of water without any reflection of the moon during the day ; and we see the moon in the sky at night and recognize its reflection in the water. But we apprehend neither formless cognitions without the forms of objects, nor external objects endowed with forms in the absence of cognitions so that we may recognize that the forms of external objects are reflected in formless cognitions. Further, how incorporeal objects like sounds, odours, and tastes are reflected in cognitions is incomprehensible.[2] We distinctly apprehend forms as belonging to cognitions ; they cannot therefore, be held to belong to objects.[3]

The object exists in the external world, while its cognition exists in the mind. There cannot be mutual contact between the external object and the internal cognition so that one may be mistaken for the other. It cannot be said that the form really belongs to the object, but the form of the object is mistaken for the form of its cognition owing to their contact with each other.[4]

The form cannot be said to be a property of the contact of the object with its cognition because there can be no such contact. The object is external while the cognition

[1] Ibid., 35. [2] Ibid., 36–9.
[3] Jñāne ca gṛhyamāṇasya katham syādarthadharmatā. ibid., 39
[4] Ibid., 40.

is internal. The object is corporeal while the cognition is incorporeal. Hence there cannot be any contact between them. The contact of the object with its cognition cannot be said to consist in their existence at the same time. In that case, the whole universe would come in contact with the cognition because it exists at the same time, and there would be nothing to restrict the cognition to its appropriate object. If a cognition were held to be in contact with its object in its entirety, and to embrace all its forms, then its constituent atoms and tastes, sounds and the like would be perceived by the cognition, on the presentation of the object to the eye—which is absurd. The contact of a cognition with its object cannot be said to consist in the mere existence of the object as an object of cognition, since we cannot comprehend the character of the object before we apprehend its forms. Nothing can be said to be an object of cognition if it is not apprehended. An object is known to have a definite form when it is an object of cognition ; and it is an object of cognition when it has a definite form. Thus there would be mutual interdependence. We cannot discriminate between the cognition and the object as they are in themselves. We never apprehend formless objects and formless cognitions. Therefore we cannot say that the form is a property of the contact of the cognition with its object.[1]

The assumption that a single form belongs to both the cognition and the object is groundless because they occupy different positions, cannot come in contact with each other, and are not recognized as distinct from each other. And because they are not recognized as distinct from each other it cannot be said that they are indistinguishable from each other owing to their likeness inasmuch as comprehension of likeness presupposes comprehension of difference.[2]

[1] Ibid., 42–9.

[2] Ibid., 55.

We need not assume the contact of objects with cognitions to account for the variety of cognitions. Objects are never found to produce cognitions. So we cannot assume that the forms of cognitions are due to the contact of cognitions with their objects. The cognition and the object are held to be formless before they come in contact with each other. Mere contact, which is formless, can never give rise to diversity of forms of cognitions. Nor can formless objects produce forms of cognitions.[1]

(6) One and the same object appears different to different individuals. The same woman appears as an object of enjoyment to an amorous man, as delicious food to a carnivorous animal, and as a corpse to an ascetic.[2] If the external object exists, it must have the same nature and should be perceived as such by all. It cannot be perceived as different by different individuals. These different appearances are different forms of cognitions which are due to different psychical dispositions (vāsanā).[3]

Further, one and the same object appears long in comparison with one object, and short in comparison with another.[4] The same object appears long to one, and short to another at the same time. But contradictory qualities cannot exist in one and the same object at the same time. But the cognitions or ideas are different in each case, and they are due to different psychical dispositions.[5] Even if the external object exists, its real nature can never be apprehended by cognitions ; the forms of cognitions never correspond to external objects ; they are always independent of them. The hypothesis of external objects is absolutely groundless.[6]

[1] Ibid., 49–51, and NR.
[2] Cf. Y.B., iv, 15 ; NM., p. 540.
[3] SV., 5 Śūnyavāda, 59, and NR.
[4] Ibid., 59. [5] Ibid., 59–61. [6] Ibid., 62–3.

Relativity of sensations is a favourite argument of the idealist. Berkeley also argues : " That which at other times seems sweet, shall, to a distempered palate, appear bitter. And, nothing can be plainer than that divers persons perceive different tastes in the same food ; since that which one man delights in, another abhors. And how could this be, if the taste was something really inherent in the food ? " [1] Thus Berkeley proves that tastes, odours, sounds, colours, and temperatures are only ideas of the mind.[2] He simply repeats Locke's argument in proving the secondary qualities to be merely subjective. He applies the same argument to the primary qualities also and proves them to be merely subjective. He says : " *Great* and *small*, *swift* and *slow*, are allowed to exist nowhere without the mind, being entirely relative, and changing as the frame or position of the organs of sense varies. The extension therefore which exists without the mind is neither great nor small, the motion neither swift nor slow, that is, they are nothing at all." [3]

§ 3. *Kumārila's Criticism of the Yogācāra Idealism*

1. (i) The Yogācāra argues that waking cognitions are false or without corresponding external objects because whatever is a cognition is false or without any corresponding reality, like dream-cognitions.[4] Kumārila urges that waking perceptions are certain and well-defined ; they establish the existence of well-defined external objects. In fact, all means of right knowledge prove the existence of external objects. To regard the objects of uncontradicted waking perceptions as mere forms of cognitions is to contradict the direct evidence

[1] *Dialogue between Hylas and Philonous*, p. 129.
[2] Ibid., pp. 124–138.
[3] *Principles of Human Knowledge*, pp. 40–1.
[4] SV., 5, nirālambanavāda, 23.

of perception.[1] The object of sense-perception and the other means of right knowledge must have an existence in the external world. The Yogācāra theory of the denial of the external reality is contradicted by the evidence of sense-perception and the other means of right knowledge.[2] The uncontradicted and well-defined waking perceptions, which bear clear testimony to the existence of external objects, are superior in strength to the Yogācāra inference which seeks to establish the non-existence of external objects.[3] All persons recognize the existence of external objects independent of their cognitions, which are facts of their experience. The Yogācāra goes against the universal experience of mankind in denying the existence of external objects.[4] It is right to deny the existence of objects apprehended by cognitions which are vitiated by some defects. But the Yogacara who denies the existence of the object of every cognition undermines his own theory, since the object of his inference also is non-existent.[5]

(ii) The Yogācāra argues that waking cognitions are without corresponding external objects like dream-cognitions and illusions. But Kumārila points out that even dreams and illusions are not without foundation in external objects. In dream-cognitions the objects which were perceived at some other time or in some other place are remembered and owing to some mental disorder under the influence of sleep they are apprehended as present here and now. The objects which are apprehended by dream-cognitions are some real external objects which were perceived in the past either in the

[1] Ibid 30, and NR; cf. NM., 543; S.B.S., ii, 2, 28.

[2] Pratyakṣādeśca viṣayo bāhya evāvatiṣṭhate, ibid., 32; cf. Śūnyavāda, 259–261.

[3] Ibid., 33, and NR.; see NR. on Śūnyavāda, 228; SD., p. 143 (Ch. S.S.); cf. T.V. on Y.S., iv, 14.

[4] Ibid., 74; cf. S.V.M., pp. 113–14.

[5] Ibid., 34, and NR.; cf. Y.B., iv, 14.

present life, or in some past life, either in the same place, or in some other place.[1] *Nyāyaratnākara* makes it more clear. "We dream only of such external objects as we perceived in the past. The only difference lies in the change of order in the time and place of the perceived. Therefore dreams cannot be said to be pure creations of fancy without any real foundation in the external world." Therefore dreams cannot be said to be totally devoid of real basis in the external world.

Alexander, in a way, corroborates the truth of Kumārila's view. He says : "The illusion of the dream consists in the disagreement of this world of dream-things with the greater world, which is the whole world of Space-Time, not limited to this particular dream-vision of it. Everything in the dream is real, the materials of it and the ways in which they are related, including the thing-hood of its things. But in the larger world they are not found in these arrangements and thus they cannot bear the test of the wider reference."[2] Modern psycho-analysis shows that "no detail in the dream is too insignificant to be neglected, and every element can be tracked by association to its source in former experience".[3] "The imagery in a dream is its manifest content, and this manifest content, according to the psycho-analysts, is not really creative. It is one of the termini in a chain of association whose other terminus can be recalled to memory when sufficient pains are taken."[4] Thus dreams are not without their counterparts in reality.

(iii) Kumārila holds that illusions also are not without a foundation in real objects. Illusions are perceptions of external objects in a wrong manner. The cause of the illusory perception of the fire-brand circle (alātacakra)

[1] Ibid., 107–9 ; cf. 50 and NR. ; SD., p. 143 ; NB., iv, 2, 34.

[2] *Space, Time, and Deity*, vol. ii, p. 215 ; cf. *Mysticism and Logic*, pp. 177-178.

[3] *A Study in Realism*, p. 76.

[4] Ibid., p. 78.

is the fire-brand whirled with extreme rapidity. The cause of the illusory perception of imaginary cities in the clouds (gandharvanagara) is a particular arrangement of clouds and the recollection of some houses perceived in the past. The cause of the "mirage" (mṛgatoya) in a desert is sand heated by the rays of the sun and reflecting them, and the recollection of the water perceived in the past. Even purely imaginary notions like "hare's horns" (śaśaśṛṅga) imply the existence of hares and horns separately in the external world. The cause of the notion is either the horns of other animals, or the peculiar character of the hare itself.[1] Kumārila is an advocate of anyathākhyāti. He looks upon illusion as misapprehension. It is wrong perception of an object. In an illusion a thing perceived somewhere in the past is remembered and is erroneously attributed to a thing perceived here and now.[2] Thus, if dreams and illusions are not totally devoid of a real substratum in the external world, waking perceptions can never be without their counterparts in the external world. In all cognitions there is some element of reality.

Alexander holds that illusions are not without their counterparts in reality. He says: "Illusory appearances do not belong to the thing of which they are appearances; and the illusion consists in their being so referred. Only in so far are they illusory; there is no illusion until an element in the appearance which does not belong to the thing is perceived as belonging to it: until, for instance, the green seen by contrast on a piece of grey paper lying on a red ground is seen as an affection of the place of the grey paper. The green by itself is not illusory; but the patch, occupied by the grey, seen as green."[3] "The illusory appearance of a thing is commonly said

[1] SV., nirālambanavāda, 109–111.
[2] *Indian Psychology: Perception*, pp. 301–2.
[3] *Space, Time, and Deity*, vol. ii, p. 209.

to be an illusion if the thing in question is actually present but misinterpreted." [1] "Illusion lies in reference of the imaginary element to the thing to which it belongs." [2] "The illusory object is as much non-mental as the real appearance. Yet it is chosen by the mind from the world of things not directly connected with the thing to which it is referred. The grey piece of paper is seen green by contrast on the red ground. The paper itself is not green. But there is green in the world. The appropriate response of the mind to green is the kind of sensory act which the mind is at the moment performing, and accordingly it sees green." [3] "We can see how illusion is possible. The object, with which the mind is brought into compresence by virtue of an act initiated by itself, is transferred from its place in the world into a place to which it does not belong. The illusion is a transposition of materials. Moreover the form of combination is also real. . . . We combine elements not really combined, but both the elements and their form of combination are features of the real world when that world is taken large enough." [4] Thus illusions are not pure creations of imagination.

(iv) Kumārila brings forward a counter-argument to prove the existence of external objects. Cognitions have real counterparts in the external world ; and these cognitions apprehending external objects are valid since they are free from contradiction, like the cognition of the falsity of a dream-cognition.[5] If the Yogācāra urges that the cognition of the falsity of a dream-cognition also is false, then the dream-cognition cannot be false, and consequently cannot serve as an instance of false

[1] Ibid., p. 210.

[2] Ibid., p. 209, n. ; cf. Russel, *Mysticism and Logic*, p. 176 ; *Our Knowledge of the External World*, p. 85.

[3] Ibid., p. 214.

[4] Ibid., pp. 214–215.

[5] SV., nirālambanavāda, 79–80.

cognition.[1] If all cognitions were equally false and without any counterparts in the external world, we could never have ideas of proximity and remoteness,[2] and reality and unreality.[3] If a cognition be false, it is sure to be contradicted. If it were false without being contradicted, there would be no restriction as to the reality or unreality of a cognition.[4] Kumārila holds that dream-cognitions are false, and they are contradicted by waking perceptions ; but waking perceptions, which are not contradicted by other cognitions, are valid. But the Yogācāra cannot distinguish between dream-cognitions and waking cognitions, since he holds them both to be false. Waking cognitions of posts and the like, which are not contradicted by other cognitions, are valid. But dream-cognitions are known to all persons to be contradicted by waking perceptions. Hence there is a difference between dream-cognitions and waking perceptions.[5]

(v) The Yogācāra may urge that waking cognitions also are contradicted by the intuitions of the yogins who realize the falsity of all things in the world. Thus waking cognitions of posts and the like are as false as

[1] Ibid., 80–1.

[2] Berkeley anticipates this objection. "It will be objected that we *see* things actually without, or at a distance from us ; and which consequently do not exist in the mind ; it being absurd that those things which are seen at the distance of several miles should be as near to us as our own thoughts." (*Principles of Human Knowledge*, p. 62.) Berkeley refutes this objection by saying that proximity and remoteness are "ideas of touch" which are suggested by "ideas of sight", both of which exist in the mind. (Ibid., pp. 62–3.)

[3] SV., 5, nirālambanavāda, 85–6. Berkeley anticipates this objection also. "It will be objected that by the foregoing principles all that is real and substantial in nature is banished out of the world ; and instead thereof a chimerical scheme of *ideas* takes place." (Ibid., p. 57.) "It will be objected that there is a great difference betwixt real fire and the idea of fire." (Ibid., p. 61.) Berkeley refutes this objection by showing that the distinction between reality and unreality is *within* consciousness. (Ibid., pp. 55–6.)

[4] SV., 5, nirālambanavāda, 87–8.

[5] Ibid., 88–91 ; cf. S.B.S., ii, 2, 28 ; SD., p. 144.

dream-cognitions. And all persons will realize the falsity of waking cognitions when they will reach the stage of the yogin. Hence it is established that waking cognitions are false since they are invalidated by the intuitions of the yogins.[1]

But Kumārila points out that such yogic intuitions are not given to mortals on earth ; we know nothing about the so-called intuitions of the gifted few who are said to have reached the yogic state.[2] An appeal to yogic intuitions is an appeal to credulity. The Yogācāra cannot show any instance to prove the real nature of the yogic intuitions which invalidate waking cognitions. But Kumārila can easily give an instance to prove that yogic intuitions have real substrata in the external world as cognitions of all persons apprehend external objects.[3]

(vi) Kumārila raises many technical objections to the Yogācāra's inference, some of which are indicated here. The Yogācāra concludes that " waking cognitions " are " without corresponding external objects ". Here both the subject and the predicate of the conclusion—or the minor term and the major term of the syllogism—are incapable of being apprehended because both of them are without counterparts in reality. Both the cognition of " waking cognitions " and the cognition of " being without corresponding external objects " are without any foundation in reality (nirālambana). And an inference with an unknown minor term or an unknown major term can never be valid. In fact, the Yogācāra who denies the reality of the major term and the minor term of his own syllogism stands self-contradicted. Further,

[1] Ibid., 91–3.

[2] Ibid., 93–4 ; see *Indian Psychology : Perception*, pp. 336–7. " Mysticism as a way of being should command our respect, if not our aspirations, but when the mystic, becoming arrogant, waves his wand before the multitude and whispers darkly that knowledge is not what it is, it is time to be on our guard against this wizardry." (*A Study in Realism*, p. 54.)

[3] S.V., nirālambanavāda, 95–6.

it is not possible to distinguish the major term from the minor term. So the conclusion of the Yogācāra cannot be valid.[1] Then, what does the Yogācāra mean by "cognition" which is the minor term of his syllogism? If he means by it a property of the soul, he himself does not recognize the existence of such a cognition. This makes his argument fallacious. If, on the other hand, he means by it mere cognition without any notion of the cognizer and the cognized such a cognition is not recognized by the Mīmāṃsaka. And this also makes the argument fallacious inasmuch as the minor term must be such as is accepted by both parties.[2] Further, the conclusion of the Yogācāra's syllogism denies the reality of the cognitum of every cognition; therefore an establishment of the reality of the object of his premises renders his own conclusion impossible.[3] If all cognitions were false, there would be no degrees of falsity, and dream-cognitions could not be regarded as more false than waking cognitions. Moral considerations of virtue and vice compel the recognition of the existence of external objects.[4] If the experiences of heaven were similar to the experiences of a dream nobody would exert himself to perform duties for the mere pleasures of a dream.[5]

2. The Yogācāra holds that the variety of impressions[6] is the cause of the variety of cognitions.[7] But Kumārila urges that there cannot be variety of impressions, since the Yogācāra cannot provide any cause of impressions. If the variety of cognitions were held to be the cause of the variety of impressions there would be mutual inter-dependence (anyonyāśraya). The variety of cognitions would depend upon the variety of impressions, and the

[1] Ibid., 35–7 and NR.
[2] Ibid., 47; see Jha's E.T., p. 126, n.
[3] Ibid., 150–2, and NR. [4] Ibid., 1–3. [5] Ibid., 11–13.
[6] "Subconscious impressions" (vāsanā) are called "impressions" here.
[7] "Cognitions" here mean "perceptions".

variety of impressions would depend upon the variety of cognitions.[1] The Yogācāra holds that consciousness in itself is pure and formless and devoid of difference; it is diversified into various cognitions by various impressions. So he cannot hold that there is a natural difference of cognitions in pure consciousness.[2] Further, there is no evidence either for the existence of impressions, or for the variety of impressions. Even granting the existence of various impressions, they would only tend to recall past cognitions and thus bring about a variety of apprehending cognitions; but they would, by no means, bring about a variety of apprehended objects.[3] When an impression is revived and appears in the field of consciousness it can bring about a mere recollection.[4] A variety of impressions, therefore, can never bring about a variety of perceptions. Cognitions are momentary; they are absolutely destroyed without leaving the least traces behind. And two momentary cognitions cannot be related to each other as the impresser (vāsaka) and the impressed (vāsya), since they never appear together in consciousness.[5] The preceding cognition cannot impress the succeeding one before it comes into existence; and, the succeeding cognition cannot be impressed by the preceding cognition, since it is destroyed. Even if the two cognitions appear together in consciousness, they are not related to each other, and consequently one cannot be impressed by the other. Hence there can be no impression (vāsanā).[6] Both the preceding cognition and the succeeding one are momentary; they cannot, therefore, operate upon each other. One cognition which is in the process of being destroyed cannot be impressed by another which

[1] SV., 5, nirālambanavāda, 178–9.
[2] Ibid., 179, and NR.
[3] Ibid., 180, and NR.
[4] Saṃvittyā jāyamānā hi smṛtimātraṃ karotyasau, ibid., 181.
[5] Ibid., 181–2.
[6] Ibid., 182–3.

also is undergoing destruction. Momentary entities cannot impress one another. It is only permanent entities that are impressed by other permanent entities ; for instance, oil is perfumed by parts of a fragrant flower, both of which are permanent and last for some time.[1]

The Yogācāra contends that if the succeeding cognition, which is durable, did not differ from the preceding cognition, there could be no impression (vāsanā) since there is no difference between them. If two cognitions are related to each other as the impresser and the impressed, they must be different from each other. But if both of them were permanent, the preceding cognition would be identical with the succeeding one because what is permanent has the same form at all times, past, present, and future ; and they could not be related to each other as the impresser and the impressed because they are identical with each other. Hence cognitions cannot leave any impressions because they are permanent according to Kumārila.[2] But the Yogācāra holds that cognitions are changing every moment, and are partly similar to, and partly different from, one another ; hence they can have impressions. Cognitions are undergoing changes every moment ; the preceding cognition differs from the succeeding one as they occur at different moments of time, and yet they are similar to each other ; hence the preceding cognition can leave an impression which modifies the succeeding one which is impressed with it and appears in the form of the preceding cognition. There need not be any operation between the preceding cognition and the succeeding one so that the former may leave an impression upon the latter. There can be no action of momentary cognitions upon one another. But still they are related to each other as cause and effect.[3]

[1] Ibid., 184.
[2] Ibid., 185–6, and NR.
[3] Ibid., 186, and NR., pp. 262–3.

Kumārila replies that cognitions, according to the Yogācāra, are momentary, and cannot, therefore, be similar to one another ; they must be absolutely different from one another. The preceding cognition cannot bring about an effect before it comes into being ; nor can it bring about an effect when it has been destroyed ; and when it is accomplished it does not continue even for a single moment. Thus there is no time when the cognition can produce its effect, since it is destroyed no sooner than it is produced. Hence the preceding cognition cannot produce any effect upon the succeeding one. Further, the preceding cognition is totally destroyed and does not leave any trace behind ; it cannot, therefore, be similar to the succeeding cognition. Similarity means the sameness of properties. But no property of the preceding cognition can persist in the succeeding one, since the former is totally destroyed. If the preceding cognition leaves an impression upon the succeeding one owing to its similarity with it, the cognition of a cow followed by that of an elephant can never leave an impression upon it because they are entirely different from each other. And the cognition of the cow being absolutely destroyed, such a cognition will never appear again because there is no impression of the cow. In fact, all cognitions being different from one another, none of them can leave an impression upon another. Further, the Yogācāra does not believe in the existence of external objects. Hence impressions cannot bring about their effects in a serial order inasmuch as they are totally destroyed, and cannot be aided by external objects or influenced by extraneous circumstances.[1]

But the realist holds that all impressions are permanent and exist in the soul ; they bring about effects in the form of recollections in a serial order because they depend upon the aid of external objects and the order

[1] Ibid., 187–192.

of thinking in the self in producing their effects ; the perception of similar objects revives the impressions of like objects perceived in the past in some other place. Thus the realist can account for the order of recollections produced by impressions with the help of external objects and the series of thoughts in the mind. But, according to the Yogācāra, nothing exists except cognitions and impressions, and impressions are totally destroyed, and cannot, therefore, bring about their effects in a serial order because they do not depend upon any other conditions.[1]

The Yogācāra holds that an effect is produced only on the destruction of its cause ; the effect cannot appear so long as the cause exists. Hence the destruction of a single cognition would bring about the destruction of all impressions based upon it ; and the cognition which springs from all these impressions and which appears in all their forms would be destroyed in a single moment. If the potentiality of a cognition is held to persist in the shape of an impression even on the destruction of the cognition which is its substratum, then it loses its momentary character, and cannot bring about any effect which appears only on the destruction of its cause.[2] If the stream of impressions is like the stream of cognitions, both being unbroken and continuous and independent of each other—then impressions cannot produce cognitions, and cognitions, again, cannot produce impressions. If there were two independent parallel streams of impressions and cognitions, impressions would produce only impressions, and cognitions would produce only cognitions, but impressions could never produce cognitions, and cognitions could never produce impressions because causes can produce only similar effects. Similar causes can produce dissimilar effects only in co-operation with adventitious

[1] Ibid., NR. on 193, pp. 164–5.

[2] Ibid., 193–6.

conditions. But the Yogācāra does not believe in anything but impressions and cognitions. Hence impressions and cognitions can never produce one another.[1]

Therefore, the so-called "impression" (vāsanā) of the Yogācāra must be assumed to be a false reality (saṃvṛtisatya), and not a true reality. And such false entities can never bring about any effects. But Kumārila believes in the existence of the permanent knower or the self; the self is the substratum of impressions which are effects of repeated cognitions. The self is the substratum of impressions; or it may be said to be the impression itself.[2] Impression consists in the transference of a part of one thing (dye) to another (cloth). But a part of the preceding cognition can never be transferred to the succeeding cognition. Hence there can be no such thing as vasana.[3] And because vāsanās cannot exist, and they do not depend upon extraneous circumstances such as external objects, time, place, and the like, they cannot be said to have causal efficiency (śakti) in producing variety of cognitions.[4] Further, vāsanās, instead of explaining cognitions or perceptions, presuppose them. Impressions (vāsanā) are the result of repeated similar perceptions. Thus impressions are preceded by perceptions; and perceptions must have apprehended external objects before in some place or other, which gave rise to impressions. Thus impressions presuppose the existence of cognitions of external objects. Hence it is not proper to deny the existence of external objects, and to account for a variety of perceptions by a variety of subconscious impressions.[5]

3. Sometimes it is argued that waking cognitions are without corresponding external objects as recollections

[1] Ibid., 196–8 and NR.
[2] Ibid., 199–200; cr. S.B.S., ii, 2, 31.
[3] Ibid., 200, and NR.
[4] Ibid., Śūnyavāda, 256–8.
[5] Ibid., 205–6.

are.[1] But recollections apprehend objects of past cognitions. There are recollections of *objects* perceived in the past, and not of past cognitions of objects. It is the recollection of the object perceived in the past that leads us to infer the existence of the past cognition. Hence recollection cannot be cited as an example of cognition without a corresponding object.[2]

Reid said: "It is by memory that we have an *immediate* knowledge of *things* past." [3] The modern realists seem to be in favour of this view. Memory is generally held to be representative knowledge of the past. It is a present act of mind representing the past. But the modern realists look upon memory as presentative knowledge. Laird holds that the object remembered is the same thing as the object perceived. He says: "The things we perceive are also the things we remember. . . . Memory does not mean the existence of present representatives of past things. It is the mind's awareness of past things themselves." [4] "Recollection appears to be the direct apprehension of the past." [5] Alexander also says: "The pastness of the object is a datum of experience, directly apprenended. The object is compresent with me *as past*." [6] Sinclair states the theory thus: "Memory is, in fact, perception, not of the object as it exists now but as it was perceived. We perceive it for ever as we perceived it then. . . . In every case of remembering we perceive, and it is only by its time element that we distinguish between memory and perception." [7] Laird roundly declares: "Things perceived and remembered are independent of the mind and directly apprehended by it." [8] If this is true, recollection cannot be cited in favour of the denial of

[1] Ibid., 51–2. [2] Ibid., 192, and NR.
[3] *Works* (Hamilton's edition), p. 339; the italics are mine.
[4] *A Study in Realism*, p. 56. [5] Ibid., p. 52.
[6] *Space, Time, and Deity*, vol. i, p. 113.
[7] *The New Idealism*, p. 25. [8] *A Study in Realism*, p. 64.

external objects. Recollection is as much direct awareness of past things, as perception, of present things. Thus Kumārila's suggestion that recollection is always of objects (arthasmṛti) is full of significance.

4. The Yogācāra holds that a cognition is both subject and object. It apprehends and is apprehended. But Kumārila points out that the act of cognition cannot cognize itself even as the act of cutting cannot cut itself. The act of cognition cannot turn round upon itself and make itself its own object. The Yogācāra may say that the cognition is self-luminous and so manifests itself; it does not depend upon anything else for its manifestation; it does not apprehend itself as an object (karma). But if the cognition were self-luminous, it would appear in such a form as "*I* am blue", and not as "*this* is blue".[1] Consciousness is different from self-consciousness. It is not directed inward to the self (pratyagātmavṛtti), but outward to the external object (parāgvṛtti).[2] Hence one and the same cognition cannot be both subject and object. There is not a single object which has such a dual character.[3]

Alexander holds that "the object of the mental act is a distinct existence (or subsistence) from the mental act. . . . Experience tells us that the mind does not experience itself as an object, but lives through its own self. The objects of which it is aware are distinct from its awareness."[4] "A mind in any mental act or process," he says, "is conscious of the appropriate object in so far as the act and the object which are appropriate to each other are in compresence, no matter how they are brought into this relation. The act of mind is the cognition, the object is the cognitum, the cognitive relation is the compresence between them. . . . The

[1] Cf. NM., p. 541; S.V.M., p. 112.

[2] Cf. Jñānād bahirbhūtasya saṃvedanāt, S.V.M., p. 112.

[3] SV., 5, Śūnyavāda, 64, and NR., pp. 287–8.

[4] *Basis of Realism*, § 3.

object is some existent distinct from the act of mind "[1] "Any experience whatever may be analysed into two distinct elements and their relation to one another. The two elements which are the terms of the relation are, on the one hand, the act of mind or the awareness, and on the other the object of which it is aware. . . . But the two terms are differently experienced. The one is experienced as the act of experiencing, the other as that which is experienced."[2] Hasan states Meinong's theory thus: "Not only thought but every cognitive activity, and not only cognitive, but all mental activity has an object. . . . It is an activity, and is directed to an object. It transcends itself, and as it were leaps over to the object, which is beyond it and independent of it."[3] Laird observes : "The process of knowledge refers beyond itself, and therefore an act of knowledge can never be aware of itself."[4] But it can be known by introspection. It is always a different act from the mental act of which it is aware.

But the Yogācāra may urge that Kumārila himself holds that the self (ātman) has the dual character of both the cognizer and the cognized. Kumārila holds that the self has a dual character ; the self is a cognizer in one aspect, and the cognized in another. The self is a conscious substance ; as conscious it is the cognizer, and as a substance it is the cognized.[5] So there is no contradiction here. But a mere cognition cannot be the cognizer. The self which is the substratum of cognition can be the cognizer ; it is apprehended by self-consciousness (ahaṃbuddhi) as a spiritual substance.[6] There

[1] *Space, Time, and Deity*, vol. ii, pp. 86–7.
[2] Ibid., vol. i, pp. 11–12.
[3] *Realism*, p. 81.
[4] *A Study in Realism*, p. 172.
[5] SV., Śūnyavāda, 67–8 ; see *Indian Psychology : Perception*, pp. 226–8.
[6] Ibid., NR. on 70, p. 289 ; see *Indian Psychology : Perception*, pp. 236 ff.

is no apprehension of the form of the apprehending cognition so that the cognition may be held to be the cognized object. The cognition may be supposed to be manifested as the instrument of cognition, or the act of cognition, or the agent of cognition, but it is never manifested as an *object* such as blue. So the cognition cannot be regarded as the cognized object (grāhya) By "cognition" we mean the act of cognition which can never apprehend itself.[1] If the cognition which appears in one form were held to apprehend another form, then the cognition could not apprehend an object though it appears in the form of a cognition. If consciousness were held to apprehend the form of a cognition though it appears in the form of an object only, the consciousness could be held to apprehend an object though it appears in the form of a cognition. In the consciousness "I know the jar" only the jar is manifested, and not the act of cognition or the agent of cognition or the self. The consciousness of the jar proves the existence of the jar. It is not an illusion. It is a right cognition. Hence the object of cognition is different from the act of cognition.[2]

If the act of cognition is identical with the object, they should not be called by different names. But the one is the act of experiencing and the other is experienced. "To use Lloyd Morgan's happy notation, the one is an *-ing*, the other an *-ed*." [3] If the cognitive act and the cognized object are different from each other, they cannot be said to be identical with each other. If they are identical with each other, and consist in one and the same cognition, there can be cognition of one of them only, either the cognitive act or the cognized object. If the same cognition were partly the cognitive act

[1] Ibid., 71, and NR., p. 290.
[2] Ibid., 72, and NR., p. 290; cf. S.V.M., p. 112.
[3] *Space, Time, and Deity*, vol. i, p. 12.

(grāhaka) and partly the cognized object (grāhya), one of them being suppressed, the other also would be suppressed, and both of them being suppressed, there would be negation of the cognition itself. Or, again, the cognition being non-different from the cognitive act and the cognized object which are different from each other, there would be difference in the cognition itself. Thus there being a difference in the cognition, the difference between the cognitive act and the cognized is established.

The Yogācāra may urge that, though there is a difference between the cognitive act and the cognized, yet the latter is not an object independent of the cognition but the cognition itself. Kumārila asserts that there is no ground for holding the cognized to be a cognition only. There is no cognition that is common to both the cognitive act and the cognized. The Buddhist does not recognize the reality of a universal which is different from individuals.[1] So he cannot admit the reality of any such distinct class as "cognition" apart from distinct cognitions. If there were such a distinct class as "cognition" different from the cognitive act and the cognized, they would be of the nature of cognition; and there would be negation of the "cognition" distinct from them, and devoid of their forms. Therefore, both the cognitive act and the cognized cannot be of the nature of cognition; only the cognitive act can be held to be of the nature of cognition; and this is admitted by both the Yogācāra and the Mīmāṃsaka. Cognitions are momentary, and appear in succession; they cannot, therefore, be related to each other as the cognitive act and the cognized. Even if the two cognitions appear simultaneously, they cannot be related to each other as the cognitive act and the cognized, inasmuch as they are independent of each

[1] *Indian Psychology: Perception*, pp. 165–172.

other. Therefore, the act of cognition and the cognized are different from each other.[1]

5. The Yogācāra identifies the object with the apprehending cognition. But if the object were identical with the cognition, the apprehension of one of them would lead to the apprehension of both.[2] But sometimes the consciousness of the object is not accompanied by the consciousness of the cognition.[3] Consciousness is different from self-consciousness. Consciousness of a jar is different from consciousness of the cognition of the jar which does not necessarily go along with the other. Consciousness does not necessarily involve self-consciousness.[4] If the object were identical with the cognition, there would be apprehension of the cognition also along with apprehension of the object; or there would be no apprehension of the object, just as there is no apprehension of the cognition. Similarly apprehension of the cognition would lead to apprehension of the object as well, especially because the Yogācāra regards the apprehending cognition as pure and formless. If the cognition were identical with the cognized object which has a definite form, such a formless cognition would not be possible; or if the object were not to be apprehended, the cognition too would not be apprehended because the object is held to be identical with the cognition.[5] Just as sometimes there is apprehension of the object without apprehension of the cognition, so sometimes there is apprehension of the cognition without apprehension of its object. Sometimes we remember a cognition without remembering its object. Sometimes we feel that we perceived something in the past but do not remember it aright. This is an instance of indefinite

[1] Ibid., Śūnyavāda, 124–151.
[2] Ibid., 73.
[3] Cf. Ibid., 79; 172–5.
[4] Ibid., 74; cf. NM., p. 542, and S.V.M., p. 113; see *Indian Psychology: Perception*, p. 239.
[5] Ibid., 75–7.

memory. If the cognition were identical with the object, the recollection of one would bring about the recollection of the other. But, as a matter of fact, there is sometimes a recollection of the cognition only without its object. Hence the cognized object (grahya) can never be identical with the apprehending cognition (grāhaka). They are entirely different from each other.[1]

6. The Yogācāra argues that the object is not different from its cognition, because there can be no cognition of anything which is not identical with it ; for instance, the cognition of " blue " cannot apprehend " yellow ". And, again, if there be no relation between the cognition and the object, the object cannot be said to be the cognized (grāhya). The Yogācāra regards the form of a cognition as the cognized object which is close to, and identical with, the cognition ; and it is for this reason that the object is cognized. Cognizability of the object by the cognition depends upon the relation between the two ; and the relation between them implies their identity with each other.[2]

To this Kumārila replies that proximity and relation are not possible in the case of a cognition for the simple reason that it is not perceived. Kumārila holds that a cognition is not perceived but inferred from cognizedness (jñātatā) of the object.[3] Proximity and relation can be said to be based on the subject-object-relationship between the cognition and the object ; the assumption of identity between them is useless.[4] Even in the absence of identity between the cognition and the object, proximity and relation between them are possible on account of their relation to each other as subject and object (viṣayaviṣayibhāva). Identity (tādātmya) consists in non-distinctness of place, while objectivity (viṣayatā) consists in being

[1] Ibid., 79–85, cf. NM., p. 544. [2] Ibid., 200 NR., p. 325.
[3] *Indian Psychology : Perception*, pp. 199–201.
[4] SV., 5, Śūnyavāda, 200.

the substratum of the result of cognition, viz. cognizedness (jñātatā).[1]

Thus Kumārila takes the relation of cognition to its object to be a unique relation called subject-object-relation (viṣaya-viṣayi-bhāva). It is unique and *sui generis*. It is different from spatial, temporal, causal, or any other objective relation. The relation of cognition to its object cannot be reduced to identity or co-essentiality. Identity is denial of relation The cognitive relation is a unique relation which makes the cognitive act apprehend the object. The cognition modifies the object apprehended by it. It produces cognizedness in the object from which the act of cognition is inferred. Kumārila is a realist. He emphatically denies identity of the cognitive act with the cognized object like any modern realist.

Laird also emphatically denies identity of the *knower*[2] and the *known*. " According to M. Bergson, true knowledge is intuition, and that, in its turn, is a process of union and becoming. . . . We know a thing by becoming it, and it is known by becoming us." Realists deny this. " Knowledge, they think, is never a kind of identity. . . . We do not become Niagara by looking at it; we do not become the past by remembering the great war. . . . On the contrary, if we became these things we could not know them at all. According to realists, the process of knowledge always implies that the mind is confronted with an object, and always implies that we are never under any conceivable circumstances identical with that object. Even when we apprehend our own experiences, the process of apprehension cannot be identical with the experience which is apprehended."[3] Thus knowledge presupposes the distinction between knower and known,

[1] Ibid., 200 NR., p. 325.
[2] Here the identity of *knowledge* with *known* is not shown.
[3] *A Study in Realism*, pp. 10–11.

and knowledge and known. Identity between them makes knowledge impossible.

Dr. Hasan beautifully describes the unique character of knowledge. " Knowledge is neither the relation of compresence, nor of causation, nor of reaction. It may presuppose compresence, it may presuppose causation, it may presuppose reaction ; it may be *of* compresence, it may be *of* causation, it may be *of* reaction ; but it is neither compresence, nor causation, nor reaction. It is *knowledge*. It is an ultimate unique fact, which has to be taken as such, and is not reducible to any other simpler facts. And this is what is meant by calling it *sui generis*." [1]

7. The Yogācāra holds that only one form is manifested to consciousness, and it is the form of a cognition. Kumārila also holds that only one form is manifested to consciousness but it is not the form of a cognition, but of an object. Here Kumārila agrees with the Naiyāyika. Kumārila agrees with the Yogācāra in advocating the presentative theory of perception ; but they advocate it in different ways. The Yogācāra, like Berkeley, holds that what we directly perceive are ideas of the mind. Kumārila, on the other hand, holds that what we directly perceive are external objects. Kumārila argues that the representative theory of perception contradicts our common experience. Ordinary people say : " The external object exists just as we perceive it " ; yet they do not hold that we perceive the form of an object after we have perceived the form of its cognition. A cognition is the means (upāya) of apprehending the object ; it presents an object to us because it is only the means of apprehending the form of the object.[2] The cognition directly presents an object to us ; it does not at first apprehend the form of a cognition, and through it the form of the object. The

[1] *Realism*, p. 162.

[2] Cf. NM., p. 541 ; S.B.S., ii, 2, 28.

cognition directly and immediately perceives external objects. So the representative theory of perception is wrong.[1]

The realists who recognize the existence of external objects pass over the apprehension of cognitions. They hold that we directly perceive external objects.[2] They do not admit the non-existence of external objects which the Yogācāra seeks to prove by inference, because we directly perceive them. Perception is of superior strength than inference.[3] The external object is never perceived to be of the same form as the internal cognition. The object is perceived as "*this* is blue"; it is never perceived as "*I* am blue", which is the true form of the internal cognition.[4] Thus both the Sautrāntika and the Yogācāra are in the wrong. The Sautrāntika wrongly holds that we infer the forms of external objects through the forms of cognitions which are directly and immediately perceived. The Yogācāra wrongly holds that we directly and immediately perceive only the forms of cognitions, and do not know the existence of external objects by any means of right knowledge. Kumārila holds that we directly perceive the forms of external objects; formless cognitions are inferred from cognizedness of external objects, which is produced in them by cognitions. Laird humorously criticizes the representative theory of knowledge. The realists "need not deny that much of our knowledge is merely representative. What they deny is, firstly, that knowledge *means* representation, and secondly that representative knowledge could occur without a direct, non-representative basis. If knowledge meant representation, the still pools would know the clouds and the trees which

[1] SV., Śūnyavāda, 226–7, and NR., p. 333.

[2] Jñānānubhavam utkramya bāhya eva pratīyate, ibid., 228.

[3] Ibid., 228, and NR.

[4] Ibid., 229, and NR.; cf. NM., p. 541; S.V.M., p. 112; S.D.S., p. 14.

they reflect. Indirect or representative knowledge, again, implies direct acquaintance at some point."[1]

8. The Yogācāra argues that, because cognition is the means of apprehending the object, it must be apprehended before there can be apprehension of its object. Kumārila urges that this argument is wrong because there are instances to the contrary. The eye is the means of apprehending colour ; but the eye is imperceptible ; it is not apprehended before colour is apprehended. Then the Yogācāra has argued that a cognition must be apprehended as soon as it is produced because there is no impediment to its apprehension. Kumārila urges that the cognition cannot be apprehended by itself ; and no other cognition has till then been produced which would apprehend it. Hence the cognition cannot be apprehended, since there is no means of apprehending it. The existence of the cognition is known by inference. It is inferred from cognizedness of the object. Or it is known by arthāpatti. If there were no cognition, we could not, in any other way, explain the existence of objects perceived by us. Hence after the object has been perceived we know the existence of the cognition as the means of right knowledge by arthapatti. Just as the eye can manifest other objects but cannot manifest itself, so the cognition can manifest other objects but cannot manifest itself. The cognition apprehends other objects but cannot apprehend itself.[2] Therefore, the cognition is not apprehended before it apprehends its object as the Yogācāra wrongly supposes. Further, he holds that all cognitions have cognitions for their objects, since there are no external objects. For him, therefore, there can be no distinction between the cognition of a jar and the cognition of this cognition, since both of them have cognitions for their objects which have no

[1] *A Study in Realism*, p. 11.
[2] SV., Śūnyavāda, 179–187.

existence distinct from them.[1] He cannot speak of apprehension of the cognition before the apprehension of an "object" by it, since he does not recognize the existence of the object.[2] If we admit apprehension of the cognition, either prior to, or simultaneously with, apprehension of the object, we shall be compelled to admit that the form apprehended belongs to the cognition, and deny the existence of the object altogether. It is for this reason that the Mīmāṃsaka seeks to prove that, though the cognition is produced before apprehension of the object, it is not apprehended before apprehension of the object; the object is apprehended before the cognition is subsequently known by inference or arthāpatti. Thus cognition of the object precedes that of its cognition.[3]

9. Kumārila argues that consciousness in itself is one and formless; the diversity of cognitions is due to the diversity of objects. So it is useless to assume forms of cognitions. Apprehending cognitions are of the nature of consciousness only; the external objects with their various forms are apprehended by them. Though the cognitions in themselves are formless, yet they apprehend a variety of objects. Cognitions are said to be of the forms of blue and the like because they apprehend these objects. The intrinsic differences among cognitions are determined by their objects.[4]

We find a similar argument in modern realism. Dr. Moore says: "We all know that the sensation of blue differs from that of green. But it is plain that if both are *sensations* they also have some point in common. What is it that they have in common? . . . I will call

[1] Ibid., 197, and NR. [2] Ibid., 230.

[3] Yugapad gṛhyamāṇe'pi nākāro'rthasya lakṣyate. Tasmād arthasya saṃbittiḥ pūrvaṃ yatnena sādhyate. Ibid., 241, and NR.

[4] Tasmāj jñānātmanaikatve grāhyabhedanibandhanaḥ. Saṃvittibhedaḥ siddho'tra kimākārāntareṇa naḥ. Ibid., 116; see NR., p. 300; cf. S.B.S., ii, 2, 28; NM., pp. 540–1.

the common element 'consciousness'. . . . We have then in every sensation two distinct terms, (1) '*consciousness*,' in respect of which all sensations are alike; and (2) *something* else, in respect of which one sensation differs from another. . . . I may be allowed to call this second term the 'object' of a sensation. . . . We have then in every sensation two distinct elements, one which I call consciousness, and another which I call the object of consciousness. This must be so if the sensation of blue and the sensation of green, though different in one respect, are alike in another: blue is one object of sensation and green is another, and consciousness, which both sensations have in common, is different from either."[1] Perry supports Moore's view. "It is evident," he says, "that 'sensation of yellow' contains over and above 'yellow', the element, 'sensation,' which is contained also in 'sensation of blue', 'sensation of green', etc."[2] Alexander says, "The acts of mind are not colourless. They are different with every variation of the object. . . . They vary according to the qualities of the object. It is not the same act of mind which apprehends green as apprehends red."[3]

10. The Yogācāra argues that one and the same object appears different to different persons. The same woman may appear beautiful to an amorous young man, loathsome as a corpse to an ascetic, and delicious to a carnivorous animal. But the same object cannot possess these diverse forms at the same time. Hence there is no external object; the different forms that are apprehended by different persons are forms of cognitions only.[4] The Yogācāra is a subjective idealist. He cannot recognize the existence of any object independent of consciousness. Likewise he does not recognize the

[1] *Philosophical Studies*, p. 17 (italics are mine).
[2] *Present Philosophical Tendencies*, p. 321.
[3] *Space, Time, and Deity*, vol. i, pp. 25–6. [4] SV., Śūnyavāda, 59.

objectivity of value independent of consciousness. He treats value as purely subjective.

Kumārila contends that the same object may possess diverse forms. A particular form is perceived by a particular individual on account of a particular psychical disposition (vāsanā) in his mind, which is stronger and more permanent than others. The same woman possesses the properties of a beautiful damsel, a dead body, and delicious food at the same time. An ascetic with his deep-rooted aversion to the world and hatred for women perceives her as a corpse. A lustful man with his strong sex instinct perceives her as a beautiful damsel—an object of enjoyment. And a carnivorous animal, accustomed to eating flesh, perceives her as a palatable lump of flesh. The determining condition of the perception of a particular form is the psychical disposition (vāsanā) which is deeply imprinted on the mind of each individual. The psychical disposition is the result of repeated similar experiences. It predisposes the mind to perceive a particular form of an object. An object is sometimes multiform. It possesses diverse forms. But a particular form is perceived by an individual, which fits in with his deep-rooted psychical disposition (vāsanā) which is awakened in his mind at the time.[1] The external object in co-operation with a psychical disposition is the cause of the perception of its particular form.[2]

The variability of appearance does not take away from the reality of an object. It depends partly upon subjective factors and partly upon objective factors. Kumārila does not treat value as purely subjective or purely objective. He makes it partly subjective and partly objective. Value resides in an object independent of consciousness. But it is appreciated by a person with an appropriate vāsanā.

[1] Ibid., 215–16, and NR.

[2] Vāsanāḥ sahakāriṇyo vyavasthākāradarśane, ibid., 215; cf. NM., p. 547; Y.B., iv, 15.

Vāsanā is a psychical disposition. It may be interpreted as desire. Value depends partly upon desire, though it is not a creation of desire.

There is a divergence of opinion on the nature and conditions of value. Some treat it as subjective and dependent on consciousness. Some treat it as objective and independent of consciousness. Others treat value as subjective, though they regard the object having value as independent of consciousness. Perry holds the last view. "Consciousness is a relation into which things enter without forfeiting their independence. To be conscious of *a* means that it is acted on in a peculiar manner ; and while this action gives *a* a new status and new connections, it does not condition the being of *a*, or give it its character as *a*. Thus if I desire *a*, it becomes a *thing desired*, and is connected in a new way with the other things which I desire, or with the things I remember, perceive, etc. ; while it nevertheless *is*, and is *a*, quite independently of this circumstance. But it is entirely conceivable that the *value* of *a* should consist in its being desired ; in other words, in that specific relationship which the desiderative consciousness supplies. We should then say that the being or nature of things is independent of their possessing value, but not that *their possessing value* is independent of consciousness. . . . Things do derive value from their being desired, and possess value in proportion as they are desired."[1] Kumārila seems to hold that value is inherent in an object independent of consciousness, but it is appreciated by a person with an appropriate psychical disposition (vāsanā) or desire. Alexander looks upon tertiary qualities neither as purely subjective nor as purely objective but as "subject-object-determinations".[2] "In every value," he says, "there are two sides, the subject of valuation

[1] *Present Philosophical Tendencies*, pp. 332–3.
[2] *Space, Time, and Deity*, vol. ii, p. 238.

and the object of value, and the value resides in the relation between the two and does not exist apart from them. The object has value as possessed by the subject, and the subject has value as possessing the object. . . . Value is not mere pleasure, or the capacity of giving it, but is the satisfaction of an appetite of the valuer. . . . Values arise out of our likings and satisfy them." [1]

11. The Yogacāra argues that one and the same object appears long in comparison with one thing, and short in comparison with another. But it cannot possess these contradictory qualities at the same time. Hence the object does not exist; the different appearances are but different ideas in the minds of the perceiving individuals.[2]

Kumārila urges that there is no contradiction among the diverse forms of the same object. The diversity of forms is due to differences based upon comparison of the object with various other objects (apekṣānibandhana). The same object may be long in comparison with one object, and short in comparison with another. Judgment and comparison may account for the diversity of appearances. So there is no contradiction here. It is wrong to argue that an object does not exist because it appears different to different individuals at the same time, or to the same individual at different times.[3] The diversity of forms may exist in the same object because they are perceived as such by different individuals.[4] The reality of an object is established by perception. Different individuals have different perceptions of the same object. This is sufficient proof of the fact that the object is

[1] Ibid., vol. ii, pp. 302–3. [2] SV., Śūnyavāda, 59; cf. Berkeley.

[3] Nānekākārasaṃvitterniräkāratvakalpanā yuktā, ibid., 218. In criticizing Berkeley, Fraser observes: "Does it follow that if extension, viewed apart from the perceptions of individuals, is 'neither great nor small', or that motion, so abstracted, is 'neither swift nor slow', they must, after conscious mind is withdrawn, be 'nothing at all'?" (Fraser's *Selections from Berkeley*, p. 41, n.)

[4] Pratītibhedāttu bahvākāratvasambhavaḥ, SV., 5, Śūnyavāda, 218.

endowed with diverse forms.[1] There is no hard and fast rule that an object can have only one form. We must take an object to be of one form or of diverse forms according as we perceive it.[2] The reality of an object is determined by the perception of it.[3] One form of an object is perceived by one, and not perceived by another. "Thus then the object will have one form or the other, according as it happens to be cognized by this or that person. Such appearance or disappearance may be based upon the differences of time, place, etc.; for instance, a well-armed man in the jungle is recognized as a huntsman, while in the midst of a town, he is only known as a policeman."[4] Though the properties of colour, odour, and the like exist separately in the same object, they are not perceived through the same sense-organ; each quality is perceived through a separate sense-organ; colour is perceived through the visual organ, odour through the olfactory organ, and so on.[5] Though the qualities of colour, odour, etc., are different from one another, they belong to the same substance, and consequently are not absolutely different from one another. Thus the substance, though in itself only one, becomes diverse, according to the diversity of the forms of its properties.[6] Similarly an object is recognized as a jar by one person, as made up of earth by another person, and so on; these qualities exist in the same object for all persons, but they are not recognized by all because their recognition depends upon the recollection of these qualities perceived in the past, and of the words that denote their classes. Recognition of an object presupposes recollection of the class to which it belongs. Different qualities of an object are recognized by different persons

[1] Saṃvitteścāviruddhānām ekasminnapi sambhavaḥ, ibid., 219.

[2] Ibid., 217–220, and NR.

[3] Samvinniṣṭhā hi vastuvyavasthitiḥ, NR. on ibid., 220.

[4] Ibid., 221, NR., E.T., p. 175, n.

[5] Ibid., 223 and 225.

[6] Ibid., 98, and NR.

because they remember different qualities perceived in the past and the classes to which they belong.[1] Thus various appearances of the same object are not inconsistent with its reality independent of its cognitions. Kumārila holds that primary, secondary, and tertiary qualities abide in the external object.

Locke appeals to the relativity of sensations to prove the unreality of secondary qualities. Berkeley also appeals to the same argument to prove the unreality of primary qualities. C. D. Broad elaborately criticizes the arguments of Locke and Berkeley under the heads of "synthetic incompatibility" in the evidence of the senses, either of one person or of different persons.[2] For example, there is the temperature test. "You put one hand in hot water and one in cold, and afterwards both in lukewarm water which will then feel hot to the cooled hand and cold to the heated one. . . . Professor Broad dismisses the temperature test on the grounds that (*a*) it does not disprove the existence of *some* temperature, and (*b*) that the two temperatures need not be thought of as occupying the same points."[3] He says: "It seems much more reasonable to conclude from the experiment that, though other bodies have temperatures, we cannot tell precisely what their degree is from that of the felt temperature of our hands, than that other bodies have no temperature at all and our own none except when we perceive it."[4] Broad says, "appearances are not perceptions of nothing but have an object just as much as do those which are supposed to be perceptions of the real." Thus variability of appearances does not disprove the reality of qualities of external objects. It proves relativity, but not unreality. This is also the contention of Kumārila.

[1] Ibid., 224.
[2] *Perception, Physics, and Reality*, pp. 8 ff.
[3] *The New Idealism*, p. 53; *Perception, Physics, and Reality*, pp. 10–17.
[4] *Perception, Physics, and Reality*, p. 13.

Hence Kumārila concludes that the non-existence of the external object is not proved by any means of valid knowledge. Perception apprehends external objects ; so it cannot prove their non-existence. Nor can inference prove it ; inference, on the contrary, proves the existence of external objects. There is no scope of verbal authority (āgama) in the denial of external objects. On the other hand, injunctions and prohibitions laid down in the Śāstras bear testimony to the existence of external objects. Analogy (upamā) cannot prove the non-existence of external objects, because the Yogācāra does not admit anything else that is similar to cognitions. Nor can presumption (arthāpatti) prove the non-existence of external objects. In fact, it proves quite the contrary. If there were no external objects there would be no differences among cognitions. Hence Kumārila concludes that there is scope for negation only in the denial of external objects ; in other words, the denial of external objects can only be denied ; the external objects do exist.[1] Moreover, practical considerations of morality and religion demand a belief in the existence of the external world and objectivity of values. Actions and their results in the world clearly prove the existence of the world.[2] Thus both theoretical and practical considerations force upon us recognition of the external reality.

§ 4. *Pārthasārathimiśra's Exposition of the Yogācārc Idealism*

Pārthasarathimiśra, a follower of Kumārila, gives a critical exposition of the Yogācāra idealism in *Śāstradīpikā*. He states the following arguments of the Yogācāra for the denial of external objects :—

(1) We have perceptions in such forms as "this is blue", "this is yellow", etc. The Yogacara asks whether

[1] SV., Śūnyavāda, 259–261, and NR., p. 343.

[2] Ibid., nirālambanavāda, 1–3, 12–13, and 72–3; see also *The Karma-Mīmāṃsā* (A. B. Keith), pp. 44–52.

in such perceptions, a mere cognition or an external object is manifested to consciousness. If it is a mere cognition, it is either perceived or inferred. If it is perceived, it must be endowed with a form, since a formless cognition is not perceived ; and the form perceived must be held to belong to the cognition inasmuch as only one form is perceived. If two forms were perceived, one of them might be held to be a form of the cognition, and the other, to be a form of the object. But we do not perceive two forms. We perceive a single form, and it must be held to belong to the cognition. The external object is not perceived ; hence it does not exist.[1] If it were existent, it would be perceived by a cognition at some time or other. But it is never perceived. In fact, the external object can never be related to cognition, and therefore cannot be perceived by it. A cognition cannot function towards an external object. It makes itself its object of cognition.[2]

(2) The parsimony of hypotheses demands that we should recognize the existence of cognitions only. It is a cognition that is manifested in the form of blue or the like.[3] It is known to all that blue, yellow, and the like are perceived. If these are regarded as cognitions which appear to be external objects owing to an illusion, it does not involve many assumptions. But if they are regarded as external objects, it involves many needless assumptions, since objects cannot be established without cognitions apprehending them. It is true that the Yogācāra assumes a single cognition to have the power of cognizing and being cognized. But the realist unnecessarily adds to the number of assumptions ; he assumes the existence of the percipient cognition and the perceptible object and their different capacities. Thus the parsimony of hypotheses is in favour of the Yogācāra idealism.[4]

(3) Pārthasārathimiśra contends that a cognition is not perceived but inferred from cognizedness (jñātatā)

[1] SD., p. 146. [2] SDP., p. 175. [3] SD., p. 146. [4] YSP., p. 147.

produced by it in the object ; and because a cognition is imperceptible it cannot be manifested to consciousness in the forms of blue and the like. Hence he concludes that external objects are manifested to consciousness in the forms of blue and the like, and cognitions are inferred from their manifestation. Thus external objects exist.[1]

The Yogacāra refutes this argument. If a cognition is imperceptible, it cannot be known by any other means of valid knowledge.[2] If a cognition were known by an inferential cognition, it would be known by another, and so on *ad infinitum*. Further, a cognition is self-luminous ; it does not depend upon any other cognition for its manifestation.[3] If a cognition were always imperceptible, its invariable concomitance with any other thing would never be perceived, and consequently it could never be inferred. Hence a cognition must be held to be perceptible.[4]

(4) The cognition cannot be said to be inferrible, since there is no mark of inference (liṅga). The external object (artha) cannot be regarded as the mark of inference which is an invariable concomitant of the object of inference. The external object is not an invariable concomitant of the cognition. The Mīmāṃsaka himself admits that external objects exist during deep sleep when there are no cognitions at all.[5]

The use of an external object (arthavyavahāra) also cannot be regarded as the mark of inference. It may be argued that the use of an object is an invariable concomitant of the cognition of the object. An object cannot be used unless it is known beforehand. It is used at times ; and the occasional use of the object presupposes the cognition of it as its cause. Hence a cognition is inferred from the use of an object. The Yogācāra urges that if the cognition of an object were inferred from its use, there would be no manifestation of cognition before the use of an

[1] SD., p. 146 SDP., p. 175. [2] SD., p. 146.
[3] YSP., p. 147. [4] SDP., p. 175. [5] SD., p. 147.

object. But, as a matter of fact, even before using a jar I may be conscious of the fact that I know the jar. Hence the cognition is directly perceived, and not inferred from the use of an object.[1]

A property of the object (arthadharma), viz. cognizedness produced by a cognition in the object also cannot be said to be the mark of inference, since there is no evidence for its existence. If a cognition were inferred from cognizedness of an object, the past and the future objects would never be cognized. They do not exist at present; therefore cognizedness cannot be produced in them by a present cognition.[2]

Hence we must admit that cognitions are perceptible, and the forms perceived belong to cognitions, and not to external objects. There is no evidence for the existence of external objects.[3]

(5) The Yogācāra further argues that the blue and the like are nothing but modes of cognition because they are cognized. Any other object which is not cognized cannot be said to be perceptible.[4] The blue and the like are cognized; they are objects of cognition. What is

[1] SD., pp. 147–8.

[2] SD., pp. 148 and 152; see *Indian Psychology. Perception*, pp. 199–210.

[3] SD., p. 148.

[4] Saṃvedyatvācca nīlāderjñānākāratvaniścayaḥ. Arthāntarasya ca grāhyalakṣaṇaṃ na hi yujyate. SD., p. 147; cf. S.V.M., p. 110; cf. Berkeley. Berkeley similarly argues: "It is indeed an opinion strangely prevailing amongst men, that houses, mountains, rivers, and in a word all sensible objects, have an existence, natural or real, distinct from their being perceived by the understanding. But, with how great an assurance and acquiescence soever this principle may be entertained in the world, yet whoever shall find in his heart to call it in question may, if I mistake not, perceive it to involve a manifest contradiction. For, what are the forementioned objects but the things we perceive by sense? and what do we perceive besides our own ideas or sensations? and is it not plainly repugnant that any one of *these*, or any combination of them, should exist unperceived?" (*Principles of Human Knowledge*, p. 35.) Likewise, "Is it not as great a contradiction to talk of *conceiving* a thing which is *unconceived*? And what is conceived is surely in the mind." (*Dialogue between Hylas and Philonous*, p. 153.)

related to a cognition is cognized. The so-called external object cannot be related to a cognition, and cannot, therefore, be cognized. Hence the blue and the like which are cognized must be modes of cognition.[1] If they are something other than cognition, they can never be cognized.[2] Even the ordinary people who say that the cognition of " blue " is produced by the blue object, tacitly admit that the object cognized is nothing but a mode of cognition.[3] They do not believe in the existence of any object which is not cognized ; and an object which is not cognized cannot be said to be an object of cognition. If the object were different from its cognition, they could not be related to each other as the cognizer and the cognized because there is no relation between them. But if the object is held to be a mere form of cognition, it can be apprehended by it ; the cognition and the object can be related to each other as the cognizer and the cognized on account of the relation of identity between them.[4] This is a stock argument of the western idealists also.

(6) Further, the object and its cognition are invariably perceived together at the same time. Hence they must be identical with each other. A jar and a cloth are different from each other ; so they are not invariably perceived together at the same time. It cannot be said that a cognition is not always perceived when its object is perceived. The object is not only perceived along with its cognition, but it is also remembered in future along with its cognition. Nothing can be remembered unless it was perceived in the past. Thus the recollection of an

[1] SDP., p. 176 ; cf. Berkeley's thesis, *Esse* is *percipi*.

[2] Kiṃ ca vedyatvādapi nīlāderjñānākāratvaṃ, na hyanātmano nīlasya pītavat vedyatā sambhavati, SD., p. 148.

[3] YSP., p. 147. Berkeley says : " The only thing whose existence we deny is that which *philosophers* call *matter* or *corporeal substance*. And in doing of this there is no damage done to the rest of mankind, who, I dare say, will never miss it." (*Principles of Human Knowledge*, p. 58.)

[4] YSP., p. 147.

object perceived in the past proves that the cognition was perceived in the past along with its object.[1]

(7) Further, the cognition is self-luminous ; it apprehends itself when it apprehends its object. The cognition is apprehended as soon as it is produced. It cannot be held that a cognition which is in itself formless assumes the form of its object when it is related to it, because a formless cognition is never apprehended. A cognition is always apprehended as endowed with a definite form. So the forms of blue and the like which are apprehended belong to cognitions, and not to external objects. Just as the forms of dream-cognitions are admitted by all to be mere forms of cognitions, so the forms of waking cognitions also should be regarded as mere forms of cognitions, and not of external objects.[2]

(8) Lastly, the cognition of blue or the like apprehends itself as its own object. It is self-contradictory to hold that a cognition apprehends an external object, because they possess contradictory qualities. Firstly, an object is inert and unconscious ; it is quite different in nature from a cognition which is a mode of consciousness. Therefore the object cannot be apprehended by a cognition. Secondly, the object is said to be permanent, while the cognition is momentary. The permanent object cannot be apprehended by a momentary cognition. Thirdly, the object is varied and multiform in nature, and possesses many qualities. It cannot, therefore, be apprehended by a single uniform cognition. Fourthly, an object is external, while the cognition is internal. Therefore, the object can never be apprehended by the cognition, because what is extra-mental cannot come into relationship with a cognition. The external object can never be apprehended by a cognition, whether it is real or unreal.[3]

[1] SD., pp. 152–3. [2] Ibid., pp. 153–4.
[3] Ajñānasthiracitratvabāhyatvāderanātmanah. Asato vā sato vāpi kathaṃ vijñānavedyatyā ? SD., p. 154.

Hence the Yogācāra concludes that a cognition apprehends itself, and not an external object; it is self-luminous: it is apprehended by itself, and not by any other cognition. There is no object other than the cognition itself; there is no other cognition to apprehend it, which is distinct from itself. It has no other object than itself; it has no other subject than itself. It manifests itself. It is its own subject; it is its own object. The distinction of subject and object is within consciousness itself, and not beyond it.[1]

§ 5. *Pārthasārathimiśra's Criticism of the Yogācāra Idealism*

(1) The Yogācāra holds that the cognition of blue does not apprehend an external object called blue. It apprehends itself. Blue that is cognized is of the nature of cognition. Pārthasārathimiśra asks what cognition apprehends that the cognition of blue cognizes itself. The cognition of blue which is said to cognize itself is not apprehended by itself. In the cognition "this is blue" there is no consciousness that the cognition apprehends itself, and not an external object; nor is there any consciousness that blue that is cognized is of the nature of cognition. In the cognition "this is blue" only *blue* is manifested to consciousness, but there is no other consciousness of any cognition. Thus in the cognition "this is blue" there is no consciousness of the cognition of blue apprehending itself as its own object. Actual experience gives the lie to the Yogācāra's theory.[2]

(2) It may be argued that the cognition cognizing itself as its own object is not apprehended by itself, but it is known by inference. It is inferred from the fact that whatever is cognized must be a mode of cognition, and

[1] Ibid., p. 154.

[2] Na hi nīlamidam ityatra svātmaparyavasāyitvaṃ nīlākārasya ca jñānātmakatvaṃ prakāśate nīlamātraprakāśanāt, SD., p. 154.

what is distinct from consciousness cannot be apprehended by a cognition and cannot, therefore, be regarded as the cognized object. It is also inferred from the invariably simultaneous perception of the object and the apprehending cognition.

Pārthasārathimiśra contends that if this inference also apprehends itself as its own object, it cannot apprehend that any other cognition apprehends itself as its own object. If the inference apprehends only itself and cannot transcend itself, it cannot possibly know anything about any other cognition. If the inference is held not to apprehend itself but something else, the cognition of blue also may be held not to apprehend itself but something other than itself, viz., the blue object. The cognition of blue manifests an external object as " this is blue " ; it cannot therefore be regarded as confined to itself only.[1]

(3) The Yogācāra wrongly argues that an external object which is distinct from its cognition cannot enter into relationship with the cognition and be apprehended by it, and thus cannot be regarded as the cognized object (grāhya). He also erroneously argues that if an external object be regarded as the object of cognition, there can be no invariably simultaneous perception of the object with its cognition. All these are contradicted by the inference of the Yogācāra himself. The inference does not apprehend itself as its own object ; but it goes beyond itself and apprehends another cognition (e.g. the cognition of blue) cognizing itself as its own object. Thus the Yogācāra tacitly admits that all cognitions do not apprehend themselves as their own objects. If the inference is held to be confined to itself and apprehending itself as its own object, it cannot prove that the cognition of blue apprehends itself as its own object. If, on the other hand, the inference is held to apprehend that the cognition of blue apprehends itself as its own object,

[1] SD., pp. 154–5.

it transcends itself and apprehends something other than itself.[1] Thus it is established that the object of cognition is something other than the cognition itself, and the cognized object is not identical with the apprehending cognition.[2]

Then, again, the act of inference and the object of inference (viz. the cognition of blue cognizing itself) are invariably perceived together at the same time. But still the Yogācāra does not hold them to be identical with each other. Then it may equally be argued that, though blue and cognition of blue are invariably perceived together at the same time, they are not identical with each other.[3] In fact, Pārthasārathimiśra holds that the object and its cognition are not simultaneously perceived as erroneously held by the Yogācāra.

(4) The cognition of nescience (ajñāna) is a fact of experience. Nescience is negation of cognition. It is cognized as an object of cognition. But though negation of cognition is cognized as the object of cognition, it is not of the nature of cognition since cognition and its negation possess contradictory qualities. This proves that an object can be cognized though it is not of the nature of cognition.[4]

(5) Recognition apprehends an object as "this is that". In recognition an object perceived is recognized as that which was perceived in the past. It manifests an object as existing in the past and the present. It apprehends the identity of an object in the past and the present. But a momentary cognition cannot apprehend a permanent object. If an object were identical with its cognition, the permanent object would be identical with a momentary recognition. But this is absurd. Hence the cognized object can never be regarded as identical with the apprehending cognition.[5]

[1] Ibid., p. 155. [2] SDP., p. 196. [3] SDP., p. 196.
[4] SD., p. 156. [5] Ibid., p. 156.

(6) Then, again, a single motley cognition (citrabuddhi) apprehends a multiform object. But if the object were identical with its apprehending cognition, the single cognition of a multiform object would be multiform. But a single cognition cannot assume many forms. Though the object is multiform and complex, its cognition is a "simple pulse of consciousness" in the language of William James.[1] To think of the cognition of a complex object as complex involves the psychologist's fallacy. Hence the cognized object must be different from the apprehending cognition.

(7) It may be urged that a single object cannot be endowed with many forms just as a single cognition cannot assume many forms, and likewise the object cannot be permanent just as a cognition is not permanent. Pārthasārathimiśra contends that the external object may be permanent or impermanent, multiform or uniform, but it can, by no means, be held to be identical with the apprehending cognition. If the object is regarded as permanent and multiform and as identical with its cognition, the cognition which is known to be momentary and uniform will become permanent and multiform. But permanence and multiformity cannot be regarded as modes of cognition ; so they must be held to be forms of the external object. The permanent and multiform object, be it real or unreal, is apprehended by a cognition not as a mode of cognition but as something other than cognition. Hence it must be external to, and independent of, the apprehending cognition.[2]

(8) Even the Yogācāra who denies the existence of external objects attributes externality to a cognition. He holds that though there is no external object, a cognition appears as if it were an external object. This externality which is attributed by him to a cognition must be admitted

[1] Ibid., p. 156.
[2] SD., p. 156.

to be something distinct from cognition.[1] It can never be regarded as identical with cognition. Hence we are compelled to admit that cognitions apprehend objects which are something other than cognitions.[2] The existence of external objects is established on the strength of the testimony of consciousness. An external object is the object of cognition. It is a fact of experience. We cannot deny the cognizability of an external object.[3]

Pārthasārathi has already pointed out that it is not possible for a cognition to apprehend itself. In the perceptions "this is blue", "this is yellow", etc., external objects which are distinct from consciousness are manifested to consciousness ; but cognitions are not manifested to consciousness in these perceptions. Cognitions are inferred from the cognizedness of external objects.[4]

Cognition cannot be said to be the object of self-consciousness (ahaṃpratyaya). The self or the knower is the object of self-consciousness.[5] A cognition is not the object of self-consciousness. Hence an external object must be regarded as the object of cognition. The cognizability of an object consists in its being the substratum of cognizedness produced in it by its cognition.[6]

(9) The Yogācāra argues that an object is identical with its cognition because they are always perceived together simultaneously. But Pārthasārathimiśra points out that when the object is perceived, its cognition is not perceived. In the perception of an object only the object

[1] Jñānātiriktaṃ ca vāhyam, SD., p. 156 ; cf. SV., nirālambanavāda, 57.

[2] Vijñānānām anātmagrāhitvaṃ balād abhyupagantavyam, ibid., p. 156.

[3] Bāhyasyaiva hi tadā saṃvedyatvaṃ darśanabalād abhyupagamyate, ibid., p. 156.

[4] Nīlādivittīnam idaṃ nīlam idaṃ pītamityanātmāvabhāsitvāt ātmāvabhāsitvābhāvāt, SD., p. 156.

[5] See *Indian Psychology : Perception*, pp. 236–7.

[6] SD., p. 157.

is manifested, and not its cognition, far less the perceptibility of the cognition.[1] The Yogācāra wrongly holds that a cognition is always directly and immediately perceived along with an object. As a matter of fact, a cognition is not at all perceived along with its object.

It is wrong to argue that the recollection of an object as perceived in the past proves that the object was perceived along with its cognition in the past. In recollection it is an *object* that is remembered ; the cognition of the object is not remembered. The recollection of an object is not a perceptual cognition because it is not produced by the sense-organs. It presupposes the previous cognition of the object which is inferred from it as its cause.[2]

(10) The objects of cognition such as blue and the like cannot be regarded as identical with cognitions because objects of inference are known indirectly through the medium of other cognitions, but cognitions are admitted by the Yogācāra to be directly perceived. If the object were identical with its cognition, the object of inference would be identical with the inferential cognition which would thus possess the contradictory qualities of immediacy and mediacy ; it would be mediate like its object, and immediate in itself inasmuch as it is directly perceived. An object is immediately known (aparokṣa) when it is directly perceived ; and is mediately known (parokṣa) when it is inferred. Thus the same object can possess the qualities of immediacy and mediacy. But the same cognition cannot possess immediacy as well as mediacy because it is always directly perceived. Hence the object can never be regarded as a mode of cognition.[3]

(11) The Yogācāra holds that permanent external objects are unreal but momentary cognitions are real ; the cognized objects are identical with cognitions ; they

[1] Arthāvabhāsasamaye saṃvidaḥ pratibhāsa eva nāsti nitarām āparokṣyam, SD., p. 160.

[2] SD., pp. 160–1 ; cf. SV., Śūnyavāda, p. 192. [3] Ibid., p 161.

are mere modes of cognition which appear to be external objects. But Pārthasārathimiśra contends that momentary real cognitions can never appear as permanent unreal objects because they possess contradictory qualities. Or permanent unreal objects cannot be regarded as identical with momentary real cognitions.[1]

(12) Further, if objects were identical with the apprehending cognitions, the past objects inferred would be identical with the inferential cognitions. But inferential cognitions exist at present while their objects existed in the past. Past objects can never be identical with present cognitions. This clearly proves that objects are not identical with the apprehending cognitions.[2]

(13) The Yogācāra argues that waking cognitions are without corresponding external objects because they are cognitions like dream-cognitions. But Pārthasārathimiśra, like Kumārila, contends that dream-cognitions are not without any real substratum in external objects. In dream-cognitions it is external objects perceived in some other time and place that are remembered owing to revival of their subconscious impressions under the influence of some unseen force (adṛṣṭa) ; but the remembered objects appear to be present here and now owing to an illusion on account of the temporary disorder of the mind because of drowsiness.[3] The contents of dreams are all objects of past experience, and are therefore real. But the connections among them are the fabrication of the mind and are unreal.[4]

(14) The Yogācāra also argues that waking cognitions are without corresponding external objects like illusions. But Pārthasārathimiśra, like Kumārila, urges that even illusions are not without a real substratum in external

[1] Ibid., p. 161.

[2] SD., p. 161.

[3] Ibid., pp. 162–3; cf. SV., nirālambanavāda, 107–9.

[4] Sarvatra saṃsargamātram asad evāvabhāsate saṃsargiṇastu santa eva, SD., p. 163.

objects. In the illusory perception of silver in a shell both shell and silver are real. Silver was perceived in the past and is remembered at present, and the memory-image of silver is erroneously attributed to the shell that is perceived here and now.[1] The Bhāṭṭa Mīmāṃsaka is an advocate of the doctrine of Viparītakhyati according to which an error consists in the apprehension of an object as something different.[2]

(15) The Yogācāra argues that waking cognitions are false and without any corresponding real objects because they are cognitions like dream-cognitions. But Pārthasārathimiśra urges that the same argument may with equal force be applied to the inference of the Yogacara himself. If waking cognitions are false because they are cognitions like dream-cognitions, then the inference also by which the Yogācāra seeks to prove the falsity of waking cognitions is false because the inference is a cognition like a dream-cognition. If the inference is held not to be false though it is a cognition, then " cognition " cannot be regarded as the true mark of inference because it is not the invariable concomitant of falsity which is the object of inference. Hence Śavara has truly said : " Only those cognitions which are produced by disordered sense-organs are false ; other cognitions are not false." Dream-cognitions are false because they are produced by the mind vitiated by drowsiness. But uncontradicted waking perceptions produced by unvitiated sense-organs cannot be regarded as false. They apprehend external objects which must be regarded as real.[3]

§ 6. *Prabhākara's Exposition of the Yogacara Idealism*

(1) The Yogācāra argues that a cognition (vitti) and an object of cognition (vedya) are invariably perceived

[1] Ibid., p. 163 ; cf. SV., nirālambanavāda, 109–111.
[2] See *Indian Psychology : Perception*, pp. 283–4 ; also p. 305.
[3] SD., p. 165 ; see also Bhāṭṭacintāmaṇi.

together. An object can never be perceived apart from its cognition ; nor can a cognition ever be perceived apart from its object. The objects, which are different from each other such as a jar and a cloth, are not invariably perceived simultaneously. Hence the blue and the cognition of blue, which are invariably perceived simultaneously, are identical with each other.[1] Thus even the perceived object which is presented to consciousness as " this " is identical with its percipient cognition.[2]

(2) Why, then, are the cognized object and the apprehending cognition manifested to consciousness as different from each other ? The Yogācāra holds that this difference is not real but apparent ; one and the same cognition appears to be bifurcated into the internal cognition and the external object owing to an illusion like the appearance of the double moon. The internal cognition appears to be an external object owing to an illusion.[3]

(3) What is the cause of this illusion of difference ? A beginningless series of subconscious impressions of difference (anādibhedavāsanā) is the cause of this illusion. Is the cognition endowed with a form produced by an external object or by the immediately preceding cognition ?

The realist holds that it is produced by an external object. Firstly, it cannot be produced by an immediately preceding cognition because an immediately preceding cognition of a jar can produce only a cognition of a jar, but not a cognition of a cloth. But, as a matter of fact, the cognition of a cloth arises after the cognition of a jar. If the cognition of a jar produced the cognition of a cloth, there would be the cognition of a cloth at a time and in a place when and where there was no cloth. But it is never found to be so. The cognition of a cloth is produced

[1] PP., pp. 57–8.

[2] Etenaiva nyāyenāhankārāspadībhūtasyāpyaṃśasya vitterabhedo yuktaḥ, ibid., p. 58.

[3] Ibid., p. 58.

at a particular time and in a particular place when and where the cloth exists. Hence an external object which is quite different from the immediately preceding cognition is the cause of a particular cognition with a definite form.[1] Secondly, if the object were not different from its cognition, there would be no distinction between right knowledge and false knowledge. If an external object did not exist, the right cognition of water would not lead to effective action (arthakriyā) in the shape of quenching of thirst, just as the false cognition of water or mirage is not followed by quenching our thirst. Hence we must admit the existence of external objects.[2]

The Yogācāra holds that the assumption of the existence of external objects is absolutely groundless. Nobody directly perceives that an external object produces the form of its cognition ; it is only assumed. Then it is better to assume that an immediately preceding cognition produces the form of the succeeding cognition because both of them are perceived. The realist has to admit the different forms of cognitions which are said to be produced by external objects. Hence it is useless to admit the forms of external objects ; the forms of cognitions may be said to be due to the cognitions of something at some time in some place. The assumption of external objects is gratuitous.

(4) The Yogācāra regards practical efficiency (arthakriyā) also as of the nature of cognition. Some cognitions are capable of effective actions, while others are incapable of effective actions. The former are right cognitions while the latter are wrong cognitions.[3]

(5) We must admit that immediately preceding cognitions have the power of producing distinct forms in succeeding cognitions. Forms of dream-cognitions are

[1] PP., p. 58 ; cf. S.V.M.
[2] PP., pp. 58–9.
[3] Ibid., p. 59.

evidently not produced by external objects. They are produced by immediately preceding cognitions. They cannot be said to be produced by external objects existing at some other time and place because they do not exist at the time when dream-cognitions are produced. Non-existent objects cannot produce anything. Hence the forms of dream-cognitions are due to subconscious impressions which are residua of previous cognitions. Cognitions and subconscious impressions form a beginningless series, and are related to each other as causes and effects.

(6) The Yogācāra does not abolish the distinction between right cognitions and false cognitions. Right cognitions are those which are capable of effective actions and are in harmony with their cognitions ; wrong cognitions are those which are not capable of effective actions or which are not in harmony with the cognitions of actions which follow them.

Cognitions are the means to the fulfilment of desires, and are subservient to actions which, again, are of the nature of cognitions. Hence the distinction between the means of right knowledge (pramāṇa) and the result of right knowledge (phala) is a distinction within cognitions. Cognitions endowed with distinct forms are related to one another as the means (pramāṇa) and the end (phala), and form a continuous stream of consciousness without a beginning. There are no external objects over and above this stream of consciousness.[1]

§ 7. *Prabhākara's Criticism of the Yogācāra Idealism*

(1) Prabhākara urges that the object and its cognition can be invariably perceived together at the same time, though they are different from each other. The cognition of blue is itself the perception of blue. If blue does not exist, it cannot be perceived. There can be no perception

[1] PP., p. 59 ; see Bṛhatī (Madras, 1934) with Ṛjuvimalā, pp. 68 ff.

of blue, if blue does not exist. But there can be perception of blue without the perception of the cognition of blue. All objects are perceived apart from their perceptions. They are perceived though their perceptions are not perceived. Perception is not necessarily perception of a cognition. Though there is a distinction between the perceived object and the percipient cognition, there may be simultaneous perception of the two, because there can be no perception without the object of perception. Hence their invariably simultaneous perception cannot prove their identity. Though cognition and its object differ from each other, they may be perceived together.[1]

(2) Even the Yogācāra, who regards the object as identical with its cognition, does not deny the consciousness of difference between them. But he regards it as illusory, and proves the identity of an object with its cognition by inference. But Prabhākara urges that perception is of superior strength than inference which cannot override the testimony of perception. Perception bears clear testimony to the difference of the object from its cognition. Hence it cannot be disproved by inference. It is wrong to hold that the cognition of difference is illusory like the illusory cognition of the double moon, because the identity of the object with its cognition is never perceived, but the identity of the moon is perceived which sublates the illusion of the double moon. One and the same moon produces two cognitions owing to the difference in the functions of the eye.[2]

(3) The Yogācāra wrongly holds that the forms of blue and the like belong to self-luminous cognitions. The forms of objects, which are manifested to consciousness as distinct from cognitions, cannot belong to cognitions.[3]

[1] PP., pp. 60–1.
[2] Ibid., p. 61.
[3] Saṃvidbhinnasyārthasya bhāsamānasyākārasya saṃvidrūpāśrayaṇānupapatteḥ, PP., p. 61.

How can formless cognitions be manifested ? If formless cognitions mean cognitions without an essence or character, there are no formless cognitions because cognitions are admitted to be of the nature of consciousness. If cognitions are said to be formless because they are devoid of the forms of blue and the like, there is no such rule that cognitions should be manifested only as endowed with the forms of blue and the like and not in any other way. When cognitions are manifested they must be admitted to be such as they are manifested.[1]

(4) The Yogācāra wrongly argues that in dreams forms of mere cognitions are manifested. In dreams cognitions appear to manifest external objects.[2] It is not impossible for dream-cognitions to apprehend external objects. Dream-cognitions are of the nature of recollections which are due to revival of subconscious impressions left by previous perceptions of external objects. Thus external objects perceived in the past and remembered during sleep are apprehended by dream-cognitions ; the recollections of objects appear to be perceptions owing to obscuration of memory (smṛtipramoṣa). In dream-cognitions mere forms of cognitions are not manifested, but external objects perceived in the past are manifested.[3]

(5) The Yogācāra argues that an external object is material, and cannot, therefore, be manifested to consciousness. But the forms which are manifested to consciousness must be the forms of cognitions which are self-luminous. This is wrong. A material object is non-luminous ; a non-luminous object which is different from self-luminous consciousness is manifested by it. A material object cannot manifest itself ; but it is manifested by consciousness.[4]

[1] PP., p. 61.

[2] Tatrāpi hi bahiravabhāsatvāt saṃvidaḥ, ibid., p. 61.

[3] PP., pp. 61–2.

[4] Aprakāśātmakasyaiva prakāśavyatiriktasya prakāśa iti prakāśādeva siddham, PP., p. 62.

(6) The Yogācāra contradicts the universal experience of mankind when he argues that waking cognitions are without corresponding external objects because they are cognitions like dream-cognitions. External objects are perceived by all to be real ; and these perceptions are not contradicted. And dream-cognitions also apprehend external objects perceived in the past and remembered during sleep as already said. Hence it is wrong to hold that external objects are not manifested, but only forms of cognitions are manifested to consciousness.[1]

(7) It is urged that a cognition cannot apprehend itself as its object just as the tip of a finger cannot touch itself. Prabhākara holds that a cognition does not apprehend itself as its object (karma), but it is self-luminous and manifests itself. If it is denied that a cognition is self-luminous because it apprehends an external object, it contradicts the verdict of consciousness. It is a fact of experience that a cognition manifests itself and an object. Those who admit that the same self is the subject and the object of apprehension on the strength of experience should not deny that cognitions apprehend themselves and their objects. Cognitions are self-luminous, and apprehend external objects.[2]

(8) Cognition is the means of right knowledge (pramāṇa) ; and outward action in the shape of acceptance, rejection, etc., is the result of right knowledge (phala). Cognition is the cause ; and external action is the effect. The Yogācāra wrongly holds that actions which are the results of cognitions are of the nature of cognitions.[3]

§ 8. *Prabhākara's Criticism of the Sautrāntika Realism*

The Sautrāntika holds that external objects produce cognitions and imprint their forms upon them so that the forms of cognitions correspond to the forms of external

[1] Ibid., pp. 62–3. [2] Ibid., p. 63.
[3] Ibid., p. 64 ; see Bṛhatī and Ṛjuvimalā, pp. 80–90.

objects. Formless cognitions cannot be manifested. So the forms of cognitions must be admitted. They are of the nature of manifestation (prakaśa). If cognitions were formless, they would have nothing to distinguish them from one another and could not apprehend different objects. But if cognitions are held to assume the forms of external objects, they can apprehend different objects. Cognitions apprehend those objects which produce them and impart their forms to them. The similarity (sārūpya) of the forms of cognitions with the forms of objects restricts different cognitions to different objects.[1]

The Sautrāntika wrongly holds that cognitions apprehend different objects because the forms of cognitions are similar to the forms of external objects. He admits that the forms of external objects are transformed into the forms of cognitions which only are perceived. The forms of external objects are never perceived. If they are never perceived they can never be known to be similar to the forms of cognitions. The existence of external objects and their similarity with cognitions cannot be said to be inferred from different forms of cognitions as their causes. Causes are not always similar to their effects. The same cause may produce diversity of effects. There is no evidence to prove that the form of the external object is similar to the form of its cognition. In fact, there is no similarity between a cognition and its object. The object is a mere aggregate of atoms ; but the cognition produced by it has the form of a gross object. The object is specific and has a distinct form ; but its cognition is generic and devoid of form. So there is no similarity between the two. If the object were cognized by a cognition owing to its similarity with it, the distinction between the percipient cognition and the perceived object would be abolished, because, in that case, the cognitions in different persons or streams of consciousness (santati)

[1] PP., p. 57.

apprehending the same object and thus being similar to one another would be cognized by one another. If what is the cause of a cognition and is similar to it were said to be cognized by the cognition, then in a serial cognition (dhārāvāhikajñāna) each previous cognition which produces the succeeding cognition and is similar to it would be cognized by the succeeding cognition. If what produces a distinct form in a cognition were held to be cognized by it, the preceding cognition which produces a distinct form in a succeeding cognition would be cognized by it.

Prabhākara holds that cognitions apprehend different objects though they are devoid of forms. What, then, is the distinctive mark of a cognition by which it is distinguished from other cognitions ? A cognition is a distinct quality of the self, which is subservient to a particular reaction to a particular object. It is self-luminous. It apprehends a particular object not because it assumes the form of the object, but because it is manifested to consciousness as conducive to a particular reaction to a particular object. Hence formless cognitions apprehend different objects.[1] Thus the Sautrāntika view is erroneous.

[1] PP., p. 60.

CHAPTER VII

THE NYĀYA-VAIŚEṢIKA REALISM

§ 1. *The Nyāya Critique of Vijñānavāda*

Vātsyāyana's Critical Exposition of Vijñānavāda

(1) The Buddhist idealist [1] argues that the realist assumes the reality of cognitions, and establishes the reality of their objects on the strength of these cognitions; but, in fact, all these cognitions are wrong, and hence they cannot reveal the real character of their objects. If they were right cognitions, the analysis of things by them could reveal the real nature of their objects. But, as a matter of fact, when we analyse things by our reason, we fail to apprehend their real character. For instance, when we analyse a cloth by our reason, we find that it is made up of yarns; when we analyse a yarn we find that it is made up of parts of a yarn; when we analyse these parts we find them to be made up of atoms; and when we analyse atoms further and further, we reach a point where nothing remains. Thus there is no object called a "cloth" over and above its constituent parts, which may be the real object of the notion of cloth. And there being no real object called a cloth, the notion of cloth must be a wrong cognition.[2] "There is no cloth apart from the yarns; and there is no yarn apart from its parts; and so on up to atoms; of atoms also we cannot perceive the real character. Hence from atom upwards, no object

[1] Vācaspatimiśra says that the *Nyāyasūtra*, iv, 2, 26, introduces the doctrine of the Vijñānavādin. (NVTT., p. 460.) But MM. Phaṇibhūṣaṇa Tarkavāgiśa thinks that the sūtra mentions the doctrine of the "Anupalambhika" or Sarvābhāvavādin. (*Nyāyadarśana* (Bengali), vol. iv, p. 122.)

[2] NBh., iv, 2, 26.

exists."[1] Thus all cognitions are wrong ; and there are no real objects of cognitions.

Udyotakara states the position of the Buddhist idealist thus : " The objects of cognition such as a jar, a cow and the like do not exist in reality, because when we examine them by our reason, we fail to apprehend them as distinct from one another.[2] The real character of objects cannot be ascertained by analysis of reason. Hence they are without any real character and incapable of being described by words.[3]

Gautama contends that the reason given above for the non-existence of external objects is invalid, since it involves self-contradiction.[4] Vātsyāyana explains it thus : If things can be analysed by reason, then it is not true that the real nature of all things is not apprehended. If, on the other hand, the real nature of things is not apprehended, then things cannot be analysed by reason. Thus to hold that things can be analysed by reason, and yet the real nature of things is not apprehended by reason involves self-contradiction.[5] Udyotakara points out the self-contradiction thus : If there can be analysis of things by reason, then all things cannot be held to be non-existent ; and if all things are non-existent, then there can be no analysis of things by reason.[6] Vācaspatimiśra says : " If the real nature of a thing is not apprehended, there cannot be analysis of it by reason."[7]

The Naiyāyika is a rationalist and a realist. He believes in the reality of the external world which is accessible to reason. The external reality is not foreign to reason ; it is capable of being known by reason. The external world is real and intelligible ; it is of such a nature that

[1] *Indian Thought*, vol. iii, p. 249. [2] NV., iv, 2, 26.
[3] S.D.S., Bauddhadarśana. [4] NS., iv, 2, 27.
[5] Buddhyā vivecanaṃ yāthātmyānupalabdhiśceti vyāhanyate, NBh., iv, 2, 27. [6] NV., iv, 2, 27.
[7] NVTT., p. 461 ; cf. Bertrand Russell : *Our Knowledge of the External World*, pp. 150–1.

it submits to the scrutiny of reason. The analysis of nature does not falsify its nature or reality. Intellectual analysis is adequate to the comprehension of the reality. Disbelief in reason makes metaphysics impossible. Thus Nyāya realism is akin to a type of modern western realism.

Thus Gautama points out that objects are apprehended by means of right cognition.[1] The real nature of things can be apprehended by analysis of reason.[2] The analysis of things by reason does lead to the distinct apprehension of things. What things exist and what things do not exist—all this is ascertained through what we apprehend by means of the instruments of right cognition. When we examine things by reason we come to determine what things exist and what things do not exist. Analysis by reason does not prove the non-existence of all things.[3] Thus intellectual analysis does not disprove the reality of the external world.

Vātsyāyana asks whether there is any proof for the non-existence of all things. If there is a proof for their non-existence, then at least the proof is real, and it contradicts the total negation of all things. If there is no proof, the non-existence of all things cannot be established. If it is established without any proof, then the existence of all things may as well be established in the same way.[4]

Gautama explains why the whole cannot be perceived apart from its parts. The whole exists in its parts. It cannot exist apart from its parts. So it cannot be perceived apart from them.[5] Vātsyāyana says that the substance that is an effect exists in its constituent causes. Therefore the effect cannot be perceived apart from its constituent causes. A cloth exists in its yarns, and consequently it cannot be perceived apart from them. Two things can be perceived apart from each other, when there is no

[1] NS., iv, 2, 29.
[2] Buddhyā vivecanād bhāvānāṃ yāthātmyopalabdhiḥ, NBh., iv, 2, 29.
[3] NBh., iv, 2, 29. [4] NBh., iv, 2, 30. [5] NS., iv, 2, 28.

relation of cause and effect, or the container and the contained between them.[1] Therefore, it is wrong to argue that a cloth does not exist because it cannot be perceived apart from its yarns, and the notion of cloth has no real counterpart for its object.

(2) The Buddhist idealist argues that the instruments of right cognition (pramāṇa) and the objects of right cognition (prameya) are as unreal as dreams and their objects. They are as unreal as magical phenomena, the illusory appearance of imaginary cities in clouds, or the mirage.[2] In dreams we apprehend objects which are non-existent. Though the objects of dreams are not real, yet they appear to be real. Similarly neither the so-called instruments of right cognition (pramāṇa) nor the objects of right cognition (prameya) are real ; but they appear to be real.[3]

Firstly, Gautama urges that there is no reason in support of this view. So it is without any foundation.[4] Vātsyāyana says that there is no reason to prove that non-existent things are apprehended by dream-cognitions. If the non-existence of the objects of dream-cognitions is said to be proved by their non-perception in the waking condition, then it follows that waking perceptions are right and the objects apprehended by them are real. If the objects apprehended by dream-cognitions are said to be non-existent because they are not perceived in the waking cognition, then it follows that the things that are perceived by us during the waking state are existent because they are perceived. Thus the reason put forward by the Buddhist idealist in support of the unreality of dream-objects proves a contrary conclusion. It proves the reality of the objects of waking perceptions. If the existence of things can be inferred from their apprehension, then only we can infer their non-existence from their

[1] NBh. and NV., iv, 2, 28.
[2] NS., iv, 2, 32–3.
[3] NBh., iv, 2, 32.
[4] NS., iv, 2, 33.

non-apprehension.[1] The non-perception of an object can prove its non-existence, only if it is admitted that its perception proves its existence.[2]

If the objects of dream-cognitions as well as waking cognitions were equally unreal, then non-perception of dream-objects during the waking state could not prove anything. Further, if all things are non-existent and unreal, the diversity of dream-cognitions cannot be accounted for. But if things are believed to be real and existent, the diversity of dreams may be traced to the diversity of these real causes.[3]

Secondly, Gautama urges that dream-cognitions have for their objects things perceived in the past, like recollection and desire.[4] Vātsyāyana says that just as recollection and desire which have for their objects real things perceived in the past, cannot prove the non-existence of such things, so dream-cognitions also have for their objects things perceived in the past, and therefore cannot prove the non-existence of their objects. It is only when dream-cognitions are compared with waking cognitions that the objects of dreams are known to be unreal. The objects apprehended by dream-cognitions are not perceived by waking cognitions. Hence they are known to be unreal. But the Yogācāra who does not recognize any distinction between dreams and waking cognitions cannot hold that the objects of dream-cognitions are unreal.[5]

Thirdly, Gautama urges that wrong cognitions are destroyed by right cognitions, just as the illusory cognitions of objects during a dream are destroyed by waking cognitions.[6] A wrong cognition is not without a core

[1] Upalambhāt sadbhāve sati anupalambhād abhāvaḥ sidhyati, NBh., iv, 2, 33. (*Indian Thought*, vol. iii, p. 255, n.)

[2] Yadyupalabdhiḥ sattvasādhanaṃ tato'anupalabdhirasattvaṃ sādhayati, NV., iv, 2, 34. [3] NBh., iv, 2, 33. [4] NS., iv, 2, 34.

[5] NBh., iv, 2, 34; cf. Bertrand Russell: "Dream-data are no doubt appearances of 'things' but not of such 'things' as the dreamer supposes." (*Mysticism and Logic*, p. 178). [6] NS., iv, 2, 35.

of right knowledge of a real thing. At the bottom of every wrong cognition there is some sort of real entity apprehended at some time in some place. No wrong cognition is entirely without any foundation in reality.[1]

We also find that there is a difference between the perception of the magician and that of his spectators. The former regards the magic as unreal, while the latter regards it as real. There is also a difference between the perception of a man at a distance and that of a man near at hand. The former regards the imaginary cities in clouds and water in a desert as real, while the latter does not apprehend them at all. Then, again, there is a difference between the perception of a sleeping man and that of a waking man. But all these differences could not be explained if all things were non-existent, and as such entirely essenceless and nameless. These differences do imply the reality of external objects.[2]

Fourthly, Gautama urges that there is a dual character in a wrong cognition owing to the difference between the real object and its counterpart.[3] The Buddhist idealist argues that the object of right cognition must be non-existent, since the object of wrong cognition is non-existent. But Vātsyāyana points out that there is a core of truth even in a wrong cognition. The object of wrong cognition is not absolutely non-existent. The object of wrong cognition has a dual character. The cognition of a post as a man has its basis in a real object, viz. a post. But its appearance as a man has for its object a real counterpart, viz. a man. In the character of a man the object is non-existent; but in the character of a post it is really existent.[4] The illusory perception of one thing as another has its basis in the perception of a real object. When a post is mistaken for a man, the illusory perception of the man has

[1] Kvacit kadācit kasyacicca bhāvānnānimittaṃ mithyājñānam, NBh., iv, 2, 35.

[2] NBh., iv, 2, 35.

[3] NS., iv, 2, 37.

[4] *Indian Thought*, vol. iii, p. 266, n.

its basis in the perception of a real man. If a person has never perceived a man, he can never mistake a post for a man. Similarly dream-cognitions also have their basis in the perception of real objects. The contents of dreams are always objects of previous perceptions.[1] Only the connections among them are the creation of imagination and are therefore unreal.[2] Hence it is wrong to hold that the instruments of right cognition (pramāṇa) and the objects of right cognition (prameya) are wrong.[3]

§ 2. *Udyotakara's Critical Exposition of Vijñānavāda*

Udyotakara gives some other arguments of the Yogācāra for the non-existence of external objects in *Nyāyavārtika*.

(1) The Yogācāra argues that objects are not different from cognitions because they are cognized, like the feelings of pleasure and pain.[4] Just as the feelings of pleasure and pain which are apprehended are not different from the apprehending cognitions and have no existence apart from the mind, so the objects also which are apprehended are not different from their apprehending cognitions and have no existence apart from the mind.

We find a similar argument in Berkeley's *Dialogue between Hylas and Philonous* to which G. W. Kaveeshwar draws our attention. " A sensation of heat or cold, it is argued at the start, is invariably accompanied by a sensation of either pain or pleasure. A sudden leap is then taken from this accepted fact of accompaniment to a conclusion regarding the identity of these two kinds of sensations. The sensation of heat or cold, it is at once concluded, is therefore nothing but such a sensation pleasurable or painful as the case may be ; and further, since neither pleasure nor pain can exist in an unperceiving thing, nor can heat and cold too exist in any

[1] NBh., iv, 2, 34. [2] Nyāyasūtravṛtti, iv, 2, 34.

[3] NBh., iv, 2, 37 ; *Indian Thought*, vol. iii, pp. 248–267.

[4] Na cittavyatirekiṇo viṣayā grāhyatvāt vedanādivaditi yathā vedanādi grāhyaṃ na cittavyatiriktaṃ tathā viṣayā api, NV., iv, 2, 34, p. 526.

external thing."[1] Berkeley says: "The intense heat immediately perceived, is nothing distinct from a particular sort of pain. . . . Because intense heat is nothing else but a particular kind of painful sensation; and pain cannot exist but in a perceiving being; it follows that no intense heat can really exist in an unperceiving corporeal substance. . . . And is not warmth, or a more gentle degree of heat than what causes uneasiness, a pleasure? Consequently, it cannot exist without the mind in an unperceiving substance, or body."[2]

Udyotakara contends that cognition is different from pleasure and pain. They are entirely different in nature. Pleasure and pain are apprehended objects (grāhya); they are apprehended by cognition. Cognition, on the other hand, is of the nature of apprehension (grahaṇa); it is a mode of apprehending pleasure, pain, and other objects. There is a difference between apprehension and the objects of apprehension. Therefore, pleasure and pain can never be identified with their apprehending cognitions.[3] An action (kriyā) and its object (karma) can never be one and the same. The object of cognition can never be identical with the act of cognition.[4]

(2) If cognitions alone constitute the reality, their variety cannot be explained. There being no internal and external causes of the variety of cognitions, there cannot arise variety in cognitions. The Yogācāra holds that the variety of waking cognitions is due to the variety of subconscious impressions (bhāvanā), like the variety of dream-cognitions; they are independent of external causes.[5]

Udyotakara urges that even subconscious impressions (bhāvanā) imply the distinction between the impresser (bhāvaka) and the impressed (bhāvya). The impresser

[1] *The Metaphysics of Berkeley*, Indore, 1933, p. 93.
[2] *Dialogue between Hylas and Philonous*, pp. 124–6.
[3] Sukhaduḥkhe grāhye grahaṇaṃ jñānamiti, NV., iv, 2, 34.
[4] Ibid., iv, 2, 34.
[5] NVTT., p. 468.

and the impressed cannot be one and the same. Further, subconscious impressions are impressions of real objects perceived in the past. Thus the argument of the Yogācāra presupposes the existence of external objects distinct from cognitions. Hence it cannot establish the non-existence of external objects.[1]

(3) The Yogācāra argues that waking cognitions are without any basis in external objects, like dream-cognitions. Waking cognitions are as illusory as dream-cognitions. Just as there are no real objects corresponding to dream-cognitions, so there are no real objects corresponding to waking cognitions.

Udyotakara gives the following criticism of this argument :—

Firstly, it has already been shown that even wrong cognitions are not entirely baseless ; they presuppose the right cognition of real objects. There can be a wrong cognition in regard to an object, only if it has already been perceived as real. Unless one has had a previous cognition of the real object, he can have no wrong cognition in regard to it. We never find a wrong cognition without a real counterpart which has already been apprehended.[2] If there are no right cognitions of real objects, there can be no wrong cognitions with regard to them. Thus waking cognitions cannot be said to be objectless like dream-cognitions which presuppose previous perception of real objects. Even dream-cognitions indirectly depend upon external objects.[3]

Secondly, there can be no distinction, for the Yogācāra, between waking cognitions and dream-cognitions, because he does not recognize the existence of external objects independent of cognitions. According to him,

[1] NV., iv, 2, 34, p. 527.

[2] Na ca niḥpradhānaṃ viparyayapratyayaṃ paśyāmaḥ, NV., iv, 2, 34, p. 527. [3] NVTT., p. 467 ; cf. *Our Knowledge of the External World*, pp. 85-6.

just as there are no real objects corresponding to dream-cognitions, so there are no real objects corresponding to waking cognitions. So for him there is no distinction between dream-cognitions and waking cognitions.

Thirdly, the Yogācāra may urge that there is a distinction between the dream-state and the waking state, because in the former the mind is deranged by sleep, while in the latter the mind is not deranged by sleep. But how can the Yogācāra know that the influence of sleep is the cause of derangement of the mind?

Fourthly, the Yogācāra may urge that there is a distinction between the dream-state and the waking state because dream-cognitions are indistinct while waking cognitions are distinct.[1] But there can be no distinction between distinctness (spaṣṭatā) and indistinctness (aspaṣṭatā) of cognitions, if there are no real objects distinct from cognitions. In fact, the cognitions produced by real objects are distinct, while those which have no real objects corresponding to them are indistinct.[2]

Fifthly, if there is no distinction between dreaming and waking, there can be no distinction between merit and demerit, virtue and vice; for just as adultery committed in a dream is not regarded as a vice, so the same act committed in the waking condition cannot be regarded as a vice. Thus there can be no moral distinction for

[1] In distinguishing sensations from images Berkeley similarly says: "The ideas of Sense are more strong, lively, and distinct than those of the Imagination." "But then our sensations, be they never so vivid and distinct, are nevertheless ideas; that is, they exist in the mind, or are perceived by it, as truly as the ideas of its own framing. The ideas of Sense are allowed to have more reality in them, that is, to be more strong, orderly, and coherent than the creatures of the mind; but this is no argument that they exist without the mind." (*Principles of Human Knowledge*, p. 54 and pp. 55–6.) Hume also holds that *ideas* (images) are mere faint copies of impressions (sensations).

[2] Berkeley holds that the ideas imprinted on our minds by God are distinct and vivid, while the ideas of our own making are faint and indistinct. According to him, God is the cause of sensations.

the subjective idealist who denies the existence of external objects, and abolishes the distinction between dreaming and waking.[1]

(4) The Yogācāra argues that even in the absence of external objects we find diversity of cognitions. The disembodied spirits who owe their existence to the fruition of similar potencies of actions have different cognitions, though there are no real objects. Some of them perceive a river full of pus, though in reality there is neither a river nor pus there. Others perceive a river as full of water ; others, again, perceive it as full of blood. Here there are no external objects ; but cognitions appear in those particular forms ; the forms of cognitions are not produced by external objects, but they are modes of consciousness itself. One and the same object, cannot have different forms ; but the diversity of cognitions in regard to the same object is simply due to the fact that there are different cognitions with different forms, though there is no external object at all. Thus the variety of cognitions does not depend upon external objects. This seems to be a silly argument. We have no direct knowledge of the experience of the so-called disembodied spirits. To appeal to their experience is to appeal to credulity.

Udyotakara asserts that this view is wrong, since it involves self-contradiction. When the Yogācāra says that a cognition itself assumes a particular form, he must explain what is meant by the cognition assuming that form. If cognitions are held to assume the forms of " river ", " water ", " blood ", etc., the Yogācāra must explain what is meant by them. If these objects do not exist at all, cognitions cannot be said to assume the forms of those objects. Further, the Yogācāra cannot explain why disembodied spirits perceive a river full of pus in one place, and not in another. They may perceive it anywhere, since cognitions may appear in these forms in any place.

[1] NV., iv, 2, 34.

Moreover, the Yogācāra cannot regard the notions of blood, pus, water, and river as wrong cognitions, because wrong cognitions also presuppose the reality of their objects somewhere. They never completely do away with their real counterparts.[1]

Udyotakara gives the following arguments for the existence of external things. Objects are something distinct from my cognitions—like cognitions in other persons or streams of consciousness—because they are possessed of generic and specific properties. They are distinct from my cognitions because they are apprehended by the instruments of right cognition. They have an existence apart from my cognitions, because they are of the nature of effects and are produced by their causes, or because they are not eternal and spring from their causes. Overt actions have an existence independent of our minds, because they are preceded by merit. If they are held to be mere ideas of the mind, the distinction between merit and demerit will be abolished.[2]

In criticizing the Yogācāra idealism in *Nyāyavārtikatātparyaṭīkā* Vācaspatimiśra repeats the arguments given by him in *Tattvavaiśāradī*.[3] He elaborates the arguments in *Nyāyakaṇikā*, a commentary on *Vidhiviveka*.

§ 3. *Jayanta's Criticism of the Yogācāra Idealism*

(1) The Yogācāra argues that a cognition assumes the form of an object. Jayanta points out that a single cognition cannot break up into subject and object. It cannot partake of the dual character of the percipient cognition and the perceived object. They are endowed with opposite and contradictory qualities, and cannot, therefore, coexist in one and the same cognition. That consciousness

[1] NV., iv, 2, 34; *Indian Thought*, vol. iii, pp. 258–262.

[2] Madīyāccittāt arthāntaraṃ viṣayāḥ sāmānyaviśeṣavattvāt santānāntaracittavat pramāṇagamyatvāt kāryatvāt anityatvāt dharmapūrvakatvācca, NV., iv, 2, 34, p. 529. See Śāntarakṣita's criticism of this argument in TS., vol. i, 2057–8, p. 576; see Chapter I. [3] See Chapter V.

is different from the object can be proved by the method of agreement and the method of difference. When external objects like blue, yellow, and white are present, cognitions of blue, yellow, and white are produced ; and when they are absent, the cognitions disappear. So cognitions of particular objects are produced by these external objects. But in the cognitions of blue, yellow, and white there is consciousness which persists even after the external objects, blue, yellow, and white are destroyed. This persisting consciousness is, therefore, quite different from external objects.[1]

There is an essential difference between a cognition and an object. A cognition is always referred to a self (ahaṅkārāspada) ; it is someone's cognition. It is, as it were, a " private property " of a particular self. But an object is accessible to all persons. It is not referred to a self. It is, as it were, a " public property " of all. A cognition is of the nature of " I " or " I know " while an object is of the nature of " this " or the known. A cognition belongs to a self and is subjective. An object is presented to the self and is objective. A cognition is a state of the self while an object is of the nature of not-self. We are conscious of blue as " *this* is blue ", and not as " *I* am blue ". Thus the form of the object is perceived as distinct from, and independent of, the apprehending cognition. It is never perceived as identical with the cognition. Further, a cognition has a hedonic tone ; it is attended by pleasure or pain. But an object has no feeling-tone ; it is not attended by pleasure or pain. Moreover, a cognition, according to the Yogācāra, is self-luminous ; it apprehends itself and is the object of its own action. But an object is not self-luminous ; it is unconscious and cannot manifest itself ; it is manifested by consciousness. Hence a cognition can never be regarded as identical with an object.[2]

[1] NM., pp. 540–1.

[2] NM., p. 541.

The Yogācāra contends that the distinction of subject and object falls within consciousness itself, so that one cognition is the subject and another cognition is the object. Jayanta urges that this is impossible. If two cognitions are simultaneously produced, they cannot be related to each other as the percipient and the perceived, like two horns simultaneously produced.[1] If two cognitions *a* and *b* are produced in succession, one of them cannot apprehend the other, since they are momentary. If *a* apprehends *b*, *a* must continue to exist until *b* is produced in order to apprehend it. Thus *a* will not be momentary ; it must have some duration. Then, again, if *b* coming after *a* apprehends it, *a* must continue to exist until *b* is produced and apprehends it. Thus two momentary cognitions can never be related to each other as the percipient and the perceived.[2]

Further, the Yogācāra appeals to the parsimony of hypotheses to prove the non-existence of external objects. The various modes of consciousness are but different forms of consciousness itself. They are not caused by external objects. The forms of cognitions serve all our purposes. The forms of external objects are needless. But Jayanta urges that we should not speak of the existence of external objects as a hypothesis. They are not assumed but actually *perceived*. They are objects of valid perception.[3] The nature of reality is established by valid knowledge.[4] So we must admit the existence of external objects.

(2) The Yogācāra argues that a cognition cannot apprehend an object unless it is apprehended by itself. Jayanta, like Kumārila, urges that this doctrine contradicts our experience. Consciousness does not necessarily involve self-consciousness. Sometimes, I know a jar

[1] Ibid., p. 546. [2] Ibid., p. 546.
[3] Pratyakṣagamye bāhye grāhye arthākāre kalpanoktiḥ kīdṛśī, NM. p. 543. [4] Pramāṇāyattā vastusthitiḥ, ibid., p. 543.

but I do not know that I know the jar. When an object is perceived it is not necessarily appropriated by the self.[1] An object (e.g. blue) which is manifested by a cognition is said to be apprehended by it. This cognition does not depend upon any other cognition for its manifestation. If it did, it would lead to an infinite regress. It cannot be said to be self-luminous and to apprehend itself, since the cognition of blue never appears as "*I* am blue". Thus a cognition neither manifests itself nor is manifested by any other cognition. But it manifests an external object.[2]

In Indian philosophy consciousness is compared to illumination (prakāśa). When an object is perceived through the eyes, the illumination produced by them called consciousness does not illumine itself but the object. The light of consciousness produced by the eyes does not manifest itself, but it manifests an external object like a colour. Here the colour is the perceived object, and the cognition which manifests the colour is the percipient cognition. As soon as the cognition of colour is produced, the colour is manifested. The cognition does not require my further apprehension of itself in order to manifest its object.[3] It is quite unreasonable to hold that an object is not apprehended by a cognition which is not apprehended. A cognition itself manifests an object, though it is not itself apprehended. As soon as a cognition is produced it manifests its object without depending upon any other cognition to apprehend it. There is a cognition of an object but no further cognition of that cognition. The essential nature of a cognition is to manifest its object.[4]

Even granted that an apprehended cognition manifests an object, it may be asked whether it manifests its object

[1] Nīlādigrāhyagrahanasamaye tadgrāhakānupalambhāt, NM., p. 544.

[2] NM., p. 541; see *Indian Psychology: Perception*, pp. 213–14.

[3] Apratyakṣopalambhasya arthadṛṣṭiḥ siddhyati. Upalambhotpāda eva arthadṛṣṭiḥ na punarupalambhadṛṣṭiḥ. Ibid., p. 541.

[4] Arthaprakāśātmaiva khalūpalambhaḥ, NM., p. 541.

as smoke manifests fire, or as light manifests a jar. If it manifests its object like smoke, the existence of the object will be inferred from its cognition that is apprehended, as the Sautrāntika holds. But the Yogācāra himself has refuted the inferribility of external objects. If a cognition directly reveals its object like light as soon as it is apprehended, we should be conscious of two forms, the form of the object and the form of the cognition. But we are never conscious of two forms in perceiving an object. When we perceive a jar and a lamp we are conscious of two things. But we are never conscious of two things when we perceive an object through a cognition.[1]

The Yogācāra argues that a cognition must itself be apprehended in order to manifest its object even as light manifests other objects when it is perceived. Jayanta urges that this is a false analogy. It is wrong to argue that what is illuminating by its nature must be illumined by something else in order to illumine other things, and therefore a cognition which manifests an object must itself be manifested by another cognition. Take, for instance, the case of the eye. It manifests an object. But it is not first perceived before it manifests an object. The eye is imperceptible, but still it manifests an object. Similarly a cognition manifests an object without itself being apprehended.[2]

The act of illuminating is illumination itself. It is wrong to argue that because a cognition illumines an object it must itself be illumined by some other cognition. The cognition illumines an object, and the cognition itself is the illumination of the object. It does not require any other cognition to illumine itself. In the apprehension of an object the cognition itself is the illumination of the object, and illumination (prakāśa) here means consciousness which does not require any other cognition to illumine it. Hence the analogy of light fails here. Light

[1] NM., p. 542. [2] NM., p. 542.

is not of the nature of consciousness, though it is of the nature of illumination. A cognition illumines an object in a quite different sense from that in which a lamp illumines an object. Both cognition and light are of the nature of illumination. But one is conscious while the other is unconscious. There is an essential difference between the two. Hence we cannot argue that just as light must be perceived in order to illumine other objects, so a cognition must be apprehended in order to manifest its objects.[1]

Then, again, it is wrong to hold that a cognition is self-luminous and as such apprehends itself. We never find a self-luminous object in the world. A cognition is said to manifest itself and other objects even as light and a word manifest themselves and other objects. But this is wrong. Light and a word depend upon other causes in manifesting themselves and other objects. But a cognition does not depend upon any other cognition in manifesting its object. A word depends upon recognition of convention in manifesting its object. And it depends upon the ear in manifesting itself. Light depends upon the eye in manifesting itself and other objects.[2] But a cognition manifests an object without itself being apprehended.[3] It manifests other objects but does not manifest itself. It is not self-luminous ; it does not apprehend itself when it apprehends other objects.[4]

(3) The Yogācāra argues that different cognitions apprehend different objects because they have different forms, and the so-called external objects are mere subjective forms of cognitions. Jayanta urges that a cognition is determinate because it apprehends a particular object. Though the cognition of blue is produced in the presence

[1] NM., p. 542.

[2] NM., p. 542.

[3] Agṛhītameva jñānamarthaprakāśakam, NM., p. 542.

[4] Jñānasya tu paraprakāśatvameva dṛśyate na svaprakāśatvamarthaprakāśakāle tadaprakāśasya darśitatvāt, NM., p. 542.

of many objects, and though consciousness is common to all cognitions of objects, still the cognition of blue is produced by a blue object and apprehends this object and not any other. The existence of the object cannot be denied. The Yogācāra argues that if a cognition apprehends an object because it is produced by it, the eye also should be apprehended by the cognition because it produces the cognition. Jayanta urges that it is certainly true that the eye produces the cognition of blue, but it is not the object of the cognition, but the instrument of the cognition. The cognition of blue is produced by a blue object and not by any other because it is the Law of Nature (vastusvabhāva) that an object should produce a like cognition.[1] The Nyāya believes in the causal theory of knowledge.

That an object produces a cognition is proved by the method of agreement and the method of difference. For instance, when a person goes to the house of Devadatta in search of him, he does not see him if he is absent. But in a moment when he comes home he sees him. Thus whenever Devadatta is present a cognition of him is present, and whenever he is absent the cognition of him is absent. So we must conclude that Devadatta is the cause of the cognition of Devadatta. External objects are the causes of different cognitions. Hence it is needless to assume the forms of cognitions.[2]

The Yogācāra erroneously holds that forms of cognitions are necessary to account for different reactions. In fact, there would be no reactions at all, if there were no external objects. We have desire for some objects and try to appropriate them. We have aversion to other objects and try to avoid them. External objects are objects of valid perception. So we must admit their existence. If external objects were not real, there would be no reactions, and if they were not different, the reactions would not be

[1] NM., p. 543.

[2] NM., p. 544.

different. Our reactions to objects in the shape of desire and aversion, acceptance and rejection, presuppose the existence of external objects.[1]

(4) The Yogācāra argues that the forms of external objects are not inferred from the forms of internal cognitions as the Sautrāntika holds, since these two forms are not manifested to consciousness. The Naiyāyika agrees with the Yogācāra in holding that we are not conscious of two forms, the forms of cognitions and the forms of external objects. But he differs from the Yogācāra in holding that we are conscious of the forms of external objects, but not of the forms of cognitions. Cognitions apprehend the forms of external objects, though they themselves are devoid of forms. The Naiyāyika holds that the form of a cognition and the form of an object are not distinctly apprehended as " this is the form of the cognition " and " this is the form of the object ". Only one form is manifested to consciousness, and it is manifested not as an apprehending cognition but as an apprehended object. Only the form of the *object* is apprehended, and not the form of the apprehending cognition. The form of the object that is manifested to consciousness is the illumination (prakāśa) of the object. And the object is always apprehended as distinct from the apprehending cognition.[2] Thus the forms of objects can never be reduced to the forms of cognitions.

The Yogācāra contends that the cognized object is not different from the apprehending cognition, and that which is regarded by the realist as the manifestation of the object is but the manifestation of its cognition. If the apprehended object were different from its apprehending cognition, it would be material and unconscious. The

[1] NM., p. 543. Puruṣapravṛttirapi niyataviṣayā, NM., p. 544.

[2] Yadyapi jñānamidamayamartha ityevamākāradvayapratibhāso nāsti tathāpyayameko'pi ākāraḥ pratibhāsamānaḥ prakāśa eva pratibhāti na prakāśakaḥ, NM., p. 541.

apprehending cognition, on the other hand, is essentially conscious, since it manifests the object. But there is not a double manifestation of the conscious cognition and the unconscious object. Hence we must hold that a material object is not manifested by a cognition, but a cognition is manifested by itself.[1] A formless cognition is never manifested. A cognition is apprehended only when it is invested with a particular form. And since determinate forms of cognitions are apprehended the assumption of external objects is absolutely needless.[2]

Jayanta urges that this argument is baseless. The means can never lead to the rejection of the end. From the existence of the means (upāya) we can never prove the non-existence of the end or object (upeya) which it seeks to realize. A colour is manifested to the eye. From this we cannot infer that the eye itself is manifested as colour, though there is no colour at all. The eye is the means of manifesting the colour, and the colour is the object that is manifested. Similarly, a cognition, which is by nature pure and formless, manifests an external object endowed with particular forms such as shape and size, liquidity, solidity, and the like according to the Law of Nature. The cognition is the means of manifesting the object, and an external object is the object of its manifestation. They are related to each other as the percipient and the perceived. Hence we can never identify them with each other.[3] The act of cognition is distinct from the object cognized by it.

The Nyāya-Vaiśeṣika, like the Mīmāṃsaka, holds that all cognitions are formless. The object cognized cannot imprint its form on the apprehending cognition. The object is not inferred from the form of a cognition as the

[1] Prakāśa eva prakāśate na jaḍaḥ, NM., p. 541.

[2] NM., p. 541.

[3] Tadidamarthasya mūrtidravatvakāṭhinyādidharmaviśeṣitātmanastadviparītasvacchasvabhāvaṃ jñānaṃ prakāśakaṃ svabhāvatvāt, NM., p. 541.

Sautrāntika holds, since an object like a jar is directly perceived. Every cognition, on the other hand, is determined by its object, since it is apprehended by the mind only when it is related to the object.[1] We have an apprehension in such a form as "I have the cognition of the *jar*" and not merely in the form "I have a cognition".[2]

(5) The Yogācāra argues that the variety of vāsanās (subconscious impressions) is the cause of the variety of cognitions, and vāsanās and cognitions are related to each other as causes and effects, like seeds and sprouts, in a beginningless series. This argument is unsound.

Firstly, what is a vāsanā? Either it is different from consciousness or not. If it is not different from consciousness, it cannot be the cause of its various determinations. Consciousness in itself is formless and indeterminate. If a vāsanā is not different from this consciousness, it must be as indeterminate as consciousness itself, and cannot be the cause of its various determinations. If, on the other hand, a vāsanā is different from consciousness and brings about its various modes, it is but an external object in disguise. It differs from an object only in name, since it is other than consciousness or extra-mental.[3]

Secondly, a vāsanā is regarded by all as a vestige or residuum (saṃskāra) left by a previous cognition of an object.[4] It is a subconscious impression. A vāsanā which is left by a particular cognition revives the memory of that cognition at some other time. Recollection is due to revival of a vāsanā, which, again, is due to a previous perception of an object. Thus a vāsanā presupposes perception of a real object. The variety of perceptions accounts for the variety of vāsanās. But the variety of vāsanās cannot account for the variety of perceptions.[5]

[1] Sarvaṃ jñānamarthanirūpyamarthapratibaddhasyaiva tasya manasā nirūpaṇāt, TBh., p. 30.

[2] TBh., p. 30.

[3] NM., pp. 547–8; cf. NK., p. 130.

[4] Vāsanā viṣayānubhavasamāhitaḥ saṃskāraḥ, ibid., p. 548.

[5] Ibid., p. 548.

Thirdly, the Yogācāra regards cognitions as momentary. So they cannot be related to one another as the perfumer (vāsaka) and the perfumed (vāsya), just as they cannot be related to one another as the apprehending cognition (grāhaka) and the cognized object (grāhya). Stable objects like oil can be perfumed by stable objects like fragrant flowers. But cognitions cannot perfume or modify one another, since they perish as soon as they are born. Of two cognitions, *a* and *b*, appearing successively in the stream of consciousness, if the preceding cognition *a* perfumes or modifies the succeeding cognition *b*, *a* must continue to exist until *b* comes into being in order to modify it. When *a* vanishes it vanishes entirely. It does not leave behind a part which may modify *b* when it emerges into consciousness.

Fourthly, the Yogācāra holds that a variety of vāsanās in a stream of consciousness brings about a variety of perceptions in it. But what regulates the order of the origin of perceptions? The vāsanā of a cow can never give rise to the perception of an elephant. The Yogācāra tries to evade the issue by invoking an infinite series of vāsanās. Even if there is an infinite series of vāsanās, the Yogācāra must explain how different vāsanās are produced and how different perceptions arise from different vāsanās. If there is no agreement between vāsanās and perceptions, any vāsanā will give rise to any perception, and this will lead to chaos in practice. We infer the existence of fire from the perception of smoke. Here the vāsanā of smoke may be said to give rise to the perception of smoke. But why does the perception of smoke lead us to the cognition of fire? Why does not the vāsanā of water bring about the perception of water at the time? This clearly shows that there is a regular order in the connection of vāsanās with cognitions.

Fifthly, vāsanās can only revive similar vāsanās and produce recollections. The like produces the like. But vāsanās can never produce perceptions. It is curious to hold that the variety of perceptions is due to the variety of vāsanās and not to the variety of external objects.

Lastly, vāsanās cannot subsist without a substratum. The Yogācāra cannot find any abode for vāsanās. Cognitions are momentary. So they cannot be the abode of vāsanās. If all vāsanās are said to subsist in a single cognition, they will perish along with the cognition. If different vāsanās subsist in different cognitions, there will be an infinite number of vāsanās and cognitions, which will lead to chaos. There is nothing like the so-called ālayavijñāna or self-cognition. If it exists, it cannot be the abode of vāsanās, since it is momentary. Again, if it be the abode of the infinite variety of vāsanās, as soon as it is destroyed all the vāsanās will be destroyed. Then when another self-cognition is produced, it will produce infinite variety of cognitions, since it is the abode of infinite variety of vāsanās. Thus there will be nothing to regulate the order of the origin of perceptions. The Yogācāra cannot adequately account for the variety of cognitions by the variety of vāsanās.[1]

(6) The Yogācāra argues that waking perceptions are mere subjective cognitions with determinate forms like illusions, hallucinations, and dreams ; they are mere forms of consciousness which are not produced by external objects. This argument is wrong, since the forms of objects are always apprehended as distinct from, and external to, cognitions.[2] Illusions (indriyajā bhrānti) always involve an element of perception. They are either due to defects of objects (viṣayadoṣa) or to disorders of sense-organs (indriyadoṣa). The illusory perception of silver in a shell cannot be explained without reference to the perception of silver at some other time and in

[1] NM., pp. 547–8.

[2] Sarvatra jñānādvicchinnasya grāhyākārasya pratibhāsanāt, NM., p. 544.

some other place, which is illusorily superimposed on the shell. Thus illusions do not disprove the existence of external objects. Even hallucinations (mānasī bhrānti), which are creatures of imagination, are not without a foundation in external objects. When an infatuated lover sees his beloved here, there, and everywhere, his imagination under the influence of intense love creates the image of his beloved whom he did actually perceive at some other time and place. Imagination cannot create anything absolutely new. It can never transcend the limits of perception. Imagination involves memory which depends upon perception. Thus even hallucinations, which are due to some disorders of the mind (antaḥkaraṇadoṣa), cannot represent absolutely non-existent objects. They also have a reference to external objects. And in dreams also there are recollections of objects actually perceived in the past.[1] Vācaspati also says that dreams are indirectly dependent on external objects.[2] Hence illusions, hallucinations, and dreams cannot disprove the existence of external objects.[3]

(7) The Yogācāra argues that an object and its cognition are invariably perceived at the same time, and therefore they are identical with each other. They are always perceived together. So they are identical with each other. Hence it is said : " Blue is identical with the cognition of blue, since they are invariably perceived together."

If the object had a separate existence apart from and independent of, its own cognition, it could be perceived by some other cognition—which is not the case. For instance, blue is never perceived by the cognition of yellow. This clearly proves that there is no difference between the percipient cognition (grāhaka) and the object of perception (grāhya).[4]

[1] NM., p. 545 ; see also *Indian Psychology : Perception*, ch. xv, xvi.
[2] NVTT., p. 467. [3] *Mysticism and Logic*, pp. 173 ff. [4] NM., p. 539.

Thus the Yogācāra argues that a perceptible object (grāhya) must be identical with the percipient cognition (grāhaka), because they are invariably perceived together. Here the identity of the object with its apprehending cognition is sought to be established on the ground of the invariably simultaneous perception of the two. But the ground is baseless. Like Kumārila, Jayanta points out that we do not always perceive them together at the same time. Sometimes we perceive them apart from each other. At the moment when we perceive an object we do not perceive the act of cognition. In the simple apprehension of the object there is simply the cognition of the object, but there is not yet appropriation of the cognition by the self. In the perception " this is blue " there is the cognition of " blue ", but no consciousness of this cognition. Consciousness does not necessarily involve self-consciousness. Then, again, sometimes there is apprehension of a cognition, but no apprehension of its object. In the cognition " I do not remember what object I perceived at that time " there is simply apprehension of a cognition, but there is no apprehension of its object. Thus sometimes we perceive an object and its cognition apart from each other. They are not invariably perceived together. Sometimes we perceive the object of perception apart from the percipient cognition, and sometimes we perceive the cognition apart from its object. Therefore, we can never argue that the object is identical with its cognition because they are always perceived together. When the Yogācāra says that the object *and* its cognition are identical, he tacitly assumes that they are different, since one and the same thing cannot be conjoined by the word " and ". Hence it is wrong to hold that cognitions apprehend their own forms, and do not take on forms from external objects.[1]

[1] NM., p. 544.

Vācaspati also urges that the apprehension of the object is different from that of its cognition. The object is apprehended by sense-perception, and its cognition is apprehended by mental perception.[1] Therefore, the object cannot be said to be identical with its cognition on the ground that they are invariably apprehended by the same act of cognition. The object and its cognition are never apprehended at the same moment. It is absurd to speak of the invariably simultaneous perception of them. Further, the apprehension of the object is not the *same* as that of its cognition. So the object is not identical with its cognition. Supposing they are *identical* with each other, they cannot be said to be perceived *together*.[2]

G. E. Moore also contends that sensation is *different* from its object. "I am suggesting," he says, "that the idealist maintains that object and subject are necessarily connected, mainly because he fails to see that they are *distinct*, that they are *two*, at all. When he thinks of yellow and when he thinks of the 'sensation of yellow' he fails to see that there is anything whatever in the latter which is not in the former. This being so, to deny that yellow can ever *be* apart from the sensation of yellow is merely to deny that yellow can ever be other than it is ; since yellow and the sensation of yellow are absolutely identical. To assert that yellow is necessarily an object of experience is to assert that yellow is necessarily yellow—a purely identical proposition, and therefore proved by the law of contradiction alone. Of course, the proposition also implies that experience is, after all, something distinct from yellow—else there would be no reason for insisting that yellow is a sensation ; and that the argument

[1] Perry says : "The object of a sensation is not the sensation itself. In order that a sensation shall be an object, it is necessary to introduce yet another awareness, such as introspection, which is not at all essential to the meaning of the sensation itself." (*Present Philosophical Tendencies*, p. 321.)

[2] NVTT., p. 467.

thus both affirms and denies that yellow and sensation of yellow are distinct, is what sufficiently refutes it.'[1]

Dr. Moore asserts that in every sensation there are two *distinct* elements, consciousness and the object of consciousness. In the sensation of blue (nīladhī) there are two distinct elements, viz. a sensation (dhī) and an object, viz. blue (nīla). "BUT sometimes the sensation of blue exists in my mind and sometimes it does not; and knowing that the sensation of blue includes two different elements, namely consciousness and blue, the question arises whether, when the sensation of blue exists, it is the consciousness which exists, or the blue which exists, or both. These three alternatives are all different from one another. So that, if any one tells us that to say 'Blue exists' is the *same* thing as to say that 'Both blue and consciousness exist', he makes a mistake and a self-contradictory mistake. . . . When the sensation exists, the consciousness, at least, certainly does exist. . . . The only alternative left, then, is that *either* both exist or the consciousness exists alone. If, therefore, any one tells us that the existence of blue is the same thing as the existence of the sensation of blue he makes a mistake and a self-contradictory mistake, for he asserts *either* that blue is the same thing as blue together with consciousness, *or* that it is the same thing as consciousness alone."

"Accordingly to identify either 'blue' or any other of what I have called '*objects*' of sensation, with the corresponding sensation is in every case, a self-contradictory error. It is to identify a part either with the whole of which it is a part or else with the other part of the same whole."[2]

Johnston's criticism of Berkeley's main argument for

[1] *Philosophical Studies*, pp. 13–14.
[2] Ibid., pp. 17–18.

the non-existence of non-mental objects equally applies to the Yogācāra's argument mentioned above. Johnston observes: "Berkeley's doctrine is defective by reason of its lack of psychological analysis; it is too undiscriminating and too facile, and it does not account for the complexity of the process of perception. . . . He never attempted any exhaustive analysis of the actual process of perception. He draws no distinction between *sensations* and *sensible qualities*; and he even identifies *sensations* and *sensible things* or *objects*. For him the word idea means at one and the same time a *sensation* in the mind and a *thing* presented to the mind. . . .What he calls ideas bear much resemblance to presentations, but in distinction from them they are presentative of nothing apart from themselves. Ideas for Berkeley are both presentations and what presentations are presentative of. He does not distinguish carefully between the actual process of perception, the particular experience in the psychical individual, and the thing or object perceived. His theory suffers seriously, in fact, from absence of psychological analysis."[1]

(8) The Yogācāra argues that an external object does not exist, since it cannot be perceived either as a composite whole or as an aggregate of parts. An external object cannot be perceived as a composite whole with an existence over and above that of its parts. A whole cannot be perceived as distinct from its parts. If two things are different from each other, they are perceived to occupy different portions of space, like a jar and a cloth. But a whole is not perceived to occupy a different space from that of its parts. We cannot perceive a whole without perceiving its parts. Therefore there is no difference between the whole and its parts; the whole is nothing but an aggregate of parts. The Buddhist does

[1] *The Development of Berkeley's Philosophy*, pp. 152–4; the italics are mine.

not admit the reality of a whole as distinct from a collection of parts.

If we cannot perceive an object as a composite whole, we cannot perceive it as an aggregate of parts either. We cannot perceive all the parts together constituting a composite whole. We perceive only those parts which are in front of us, but not the hind and lower parts. When we perceive a cloth we perceive one thread after another, from one end to the other, and thus perceive the cloth as a mere bundle of threads. But we never perceive the cloth as a composite whole distinct from the constituent threads.

Further, the whole cannot exist in its parts. It cannot exist in its entirety in one part. If it exists entirely in one part, it is exhausted in it, and cannot exist in other parts. Nor can it exist partially in each part. If it exists partially in all the parts, it is an unconnected whole. The whole existing in one part cannot be connected with the whole existing in another part. Therefore, the whole existing partially in its parts is a mere conglomeration of unconnected parts.[1]

Thus the whole can neither exist entirely in each part ; nor can it exist partially in all the parts.

Further, the perception of unity is a mere fiction of imagination.[2] We perceive the different parts of a complex object in the same way as we perceive the cavalry and the infantry as an army, or as we perceive the different kinds of trees as a forest. Just as in the perception of an army or a forest the perception of unity is imaginary, so the perception of many parts as a single object is imaginary. In these perceptions we do not distinguish different parts from one another, and consequently perceive them as one. In fact, the perception of an object as a jar is nothing but the perception of its

[1] NM., p. 549.
[2] Ekākārā tu pratītirvikalpamātram, NM., p. 549.

different parts together. Hence the jar is not distinct from its parts ; it is a m re collection of atoms (anusañcayamātra) ; it is not a composite whole. And if we reflect on the nature of a collection, and consider whether it is distinct from, or identical with, the constituent atoms, we find that a collection of atoms is not distinct from the atoms. Thus all things are finally reduced to atoms ; they are nothing but atoms pure and simple. And atoms too have six parts, since they are made up of six surfaces coming in contact with one another. Thus atoms, too, being composed of six supersensible subtle parts, are nothing but fictions of imagination. For these super-fine atoms, which are the ultimate elements of all things, do not serve any practical purpose. Hence the so-called external objects can neither be perceived as composite wholes nor as aggregates of atoms. Therefore they are mere abstractions or constructs of imagination. They are ideas of the mind.[1]

The Yogācāra argues that an external object does not exist, because it cannot be perceived either as a composite whole or as an aggregate of parts. This is a curious argument. The nature of reality is sought to be established on the basis of abstract speculation and not on that of experience. The whole is an object of valid uncontradicted knowledge. What is the good of this childish prattle about its non-existence ? If the whole is known by any means of valid knowledge, it is useless to consider the alternatives as to how it exists in the parts.[2]

Indeterminate perception is a means of valid knowledge. It apprehends a manifold object with generality, substantiality, quality, and action, but without a name.[3] We cannot define the nature of its object. By means of

[1] NM., p. 549. [2] NM., pp. 549–550 ; cf. Śaṅkara.
[3] Ibid., p. 550 and p. 99 ; *Indian Psychology : Perception*, p. 42.

indeterminate perception we perceive a complex object as a whole without clearly discriminating its parts. By determinate perception we analyse it into its parts and distinguish them from one another. The perception of unity may be false in some cases (e.g. the perception of an army) due to the presence of a hindering condition (e.g. distance). But from this we cannot conclude that in all cases the perception of unity must be false. Thus the perception of the whole is established by uncontradicted perception.[1]

The Yogācāra argues that the whole does not exist because it is not perceived apart from its parts. The Naiyāyika replies that this does not prove that the whole does not exist, but that the whole inheres in the parts. The whole can never exist apart from its parts. Therefore it cannot be perceived as occupying a different space from that of its parts. The whole is perceived along with its parts, since it inheres in its parts. But when we fix our attention on the parts and discriminate them from one another, we lose sight of the whole.

The whole exists in the parts together. It does not exist in each part, as the universal (jāti) exists in the particular (vyakti). The whole is actually perceived as existing in the parts. The perception of the whole is faultless. So it is needless to raise the question how the whole can exist in the parts. Abstract speculation cannot override valid experience. A cognition, which is produced by unvitiated sense-organs, which is not contradicted by any valid knowledge, and which is not tainted by any doubt, can never be regarded as false.[2]

The whole is not perceived in the same way as an army or a forest is perceived. There is a hindering condition (distance) in the perception of an army or a

[1] Ibid., p. 550.

[2] NM., pp. 550–1. Aduṣṭakaraṇodbhūtamanāvirbhūtabādhakam. Asaṃdigdhaṃ ca vijñānaṃ kathaṃ mithyeti kathyate, ibid., p. 551.

forest. But there is no hindrance in the perception of the whole. When an assemblage of soldiers is perceived together from a distance, it is perceived as an army. Similarly when a collection of different kinds of trees is perceived together from a distance, it is perceived as a forest. But the perception does not depend upon the perception of the constitutent atoms. If the perception of a cloth is said to depend on the perception of a collection of threads, it may be asked on what the perception of a thread depends, which too depends upon its own parts. These parts too depend upon their own parts, until at last we reach the atoms. These atoms are the ultimate constituents of a cloth, just as soldiers or trees are constituents of an army or a forest. But the atoms cannot be perceived like soldiers or trees, since they are supersensible. Thus the perception of the whole does not depend upon the perception of atoms.[1] Hence it is proved that the whole is an object of perception, though its constituent atoms are not perceived owing to their subtlety. But the existence of eternal and indivisible atoms can be inferred from their effects. Hence an external object must exist as an undeniable object of uncontradicted and undoubted perception.[2]

(9) Lastly, the Yogācāra argues that one and the same object appears different to different persons.[3] For example, a young woman appears as a beautiful damsel to an amorous person ; she appears as no better than a corpse to an ascetic ; and she appears as delicious food to a carnivorous animal.[4] The same object appears short in comparison with one thing, and long in comparison with another. What, then, is the real nature of the

[1] NM., p. 551.
[2] NM., pp. 549–551 ; see also NVTT., pp. 274 ff.
[3] Cf. Y.S., iv, 15.
[4] NM., p. 540 ; cf. Y.B. and T.V., iv, 15 ; SV. ; Śūnyavāda, 59.

object in itself?[1] The Yogācāra replies that there is no real object at all independent of cognitions. The different appearances of the so-called external object are nothing but cognitions which are subjective modes of consciousness.

There is no need of assuming the existence of external objects. They do not explain anything. It is sufficient to admit the reality of cognitions, the variety of which is due to the variety of subconscious impressions (vāsanā) within the stream of consciousness itself. Cognitions themselves take on different forms owing to revival of subconscious impressions. This assumption does not involve any self-contradiction. But the existence of external objects distinct from, and independent of, determinate cognitions, is a useless hypothesis. Hence, cognitions alone are real, which appear as a variety of objects. The distinction of the object of knowledge (prameya), the instrument of knowledge (pramāṇa), and the result of knowledge (pramiti) is within consciousness itself. The modification of consciousness into the form of an object is the object of knowledge (prameya). The apprehending mental mode or cognition is the instrument of knowledge (pramāṇa). And apprehension of cognition by itself or self-conscious awareness is the result of knowledge (pramiti). One and the same cognition appears to be diversified into knower, known, and knowledge owing to nescience (avidyā). On the destruction of avidyā all these distinctions will melt away in the formless, transparent, transcendental consciousness.[2]

Locke offers a similar argument to prove that secondary qualities such as heat and cold, taste, odour, sound, and colour are ideas of the mind. Berkeley puts his argument thus: " It is said that heat and cold are affections only

[1] NM., p. 540.
[2] Ibid.

of the mind, and not at all patterns of real beings existing in the corporeal substances which excite them, for the same body which appears cold to one hand seems warm to another. . . . Again, it is proved that sweetness is not really in the sapid thing, because the thing remaining unaltered the sweetness is changed into bitter, as in the case of a fever or otherwise vitiated palate." [1] So heat and cold, taste, and other secondary qualities are ideas of the mind. Berkeley applies the same argument to the primary qualities such as extension, figure, motion, and the like, and proves that they also are ideas of the mind. He says : "Why may we not as well argue that figure and extension are not patterns or resemblances of qualities existing in matter, because to the same eye at different stations, or eyes of a different texture at the same station, they appear various, and cannot therefore be the images of anything settled and determinate without the mind?" [2] Thus both Locke and Berkeley suppose that if an object appears various to the same person or to different persons, it must be an idea of the perceiving mind. The Yogācāra also holds the same view.

The Yogācāra argues that there is no external object, since one and the same object appears different to different individuals. If there were an external object, it would appear to be the same to all individuals. But it does not appear to be the same. It appears different to different individuals. Hence these different appearances are ideas of the percipient minds. They are creations of the mind. It is the vāsanā or psychical disposition of the mind that creates its own appropriate object.

Like Kumārila, Jayanta urges that this does not prove the non-existence of the external object. The

[1] *Principles of Human Knowledge*, p. 42.
[2] Ibid., p. 42.

object exists. It has different powers to produce different cognitions in different minds.[1] For example, a woman has the power of satisfying the hunger of a carnivorous animal. She has also the power of satisfying the lust of an amorous person. She has also the power of satisfying the instinct of hatred of an ascetic. Different cognitions are not produced in different minds irrespective of subsidiary conditions. Every individual has a peculiar psychical disposition (vāsanā) owing to his emotional attitude or instinctive tendency, which colours all his cognitions. These psychical dispositions differ in different individuals. So the same object produces different cognitions in different individuals. The object is not the only cause of the cognitions produced by it in different minds. It is the principal cause. The psychical disposition (vāsanā) of the self which reacts to the object and apprehends it is a subsidiary condition. The self does not passively receive the impressions produced by the object. It actively reacts to the object and apprehends it according to its own psychical disposition at the time.[2] Hence the same object does not produce the same cognition in all minds.

The Yogācāra may contend that it is needless to assume the existence of an external object, since different psychical dispositions are causes of different cognitions. The Naiyāyika replies that the object is not assumed,

[1] Arthasyānekaśaktitvānnāvahantyarthaśūnyatam. N.M., p. 547. Bertrand Russell concludes from the various appearances of the same object that " what the senses *immediately* tell us is not the truth about the object as it is apart from us, but only the truth about certain sense-data which, so far as we can see, depend upon the relations between us and the object. Thus what we directly see and feel is merely ' appearance ', which we believe to be a sign of some ' reality ' behind. But if the reality is not what appears, have we any means of knowing whether there is any reality at all ". (*The Problems of Philosophy*, pp. 23–4.)

[2] Pratiprāṇiniyatānekavidhavāsanāsahakārisāpekṣo hi tasya jñānasyātmalābhaḥ, NM., p. 547.

but it is actually perceived.[1] The object is manifold in nature. It has various characters of which it reveals that only to an individual, which fits in with his psychical disposition. Thus we assume the existence of different vāsanās in different minds in order to account for different appearances of the same object. The existence of the object is undeniable, since it is an object of direct perception.[2] Jayanta has borrowed this argument from Kumārila.

§ 4. *Résumé of the Nyāya Criticism of Vijñānavāda*

Mahāmahopadhyāya Phaṇi Bhūṣaṇa Tarkavāgīśa, the author of *Nyāyadarśana*, a monumental work in Bengali on ancient Nyāya, gives the following summary of the Nyāya arguments against the subjective idealism of the Yogācāra :—

(1) The Yogācāra argues that an object of cognition is identical with the apprehending cognition. A cognized object must be of the nature of cognition ; the apprehension of the cognition is the apprehension of its object ; there can be no apprehension of an object apart from the apprehension of its cognition. This argument is wrong. There is no evidence to prove that the object of cognition is identical in reality with the cognition. The apprehension of the object is different from the apprehension of the cognition. The object is always apprehended as something different from the cognition. The object is the objective (karma) of the act of cognition (kriyā). An act and its object cannot be identical with each other. Therefore the act of cognition cannot be identical with the object of cognition, even as the act of cutting cannot be identical with the object of cutting. Further, if the object does not exist, the cognition also

[1] Na hyarthaḥ kalpyate api tu pratibhāsate eva, ibid., p. 547.

[2] Ibid., p. 547 ; see also Udayana's elaborate criticism of *Vijñānavāda* in Ātmatattviveka, pp. 52 ff. (Jīvānanda's edition, Calcutta).

cannot exist, since there is no cognition without an object.

(2) The Yogācāra argues that external objects do not really exist; they are, in reality, mere forms of cognitions; they have existence only as cognitions. But mere forms of cognitions appear like external objects. This is an absurd argument! If there are no external objects at all, it cannot be said that cognitions appear like external objects. The appearance of externality presupposes the reality of external things. Unless external things exist and are known, cognitions cannot be held to appear like external objects.

(3) If objects of cognition do not exist at all, there can be no variety of objects. And if there is no variety of objects, there can be no variety of cognitions. The variety of cognitions or perceptions (jñānavaicitrya) can be explained only by the variety of external objects (viṣayavaicitrya).

(4) The Yogācāra holds that the variety of perceptions is due to the variety of subconscious impressions which form a beginningless series and are rooted in nescience (avidyā). This argument involves *hysteron proteron*. The variety of subconscious impressions is due to the variety of perceptions of external objects. Perceptions are the causes of subconscious impressions. Subconscious impressions are not the causes of perceptions.

(5) It cannot be held that momentary cognitions are produced in particular forms which are only modifications of cognitions. There is no cause of the production of such momentary cognitions with particular forms. Cognitions which exist only for one moment and are destroyed in the second moment cannot be said to be the material cause of other cognitions.

(6) The Yogācāra admits the reality of a series of momentary cognitions only, and cannot, therefore, account for recollection. One momentary cognition

cannot remember another past momentary cognition which it never experienced. The series of self-cognitions (ālayavijñāna) cannot be said to remember momentary cognitions, because self-cognitions also are momentary like object-cognitions (pravṛttivijñāna). If the series of self-cognitions (ālayavijñāna) be held to be permanent, the doctrine of momentariness is contradicted.

(7) If there are no objects distinct from cognitions, all objects should be apprehended as cognitions of cognitions. But, as a matter of fact, when we perceive objects, we never feel that we have cognitions of cognitions, but of external objects. We perceive objects as distinct from cognitions.

(8) The Yogācāra likens waking cognitions to dream-cognitions and argues that waking cognitions are without any basis in external objects like dream-cognitions because they are cognitions. Waking cognitions are essentially different in nature from dream-cognitions. Further, dream-cognitions, though erroneous, are not absolutely without a foundation in external objects. They are ultimately founded in external reality. Perceptions of external objects leave subconscious impressions in the mind. These are revived in the dream-state and combined in a fantastic manner. The contents of dream-experience are always reproductions of past perceptions of external objects. Therefore they have a foundation in external objects. Further, all waking cognitions cannot be said to be unreal. If all cognitions were equally false under all circumstances, there would be no true cognitions at all. And if there are no true cognitions, we cannot speak of wrong cognitions. Cognitions are ascertained to be wrong only in comparison with previous true cognitions of objects. It is absolutely unmeaning to speak of all cognitions as wrong.

(9) If there be no true cognitions, there can be no

pramāṇa, for pramāṇa is only the instrument of right knowledge. If there be no instrument of right knowledge, nothing can be established. If something is established without any instrument of right knowledge (pramāṇa), its contradictory can as well be established in the same way. The Yogācāra establishes his position with the help of inference which is a kind of pramāṇa. If all cognitions are false, then inference also is false. How, then, can he prove the truth of his position by means of inference which is wrong? Further, perception is of superior strength than inference. Inference which contradicts perception cannot be regarded as valid. External objects are directly perceived. Hence their non-existence cannot be proved by inference.

(10) The objects are perceived as external (bāhya) and extended (sthūla). Externality and extension which are perceived in objects cannot be the property of cognitions. They cannot be said to be forms of cognitions. They do not exist in cognitions, and consequently cannot be said to be the forms of cognitions. Further, everything is momentary according to the Buddhist. Therefore an external object, even if it exists, must be momentary. This is the doctrine of the Sautrāntika and the Vaibhāṣika. If the object of which extension is perceived after its intercourse with the visual organ be momentary, it cannot endure till its extension is perceived. Hence the extension of a momentary object cannot be perceived.

(11) The Yogācāra holds that in the illusory cognition of silver, the mere cognition of silver appears to be an external object. But, according to him, there are no external objects at all apart from cognitions; therefore he is committed to the doctrine that one cognition appears as another cognition in an illusion. But the Yogācāra holds that in an illusion a cognition is attributed to an imaginary external object, though it is unreal

apart from a cognition. The cognition of silver is attributed to an imaginary external object ; so it appears to be an external object. But if an external object is absolutely non-existent as external, it is unmeaning to speak of a cognition appearing like an external object. When the Yogācāra speaks of a cognition appearing like an external object, he tacitly assumes the existence of an external reality and undermines his own position.

(12) An illusion is due to similarity between the object which is the substratum (adhiṣṭhana) of the illusion and the object which is erroneously ascribed (āropya) to the substratum. For instance, the illusion of silver in a shell is due to similarity between silver that is attributed to the shell and the shell which is the substratum of the illusion. But the Yogācāra does not recognize the reality of external objects. The so-called external object to which the cognition of silver is attributed is unreal and imaginary. There can be no similarity between a real cognition and an unreal object. Hence there can be no illusion. If it be held that there is some similarity between an unreal and imaginary external shell and the real cognition of silver, then there can be similarity also between the imaginary shell and the real cognition of a man so that there may be an illusion of a man in a shell. There is no reason why an illusion of a man in a shell is not possible. The Yogācāra replies that different cognitions are uniformly produced in the forms of different objects. A particular cognition appears in a particular form, and not in all forms on account of its particular nature. So a cognition of silver is produced in an unreal and imaginary shell by its own inherent nature. All sorts of cognitions are not produced in an unreal object. A particular nature (svabhāva) or power (śakti) regulates the production of particular cognitions in unreal and imaginary objects. Similarity between an illusory cognition and an unreal object does not

regulate it. Then the question arises whether the so-called nature of a cognition is self-existent and independent or springs out of something which regulates the nature of the cognition. If the specific nature of the cognition is of the nature of a cognition, it also must have another specific nature which is its cause, and so on *ad infinitum*. Thus the Yogācāra is ultimately committed to an assumption of infinite series of natures or powers of cognitions, which is absurd![1]

§ 5. *The Vaiśeṣika Exposition of the Yogācāra Idealism*

Śrīdhara outlines the Yogācāra subjectivism and its arguments in *Nyāyakandalī*.

Firstly, the Buddhist is committed to the doctrine of momentary existence. The so-called object and the cognition produced by it are momentary. The main question in a theory of knowledge is how an object is cognized by its cognition.

It is cognized by the cognition either when it comes into existence, or before it comes into existence. It cannot be cognized before it comes into existence, since it is non-existent. It cannot be cognized even when it comes into existence, since it does not endure for more than one moment. So it cannot be cognized in either case.

The object, though past and non-existent, may be said to be cognized by a cognition because it gives rise to the cognition. This is wrong for two reasons. In the first place, the object is not cognized as past but as *present*.[2] In the second place, the sense-organs also

[1] *Nyāyadarśana* (Bengali), vol. iv, pp. 166–9.

[2] Alexander's account of the process of perception is not free from the causal theory of knowledge. "If the object (event) is the cause of the act which apprehends it, evidently then the apprehension is posterior in time to the object (event) of which it is the apprehension. My act of knowing is an effect of the sensum which actuated it and which is therefore prior in time to it. The object is essentially a process, a piece of space-time, of pure motion. It sends an influence to me. But before it

produce the cognition, but they are not cognized. In fact, the sense-organs, which are not identical with their sites (adhiṣṭhāna) are imperceptible.

It may be said that the nature (svabhāva) of the object produced by its assemblage of causal conditions is such that it alone is apprehended by the cognition, even though the object and the sense-organs alike are the causes of the cognition ; and the cognition apprehends the object as present, though it is past and non-existent inasmuch as the cognition comes into existence immediately after the object.

The Yogācāra repeats the same objection. The object cannot be said to be apprehended by the cognition because it is the cause of the cognition. The sense-organs also are its cause. But they are not apprehended by the cognition.[1]

The object may be said to be cognized by the cognition which does not really cognize the object but cognizes itself. This is a curious argument ! The cognition apprehends itself. It does not apprehend the object. Yet it is incomprehensible why the object is apprehended by the cognition.

It may be said that the object which produces the cognition is apprehended by it, though the cognition apprehends itself. This is the Law of Nature that the cognition produced by an object apprehends the object, though the object has gone out of existence, and the cognition has nothing to apprehend but itself. No one can object to the Law of Nature.

reaches me and causes me to perçeive the object, the object is no more. Yet I perceive the object. The object I perceive, is therefore a past object, however strange the assertion may look. Alexander fully accepts this conclusion. Perception is a kind of memory, says he. (*Mind*, 1912, p. 3, note.) But curiously enough it is a memory of something which never has been experienced. And this puts his whole realism in jeopardy." (*Realism*, pp. 158–9.)

[1] NK., pp. 122–3

The Yogācāra contends that when an object produces a cognition, production is one only ; and it is not a property of the cognition and the object both. It is a property of the cognition only. So it cannot restrict the cognition to the particular object.

It may be said that the object cannot be apprehended by the cognition, since the cognition is a property of something else. But the mutual relation of cognizer (grāhaka) and cognized (grāhya) between the cognition and the object follows from their mutual relation, and not from the one-sided relation to one of the members related.

Further, the past and the future objects cannot produce cognitions at present, since they are non-existent. But still they are apprehended. Therefore an object cannot be said to be apprehended by a cognition because it produces the cognition. The causal theory of knowledge is unsound.

The relation of cognizer (grāhaka) and cognized (grāhya) cannot be said to follow from the subject-object-relationship (viṣaya-viṣayi-bhāva) between the cognition and the object. The two relations are not distinct ; they are one and the same. The character of the cognized (grāhyatva) does not in any way differ from that of being the object of cognition, and that of the cognizer does not in any way differ from that of being the cognition of the object. Hence the relation of cognizer and cognized cannot be said to follow from the subject-object-relation between the cognition and the object.

It may be held that it is the very nature (svabhāva) of a cognition to apprehend a particular object. What is the cause of this nature ? If it is not due to any cause, it cannot restrict the cognition to a particular object. If it is due to some cause, it is needless to speak of the nature of a cognition, which restricts it to a particular object. In fact, we do not find any other cause than production. The cognition is produced. The production determines its nature. And its nature restricts it to a particular object.[1] But the Yogācāra has already shown that what produces a cognition need not necessarily be apprehended by it.

Secondly, what is cognized by a cognition is not different from it like the cognition itself.[2] Just as the cognition is self-luminous and does not differ from the cognition which apprehends it, so the so-called object does not differ from the cognition which apprehends it. We find that blue and the like are apprehended by cognitions. If they were different from the cognitions, they could not be apprehended by them because of the absence of identity (tādātmya) between them, which is the necessary condition of cognizability. It has already been proved that causality is not a condition of cognizability. An object is not apprehended by a cognition because it gives rise to it. If the object is apprehended by a cognition, though it is different from it and bears no relationship to it, then anything will be apprehended by every cognition, and there will be nothing to restrict a cognition to a particular object. In fact, it will lead to total confusion. Non-difference or identity is the necessary condition of cognizability.

Not only the object is non-different from cognition, but also the subject is so. The distinction of the cognizer (grāhaka), the cognized (grāhya), and cognition (saṃvitti) is an illusory appearance like the appearance of the double moon.[3]

But the cognition of an object (e.g. blue) always appears with the form of the object.[4] If there is no external object, what is the cause of the form which

[1] NK., pp. 122–3. [2] Cf. TV., iv, 14, p. 293; S.D.S., p. 13.
[3] NK., p. 126.
[4] Arthabuddhistadākarā sā tvākāraviśeṣaṇā, ibid., p. 126.

appears in the cognition? The blue *object* cannot be its cause because it is never perceived; it is always beyond the range of sense-perception.[1] Berkeley also similarly argues that matter as conceived by philosophers is never perceived, and consequently it does not exist. "As for our senses," he says, "by them we have the knowledge *only* of our sensations, ideas, or those things that are immediately perceived by sense, call them what you will: but they do not inform us that things exist without the mind, or unperceived, like to those which are perceived."[2]

It may be said that we may assume the existence of the object from its effects. Then we may as well assume a diversity of powers in the immediately preceding cognition itself which is actually perceived. It can account for the diversity of forms in dream-cognitions also which cannot be produced by objects existing in some other place and at some other time, since none of them exist at the time. Therefore, the form of blue which appears in a cognition is not due to an external object, but to a potency of the immediately preceding cognition.[3] Berkeley also gives a similar argument. "What reason can induce us to believe the existence of bodies without the mind, from what we perceive, since the very patrons of Matter themselves do not pretend there is any *necessary* connection between them and our ideas? . . . The supposition of external objects is not necessary for the producing our ideas; since it is granted they are produced sometimes (e.g. in dreams, frenzies, and the like), and might possibly be produced always in the same order we see them in at present, without their concurrence."[4]

But there is a difference between Berkeley and the

[1] Arthasya sadā atīndriyatvāt, ibid., p. 126.
[2] *Principles of Human Knowledge*, p. 45.
[3] NK., p. 126. [4] *Principles of Human Knowledge*, p. 45.

Yogācāra. Berkeley accounts for waking perceptions by the agency of God external to finite spirits. But the Yogācāra accounts for them by the powers of the immediately preceding cognitions or vāsanās within the stream of consciousness itself. Both of them account for dreams by cognitions.

The Yogācāra's formal argument may be stated thus: Whatever is a cognition is without a foundation in an external object, like a dream-cognition. Waking cognitions of pillars and the like are cognitions. Therefore they are without a foundation in external objects.[1]

Thirdly, there is non-difference between the apprehending cognition (vedaka) and the apprehended object (vedya) because they are invariably apprehended together. Blue is different from yellow. So they are never apprehended simultaneously. Difference is concomitant with the absence of being always apprehended at the same time. Not-difference is concomitant with being always apprehended together. An object and its cognition are always apprehended together. Therefore they are non-different from each other.[2]

§ 6. *The Vaiśeṣika Criticism of the Yogācāra Idealism*

Śrīdhara refutes all the above arguments.

(1) The first argument is that the object cannot be apprehended by a cognition. It is not cognizable. Even granting that it cannot be apprehended, this does not prove that it does not exist. It may exist but may not be perceived. It may not be perceived owing to some hindrances such as remoteness and the like. Therefore, if a thing is not perceived, it does not follow that it does not exist.[3]

Śrīdhara asks how the form of a cognition recognized by the Yogācāra is perceived. It is not the cause of the cognition, since the two are non-different from each

[1] NK., p. 127. [2] NK., p. 125. [3] Ibid., p. 127.

other. So it cannot be perceived as the cause of the cognition. It does not impart its form to the cognition and cannot be perceived as such, since two forms are not perceived in any cognition. It cannot be perceived as mere cognition, since in deep sleep cognition is not perceived, though it continues at the time. If the form of a cognition is said to be perceived because it is manifested, what constitutes its manifestation may be asked. Its manifestation (avabhāsa) may be said to consist in the fact that it enables the cognition to lead to effective reactions in the shape of acceptance or rejection or indifference. Śrīdhara replies that the external object also is capable of being accepted, rejected, or treated with indifference. So it is manifested. It cannot, therefore, be regarded as not cognizable.[1]

(2) The second argument of the Yogācāra can be easily disposed of. An object is cognized by a cognition not because it is non-different from the cognition, but because it is the nature of a cognition to apprehend the object which stimulates a sense-organ and gives rise to it.[2] An object is apprehended by a cognition by its very nature ; and a cognition apprehends an object by its very nature. Apprehension of an object by a cognition is governed by the Law of Nature. The object and its cognition are distinct from each other.[3]

Vācaspati also holds that the nature of a thing does not depend upon any other condition. An object is apprehended by its cognition by its very nature. It does not depend upon any other condition in order to be apprehended.[4] But how can an object be apprehended by a cognition without being related to it ? A relation between two terms does not require any other relation to relate itself to them. If it requires another relation

[1] NK., pp. 126–7. [2] Ibid., p. 128. [3] Ibid., p. 124.
[4] Svabhāvataścārthasya jñānamiti na tadīyatve anyadapekṣate, NVTT., p. 465.

to relate it to the relata, that relation too will require another relation to relate it to the relation, and so on *ad infinitum*. So just as a relation between two terms does not depend upon any other relation, so a cognition apprehends an object without depending upon any other relation. A particular cognition apprehends a particular object only by its very nature. And the Law of Nature is the ultimate limit of explanation. The cognitive relation is a unique relation which cannot be accounted for.

It may be asked how the cognition of colour apprehends colour without modifying the object in any way. The act of cognition which is the instrument of knowledge (pramāṇa) does modify the object inasmuch as it brings about reaction to the object in the shape of acceptance, rejection, or treatment with indifference. It does not produce any other effect in the object. Hence a cognition which by its very nature apprehends an object does not depend upon any other condition to execute its function. A particular cognition apprehends a particular object and is restricted to it.[1]

Udayana also holds that " there is a *svarūpasambandha* between a cognition and its object by virtue of which the former is the subject (viṣayin) and the latter is the object (viṣaya). There is no *tertium quid* in the form of cognizedness between a cognition and its object. The natural relation between a cognition and its object by virtue of which the former apprehends the latter is called *viṣayatā*. . . . Objectivity (viṣayatā) constitutes the *svarūpasambandha* between a cognition and its object." [2] Haridāsa roundly declares that a particular nature determines the relation of a cognition to its object.[3]

[1] Ibid., pp. 465–6.

[2] *Indian Psychology: Perception*, p. 206; Nyāyakusumāñjali (with Haridāsī ṭikā), iv, 2–3.

[3] Svabhāvaviśeṣa eva viṣayatāniyāmakaḥ, ibid. (Jivānanda's edition, Calcutta, p. 64).

There is a *svarūpasambandha* between them.[1] *Svarūpasambandha* is a unique relation. It cannot be reduced to any other relation. The cognitive relation is unique and *sui generis*. It is quite different from relations among physical things such as causality and the like. It is not conjunction as Rāmānuja holds. It is not compresence as Alexander holds. It is not causality and resemblance as the Sautrāntika holds. It is quite different from intersubjective and inter-objective relations. " Knowledge should be regarded as foundational, and we should not seek to represent what is foundational by the analgoy of anything but itself."[2] Keith rightly observes: " Cognition must not be regarded as transforming what it cognizes ; to be cognized is no quality of the object but a relation *sui generis* (*svarūpasambandha*) existing between the object and cognition."[3]

The Yogācāra argues that the so-called object is unconscious and cannot, therefore, be manifested or apprehended. Śrīdhara urges that there is no royal command to the effect that an unconscious thing cannot be manifested! It *is* actually perceived. It is a fact of experience. So it cannot be challenged. Just as the act of cutting is related to the thing that is cut, and is yet distinct from it, so the act of cognition is related to an object cognized, and is yet distinct from it.

(3) The third argument of the Yogācāra does not prove the non-existence of an external object. Even if the blue object and the cognition of blue are invariably apprehended simultaneously, it does not prove that the object does not exist. Even if it exists, it may be apprehended together with its cognition. It may be the very nature of a cognition to apprehend an external object. And because the cognition is the means of apprehending

[1] Ghaṭajñānayoḥ svarūpa eva sambandhaḥ, ibid., p. 65.

[2] A. C. Mukherjee, *Self, Thought, and Reality*, p. 301.

[3] *Indian Logic and Atomism*, p. 46.

the object, whenever one is apprehended the other also may be apprehended.[1] Whenever we perceive a blue object, what is cognized as blue is perceived as something external, while the cognition of blue is perceived as something internal. Therefore the blue object can never be regarded as identical with its cognition.[2] If the cognized object were identical with its cognition, it would be apprehended as " *I* am blue ", and not as " *this* is blue ".[3] This clearly shows that it is something distinct from cognition, which is presented to it. The Yogācāra may argue that some cognitions are apprehended in the form of " I ", and others, in the form of " this ", though both the forms are inherent in cognitions themselves. Srīdhara urges that there is no particular cognition in the form of " I " as there is a cognition in the form of " blue ". What is perceived as " I " by one person is perceived as " you " by another. There is no fixity in the cognition of " I ". But there is a fixity in the cognition of " blue ". Therefore the cognition of " I " is not on a par with the cognition of " blue ". The self is distinct from the not-self. An object can never be reduced to a quality of the self.[4]

The Yogācāra may argue that the distinction of subject and object within a cognition is an illusory appearance. One undivided cognition *appears* to be polarized into subject and object, though really it is devoid of all distinction within itself.[5] Śrīdhara urges that the distinction between subject and object is directly perceived, and consequently should be regarded as real. Even granting that the distinction is an illusory appearance, how can it be proved? If it is proved by inference, then it involves the fallacy of mutual dependence. An

[1] NK., p. 128; cf. NM., p. 541.
[2] NK., p. 128; cf. NM., p. 541; S.D.S., p. 14; S.V.M., p. 113.
[3] NK., p. 129; cf. NM., p. 541; S.D.S., p. 14; S.V.M., p. 112.
[4] NK., p. 129; cf. S.V.M., p. 112.
[5] Jñānasyābhedino bhedapratibhāso hyupaplavaḥ, NK., p. 129.

inference is possible only when perception has already been proved to be valid, and the Yogācāra proves perception to be invalid by means of inference. Thus there is arguing in a circle.[1] This argument of Śrīdhara has already been elaborated in the Jaina criticism of subjective idealism. It is interesting to note that Mallisena borrowed this argument in all its details from Śrīdhara's *Nyāyakandalī* in almost the same language.[2]

Further, if an object were nothing but the form of a cognition, it could be apprehended only by the cognition in which the form is manifested. Thus it would be the "private property" of a particular person. It could not be open to the perception of all. But, as a matter of fact, we find that the *same* object is perceived by many when they turn their attention towards it. What is perceived by you is perceived by me also. Therefore the object cannot be regarded as identical with the form of a cognition.[3]

Just as the Yogācāra cannot account for the *sameness* of the object of perception, so Berkeley also cannot account for it. Fraser rightly says : "Perfect similarity in the sense-phenomena manifested, not objective numerical identity, constitutes 'sameness' in sensible things, according to Berkeley."[4] "*Same* may mean," says Johnston, "either (1) numerically identical, i.e. the same, or (2) numerically distinct, i.e. similar. When the plain man says that ten men look at the moon he means that the object perceived by the ten men is one and the same, is numerically identical. But Berkeley's theory implies that when ten men look at the moon each man has a presentation of his own in his mind, numerically distinct from those of the others. In the former case one moon is seen, in the latter ten. Berkeley believes

[1] NK., p. 129; cf. S.D.S., p. 14.
[2] Cf. NK., p. 129, lines 12–21, with S.V.M., p. 113, lines 14–25.
[3] NK., pp. 127–8. [4] *Selections from Berkeley*, p. 67, n.

that the ideas men have in looking at what is commonly called the same thing are numerically distinct. But men realize that these numerically distinct ideas are similar : 'they agree in their perceptions.' And Berkeley says it is of no consequence whether we attend to the *agreement* of the presentations and call them the *same*, or regard the *diversity* of the persons who have the presentations, and call them *different*. He thus reduces all sameness or identity to *similarity*." [1] This criticism equally holds good against the Yogācāra doctrine.

The Yogācāra argument that waking perceptions are without a foundation in external objects like dream-cognitions, is invalid because the instance is not established. Dream-cognitions also are not confined to themselves ; they have their real counterparts in external objects. During dreams only those things are apprehended which were actually perceived in the past at some other time and place ; they reappear in consciousness because of the revival of the subconscious impressions left by the previous perceptions. Thus dream-cognitions have their real counterparts in the external world. Therefore waking cognitions cannot be regarded as devoid of a foundation in the external world.[2]

Śrīdhara urges that an external object is directly perceived at a particular time and in a definite portion of space. This perception sets aside all arguments brought forward by the Yogācāra to prove the non-existence of the object. The perception of an object at a particular time and in a definite portion of space can never be explained by the theory of vāsanā or subconscious impression or a potency inherent in the cognition itself.[3] Thus the Yogācāra theory of subjective idealism is unsound.

[1] *The Development of Berkeley's Philosophy*, pp. 155–6.

[2] NK., pp. 128–9 ; cf. SV., nirālambanavāda, 107–9 ; SD., p. 143 ; NBh., iv, 2, 34.

[3] NK., p. 130 ; see G. N. Jhā's E.T., pp. 265–284.

§ 7. *The Nyāya-Vaiśeṣika Criticism of the Sautrāntika Realism*

The Sautrāntika holds that the object, which produces a cognition and imparts its form to it, is apprehended by it. The cognition must be admitted to have the form of the object. It is not devoid of form. The form of the cognition represents the form of the object. The Sautrāntika is an advocate of the representative theory of perception. He recognizes three elements involved in the perception of an object, viz. the act of cognition, the form of the cognition, and the object with a form (e.g. blue). Consciousness is common to all acts of cognition. They are specialized by their forms. The forms of cognitions correspond to those of their objects. If cognitions were pure, formless consciousness, they would have nothing to restrict them to particular objects, and there would be no specific cognitions of blue, yellow, and the like. Hence it must be admitted that cognitions are invested with specific forms by their objects ; the forms of objects are the evidence of the existence of their specific cognitions. The specific form of a cognition brings about a connection between the cognition and a particular object. It enables the cognition to apprehend a particular object. The sense-organs are the common factors in the production of cognitions. Therefore they cannot specialize the cognitions. It is the form of the object that gives a specific form to the cognition. A formless cognition cannot apprehend an object because it has no special power to apprehend it. The mere being of pure consciousness cannot apprehend an object, since it is common to cognitions of all objects. It can apprehend an object only when it is invested with the specific form of the object.[1]

It is misleading to compare the Sautrāntika realism

[1] NK., p. 123.

with any of the various types of contemporary realism. But still the conception of the *form* (ākāra) of a cognition may roughly be compared with Meinong's conception of the *content* of an act of cognition. "Meinong holds that the three elements involved in the perception of an object are the act of thought, the content of the act, and the object. The act is the same in any two cases of the same kind of consciousness : thus, if I perceive a cow or if I perceive a horse, the act of perceiving is exactly similar on each occasion. What is different, however, is the content of my perception, this being a cow-content in the case of the first perception and a horse-content in the case of the second. The content is again clearly distinguished from the object, since it must exist in my mind now while the object may be out in the field." [1] A cognition is an *act* of cognition. Its form is its *content*. The form of an object is the *sense datum*. And the object is the *physical object*.

Śrīdhara contends that there is nothing to prove that an object is apprehended by a cognition because it imparts its form to the cognition. If the blue object is apprehended only by the cognition of blue by its very nature, it is the Law of Nature (svabhāvaniyama) that governs the relation between a cognition and an object. A specific object is apprehended by a specific cognition by its very nature, not because it imprints its form on the cognition. When a cognition is produced by an object in intercourse with a sense-organ, it appears as apprehension of that object which stimulates the sense-organ and gives rise to the cognition ; the object also is apprehended by the cognition because it is the very nature of the object to be apprehended while the sense-organ which is an accessory condition of the production of the cognition is not apprehended. The relation of the act of cognition to its object is governed by the Law of

[1] C. E. M. Joad, *Introduction to Modern Philosophy*, p. 14.

Nature. The cognitive act apprehends its object by its very nature without being invested with the form of the object. The restriction of a cognition to its object is due to the nature of the cognition itself, and not to its form.[1]

The Nyāya-Vaiśeṣika denies the form or content of the act of cognition which directly apprehends its object in the process of perception. The Jaina, the Mīmāṃsaka, and some Vedāntists also hold the same doctrine. But they all recognize the existence of the object independent of the act of cognition of the individual self, whatever the ontological nature of the object may be. The Yogācāra, on the other hand, recognizes only the act of cognition (vijñāna) with its content or form (ākāra), but not the external object. He regards the content or form of the cognition itself as the object of the cognition.

[1] NK., p. 124.

CHAPTER VIII

THE VEDĀNTA CRITIQUE OF SUBJECTIVE IDEALISM

§ 1. *Absolute Idealism and Subjective Idealism*

In *Advaitabrahmasiddhi* Sadānanda Yati draws a distinction between the subjective idealism of the Yogācāra and the absolute idealism of Śaṅkara. Both are idealists. They recognize the ontological reality of consciousness (vijñāna) only. But there is a substantial difference between them. The Yogācāra holds that cognitions are many and non-eternal. But Śaṅkara holds that there is only one, eternal, universal consciousness or Brahman. The former is a subjective idealist or sensationist. The latter is a monist or absolute idealist. The discrete, momentary cognitions in individual streams of consciousness (santāna) constitute the reality of the Yogācāra. The one, eternal, universal consciousness or Brahman constitutes the reality of Śaṅkara. The Yogācāra is a subjective idealist. He reduces the so-called external objects to mere cognitions of the individual minds or psychic continua. He is a sensationist like David Hume and J. S. Mill. He does not recognize the existence of the permanent self apart from a series of momentary sensations, feelings, and ideas. Nor does he admit the reality of external objects distinct from, and independent of, subjective cognitions. He is emphatic in his denial of external objects. They are nothing but internal forms of cognitions which appear to consciousness like external objects owing to an illusion. Śaṅkara, on the other hand, recognizes the existence of external objects distinct from, and independent of, subjective cognitions. He is emphatic in asserting the existence of external objects. His absolute idealism is not mentalism or subjectivism. He recognizes the Absolute (Brahman) alone as the ontological reality. The Absolute is pure identity. It is not identity-in-difference like the Absolute of Hegel. But still Śaṅkara is not prevented from recognizing the empirical reality (vyāvahārikasattā) of external objects and individual souls (jīva). Deussen rightly observes : " Just as Kant, along with transcendental idealism, maintained the empirical reality of the external world, and defended it against Berkeley, so the Vedāntins are not prevented by their doctrine of Ignorance as the foundation of all Being expanded in name and form from maintaining the reality of the outer world against the Buddhists of idealistic tendencies." [1] Śaṅkara recognizes only the empirical reality of the external world and the individual souls. The external objects are real for all practical purposes of our life. They serve all practical needs. But they are unreal from the standpoint of the Absolute. When the individual soul (jīva) transcends its limitations (upādhi) and realizes its identity with Brahman, it loses all sense of plurality. The jīvas and external objects are not real *sub specie æternitatis* in the language of Spinoza. They have only an empirical reality.

The Yogācāra regards the objects of perception such as blue and the like as internal forms of cognitions only which appear like external objects. Śaṅkara, on the other hand, admits the empirical reality of external objects such as blue and the like, which are distinct from cognitions and indefinable (anirvacanīya) in nature.[2] Further, according to Śaṅkara, empirical objects are

[1] *The System of the Vedanta*, p. 241.

[2] Na hi brahmavādino nīlādyākāraṃ vittim abhyupagacchanti, kiṃtvanirvacanīyaṃ nīlāditi. Bhāmatī, ii, 2, 28, p. 541.

known through their practical efficiency (arthakriyā). But, according to the Yogācāra, objects are mere determinations of cognitions which have practical efficiency.[1]

Jayanta Bhaṭṭa also distinguishes between the absolute idealism of Śaṅkara and the subjective idealism of the Yogācāra. Both of them are idealists. They recognize the reality of consciousness only. They deny the absolute reality of anything independent of consciousness. But there is a world of difference between them. Śaṅkara's absolute reality is one, undifferenced, eternal consciousness. The Yogācāra's absolute reality is a plurality of momentary cognitions with no permanent self abiding in them and with no external objects to produce them. He does not admit the reality of one, infinite, eternal, self-luminous consciousness or Brahman, but of a beginningless series of momentary cognitions which appear and disappear in individual minds or streams of consciousness.[2]

§ 2. *Śaṅkara's Exposition of the Yogācāra Idealism*

Śaṅkara does not give a detailed exposition of the subjective idealism of the Yogācāra. Neither his exposition nor his criticism seems to be thorough and searching. He states the following arguments of the Yogācāra for the non-existence of external objects :—

(1) Firstly, if external objects exist, they are either simple atoms or complex bodies composed of atoms. Atoms are imperceptible. They are too subtle to be perceived. Imperceptible atoms cannot be perceived as gross objects such as pillars and the like. Atoms cannot produce cognitions of gross objects. External objects cannot, therefore, be of the nature of simple atoms. Nor can they be complex aggregates of atoms. If they are aggregates of atoms, they are either different or non-different from the atoms which compose them.

[1] Advaitabrahmasiddhi (Bib. Ind.), p. 93. [2] NM., pp. 536–7.

If they are different from atoms, they cannot be regarded as aggregates of atoms. If they are non-different from aroms, they cannot produce cognitions of gross objects such as pillars and the like. External objects cannot, therefore, be complex aggregates of atoms. They are neither simple atoms nor complex bodies. Hence they do not exist.[1]

(2) Secondly, consciousness is common to all cognitions ; they are not different from one another in so far as they are states of consciousness ; they undergo modifications according to their objects and are distinguished from one another by their different forms. The cognitions which are of a uniform nature as consciousness are specified by their objects so that we have now the cognition of a post, now the cognition of a wall, now the cognition of a jar, and so on. This is not possible without some distinction on the part of cognitions. The realist must, therefore, admit that there are different forms of cognitions corresponding to the forms of their objects (viṣayasārūpya). If cognitions had not the same forms as those of their objects, every cognition would be able to apprehend all objects.[2] So cognitions must have different forms. But if we admit the different forms of cognitions, it is needless to assume the existence of external objects as their objective counterparts. The Law of Parsimony demands that we should admit the existence of different cognitions only, but not of the external objects because the former alone serve our purpose.[3]

(3) Thirdly, we always apprehend an object (viṣaya) and its cognition (jñāna) together. Hence they are identical with each other.[4] Whenever we perceive an

[1] S.B.S., ii, 2, 28.
[2] Ratnaprabhā on S.B.S., ii, 2, 28.
[3] S.B.S., ii, 2, 28.
[4] Sahopalambhaniyamādabhedo viṣayavijñānayorāpatati, ibid., ii, 2, 28.
p. 544.

object we perceive also the cognition of the object. If any of the two is not perceived, the other also cannot be perceived. We cannot perceive an object without perceiving its cognition, and we cannot perceive the cognition of an object without perceiving the object itself.[1] And because an object and its cognition are always perceived together they must be regarded as identical with each other. If they were distinct from each other, they could be perceived apart from each other. So there are no external objects.[2]

(4) Fourthly, our waking perceptions can be explained without the hypothesis of external objects like dream-cognitions. Waking cognitions are on the same footing with dream-cognitions, reveries, and hallucinations, since they do not differ from each other so far as they are of the nature of cognitions. And even as dream-cognitions appear as apprehending cognitions (grāhaka) and apprehended objects (grāhya), although there are no external objects corresponding to them, so our waking perceptions also are independent of external objects. The distinction of subject and object is within consciousness itself in waking perceptions as in dream-cognitions.[3] The distinction of the cognizer (pramātṛ), the instrument of cognition (pramāṇa), the result of cognition (pramiti), and the object of cognition (prameya) falls within consciousness. None of these factors indispensable for knowledge is outside consciousness. They are nothing but consciousness pure and simple.[4] The distinction among these factors of knowledge is imaginary. It is imagined by the intellect (buddhiparikalpiṭa) for practical purposes.[5]

(5) Lastly, we cannot account for the variety of

[1] Na hyanayorekasyānupalambhe'nyasyopalambho'sti, ibid., ii, 2, 28, p. 544.

[2] S.B.S., ii, 2, 28.

[3] Ibid., ii, 2, 28; cf. Bhāmatī, ii, 2, 28.

[4] Ibid., ii, 2, 28; cf. Advaitabrahmasiddhi (Bib. Ind.), pp. 92–5.

[5] Bhāmatī, ii, 2, 28.

perceptions (pratyayavaicitrya) if there are no external objects. The Yogācāra holds that it is due to the variety of subconscious impressions (vāsanāvaicitrya). In the beginningless cycle of existence (saṃsāra) perceptions and subconscious impressions are related to each other as causes and effects even as seeds and sprouts are related to each other as causes and effects. There is mutual causality between the two. Just as seeds produce sprouts, and sprouts, in their turn, produce seeds, so perceptions produce subconscious impressions, and these impressions, again, produce other perceptions. Thus the variety of perceptions is due to the variety of subconscious impressions. Both the realist and the subjective idealist agree in holding that dream-cognitions are due to the variety of sub-conscious impressions, and not of external objects. But they differ in their explanation of the variety of waking perceptions. While the realist explains it by the variety of external objects, the Yogācāra explains it by the variety of subconscious impressions. He does not postulate the existence of external objects to account for waking perceptions. But the question is how internal cognitions assume the forms of external objects. The Yogācāra holds that the forms of internal cognitions appear to us as forms of external objects owing to an illusion.[1]

§ 3. *Śaṅkara's Criticism of the Yogācāra Idealism*

(1) Firstly, Śaṅkara does not offer any direct criticism of the first argument of the Yogācāra that an external object cannot exist, for if it exists it must be of the nature of atoms or an aggregate of atoms but it can be neither. Śaṅkara urges that an external object does exist since it is distinctly perceived by all. In every act of perception we do perceive an external object such as a post, a wall, and the like. We cannot deny the

[1] S.B.S., ii, 2, 28.

existence of an external object which is actually perceived.[1] It is as absurd to deny the existence of an external object which is actually perceived through a sense-organ as to deny the act of eating and feeling satisfied when one is actually taking his meal and feeling pleasure.[2] In other words, our perception clearly testifies to the existence of an external object. Berkeley argues that the existence of a sensible object consists in being perceived —*esse* is *percipi*—and therefore it is an idea of the mind. Śaṅkara, on the other hand, argues that an object is perceived because it actually *exists* external to the mind ; an object is distinctly perceived as existing independent of the act of perception. No one can argue a fact of experience out of existence.

The Yogācāra may argue, like Berkeley, that he does not deny the consciousness of an object, but he denies the consciousness of an object as distinct from the act of cognition; we never perceive an object as distinct from the act of perception ; hence they are identical with each other.[3] Śaṅkara replies that the Yogācāra gives here a false account of the testimony of consciousness. Our perception clearly testifies

[1] Upalabhyate hi pratipratyayaṃ bāhyo'rthaḥ. . . . Na ca upalabhyamānasyaivābhāvo bhavitum arhati, S.B.S., ii, 2, 28, p. 548.

[2] Cf. Bhāmatī, ii, 2, 28, and Advaitabrahmasiddhi (Bib. Ind.), p. 99. Berkeley refutes the objection that " it sounds very harsh to say that we eat and drink ideas, and are clothed with ideas " thus : " We are fed and clothed with those things which we perceive immediately by our senses. . . . We eat and drink and are clad with *the immediate objects of sense, which cannot exist unperceived or without the mind.*" (*Principles of Human Knowledge*, p. 60.)

[3] Nanu nāhamevamevaṃ brabīmi na kañcidarthamupalabhe iti kintu upalabdhivyatiriktaṃ nopalabhe iti brabīmi, S.B.S., ii, 2, 28, p. 548. Similarly Berkeley says : " That what I see, hear, and feel *doth exist*, that is to say, is perceived by me, I no more doubt than I do of my own being. But I do not see how the testimony of *sense* can be alleged as a proof for the existence of anything which is *not perceived by sense.*" (*Principles of Human Knowledge*, p. 61.) " That the things I see with my eyes and touch with my hands do exist, really exist, I make not the least question. The only thing whose existence we deny is that which *philosophers* call *matter* or *corporeal substance.*" (Ibid., p. 58.)

to the existence of an object independent of the act of perception. The externality of the object to our perception must be admitted on account of the very fact of perception.[1] No one perceives a post, or a wall as a mere perception but as an object of perception.

Even the Yogācāra tacitly assumes the existence of external objects when he argues that internal cognitions appear as if they were external objects, though really there are no external objects. If he had no idea of externality at all, he could not assert that internal cognitions appear as if they were external objects. We can assert that a post appears like a man only when we already know what a man is. So we can assert that internal cognitions appear as if they were external objects only when we already know what external objects are. If external objects do not exist at all and are never perceived, the Yogācāra cannot assert that internal cognitions appear like external objects. It is as absurd as to assert that Viṣṇumitra appears like the son of a barren mother! Hence if we accept the clear testimony of our consciousness we must admit that in an act of perception the object is manifested to consciousness as something really external, and not as if it were external.

But the Yogācāra may contend that, because it is not possible for an external object to exist he holds that an object of perception which is nothing but a subjective cognition appears as if it were external. To this Śaṅkara replies that the Yogācāra has no right to reject the clear testimony of consciousness and rely on abstract arguments. Reasoning must be based on the facts of experience ; it must not wander away from them and spin out a system of philosophy which has no foundation in reality. Experience cannot be made to conform to reasoning. Reasoning must be based on experience.

[1] Upalabdhivyatireko'pi balādarthasyābhyupagantavyaḥ upalbdhereva, S.B.S., ii, 2, 28, p. 548.

The possibility or impossibility of an object depends only upon the operation or non-operation of the means of right knowledge,[1] while the operation or non-operation of the means of right knowledge does not at all depend upon the abstract possibility or impossibility of an object. Whatever is apprehended by perception and the like is possible ; and whatever is not apprehended by any means of right knowledge is impossible. Is, then, an external object possible ? Certainly it *is* possible since it is apprehended as existing external to, and independent of, consciousness by all the means of right knowledge such as perception and the like. What is clearly apprehended by all the means of right knowledge can never be held to be impossible.[2] Possibility is determined by actuality. Actuality is not determined by possibility. The Yogācāra goes against the unequivocal deliverance of consciousness when he argues that an external object is not possible because it is neither different nor non-different from atoms. Śaṅkara proves the existence of an external object on the strength of the clear testimony of consciousness. He does not rebut the dilemma of the Yogācāra. He simply points out that the Yogācāra contradicts the verdict of consciousness when he denies the existence of an external object on the strength of abstract arguments. He has no right to reject experience in favour of an idle dilemma to prove the non-existence of an external object.

(2) Secondly, the Yogācāra argues that cognitions are said to have the same forms as those of their objects, but since the different forms of cognitions are sufficient for practical purposes of our life, it is needless to assume the different forms of the so-called external objects.

[1] Pramāṇapravṛttyapravṛttipūrvakau sambhavāsambhavau, S.B.S., ii, 2, 28, p. 549.

[2] Sarvaireva pramāṇairbāhyo'rtha upalabhyamānaḥ kathaṃ na sambhavati, ibid., ii, 2, 28, p. 549.

The different forms of cognitions are necessary, and they are facts of experience. But the different forms of the so-called external objects are absolutely unnecessary, and to assume their existence is a gratuitous hypothesis.

But Śaṅkara urges that cognitions cannot have the same forms as those of external objects if the objects do not really exist. Moreover, the objects are actually perceived as external to, and independent of, the act of perception, and so their existence can never be denied.[1] We cannot legitimately invoke the Law of Parsimony to deny the existence of the facts of actual experience.

Reid appealed to the common sense of mankind to prove the existence of the external world. " The universal belief of mankind is," he says, " that the immediate object of the mind in perception is the material reality itself, and that as we perceive that object under its actual conditions, so we are no less conscious of its existence, independently of our minds, than we are conscious of the existence of our own mind, independently of external objects."[2] The modern realists also appeal to " that primordial common sense which believes in a world that exists independently of the knowing of it".[3] " My experience," says Alexander, " declares the distinct existence of something as non-mental. . . . The distinct existence of my object from my mind is attested by experience itself. This is a truth which a man need only open his eyes to see."[4]

(3) Thirdly, the Yogācāra argues that we invariably apprehend an act of perception and an object of perception together. We never perceive an object of perception apart from the act of perception. So they are identical with each other : the object is not distinct from its cognition.

[1] Asati viṣaye viṣayasārūpyānupapatteḥ, bahirupalabdheśca viṣayasya, ibid., ii, 2, 28, p. 549.

[2] *Works*, p. 964.

[3] *The New Realism*, p. 10.

[4] *Space, Time, and Deity*, vol. i, p. 16.

But Śaṅkara urges that inseparability in perception is no proof of identity. It is true that an object of perception can never be perceived apart from the act of perception. But from this it does not necessarily follow that an object is identical with its cognition. All that it proves is that the cognition is the means (upāya) and the object is the end (upeya) so that there can never be a cognition unless there is an object. There can be no cognition without an object because it is the means of apprehending an object.[1] If the object is non-existent the cognition cannot apprehend anything. Cognition without an object is impossible.[2] The very existence of cognition presupposes the existence of an object. So there can be no perception unless there is an object of perception. Thus an object of perception can never be identical with an act of perception ; they are distinct from each other.

Govindānanda argues that the distinction between an object and its cognition is clearly perceived by the self. So their identity can never be proved by the fact that they are always perceived together. A visible object such as colour is always perceived together with light ; it can never be perceived apart from light. But still colour is not identical with light. Likewise an object is never perceived apart from its cognition. But this does not prove that an object is identical with its cognition. They are always perceived together because there is a uniform relation between them, the cognition being the percipient subject (grāhaka) and the object being the perceived object (grāhya). The perceptible object is not identical with the percipient cognition : they are distinct from each other. But though they are distinct

[1] Sahopalambhaniyamo'pi pratyayaviṣayayorupāyopeyabhāvahetuko nābhedahetuka ityabhyupagantavyam, S.B.S., ii, 2, 28, pp. 549–550 : cf. NM., p. 541.

[2] Cf. Jaina and Rāmānuja.

from each other they are related to each other as the percipient and the perceived.[1]

Moreover, Śaṅkara argues that consciousness is common to different cognitions ; the difference in their contents is due to the difference in their objects. Different objects modify consciousness in different ways, and give rise to different cognitions. In the cognition of a jar and the cognition of a cloth there is a difference between the jar and the cloth which are the objects of the cognitions and qualify consciousness in different ways ; but there is no difference in the consciousness which is common to both the cognitions and is qualified by the objects, even as in a black cow and a white cow there is a difference between blackness and whiteness which are the qualifications of the class-essence of cow (gotva), but there is no difference in the class-essence of cow which is common to both. Thus the consciousness which is qualified by different objects such as a jar and a cloth is different from the objects, and the objects also which qualify consciousness in different ways are different from consciousness.[2] Again, the same object gives rise to two cognitions. We have the perception of a jar and the recollection of it. Thus an object can never be of the nature of consciousness. Consciousness and object can never be identified with each other ; they are different from each other. If there were no external objects there would be no difference in acts of cognition. The variety of cognitions is due to the variety of objects.

Further, the Yogācāra is an advocate of the doctrine of momentariness. So he regards all ideas as momentary ; they cannot last for more than one moment. Hence two successive momentary cognitions which vanish as soon as they become objects of consciousness cannot be related to each other as the apprehending subject

[1] Ratnaprabhā on S.B.S., ii, 2, 28.

[2] Cf. G. E. Moore, *Philosophical Studies*, p. 17.

(grāhaka) and the apprehended object (grāhya). When the cognition *a* has come into existence the succeeding cognition *b* has not yet come into being. So *a* cannot apprehend *b* and *b* cannot be apprehended by *a*. And the succeeding cognition *b* can never apprehend the preceding cognition *a*. Thus the distinction of subject and object can never fall within consciousness as wrongly held by the Yogācāra.

Moreover, the Yogācāra recognizes the existence of cognitions because they are perceived. Śaṅkara urges that he should equally recognize the existence of external objects because they also are perceived as independent of cognitions.[1] External objects are no less perceived than cognitions. So they have as much claim to existence as cognitions. But the Yogācāra may argue that cognitions are self-luminous while the so-called external objects are not so. In other words, cognitions apprehend themselves. So the Yogācāra admits the existence of cognitions but not of the so-called external objects. But Śaṅkara urges that cognitions cannot be regarded as self-luminous or self-apprehending, for acts of cognition can no more be objects of their own activity than fire can be the object of its own activity, viz. burning. The act of cognition must, by its very nature, be distinct from the object of cognition ; they can never be identical with each other. It is self-contradictory to hold that a cognition acts upon itself and apprehends itself as its own object. It is very strange that the Yogācāra refuses to admit the existence of an external object though everyone perceives it through a cognition which is distinct from the object itself.

The Yogācāra may argue that if cognitions are not self-luminous but are apprehended by something distinct from them, that also will require something else to apprehend it and so on *ad infinitum*. Thus it will commit

[1] Vijñānamanubhūyate iti cet, bāhyo'pyartho'anubhūyate eveti yuktamabhyupagantum, S.B.S., ii, 2, 28, p. 551.

us to infinite regress. But Saṅkara replies that cognitions are apprehended by the witness self (sākṣin) which is self-luminous. Cognitions are fleeting but the witness self is permanent. Cognitions are presented to the self, but the self is self-luminous. So there is no infinite regress in the Vedāntist doctrine. The witness self and cognitions are essentially different in nature so that they are related to each other as the knowing subject and the known object. No one can deny the existence of the self since it is the very presupposition of all experience. It bears testimony to its own existence. The individual cognitions, according to the Yogācāra, are discrete and momentary ; they come into being and pass away. Hence they must require one, permanent, intelligent principle or the self to witness the production and destruction of all these cognitions which are not self-luminous.[1]

(4) Fourthly, the Yogācāra likens waking perceptions to dream-cognitions and explains them both by subconscious impressions (vāsanā) without the help of external objects. But Śaṅkara points out that there is a false analogy here. Dream-cognitions are essentially different in nature from waking perceptions. Dream-cognitions are contradicted by waking perceptions. But waking perceptions are not contradicted by any other empirical experience. Besides, dream-cognitions are of the nature of recollection while waking perceptions are of the nature of perception. And the difference between recollection and perception lies in the fact that the former arises in the absence of an external object while the latter arises in the presence of an external object. Thus waking perceptions can never be explained without the help of external objects.[2]

(5) Lastly, the Yogācāra argues that the variety of cognitions (jñānavaicitrya) is not due to the variety of

[1] S.B.S., ii, 2, 28 ; cf. Green.

[2] Ibid., ii, 2, 29.

external objects but to the variety of subconscious impressions (vāsanāvaicitrya). But Śaṅkara urges that on the Yogācāra view there can be no subconscious impressions at all since they arise from perceptions of external objects which are denied by him. When perceptions of objects pass out of the field of consciousness they leave subconscious impressions behind in the mind. But if there are no perceptions of external object at all, there can be no subconscious impressions. The variety of subconscious impressions is due to the variety of perceptions of objects.[1]

Govindānanda elaborates the argument of Śaṅkara further. We have perceptions of new objects without subconscious impressions; they are never produced by subconscious impressions without external objects. There are subconscious impressions when there are already perceptions of external objects and there are no subconscious impressions when there are no previous perceptions of external objects. Thus the Yogācāra in trying to account for the variety of perceptions by the variety of subconscious impressions is tacitly assuming the existence of external objects without which subconscious impressions are not possible.[2]

The Yogācāra assumes the hypothesis of an infinite series of subconscious impressions and perceptions related to each other as causes and effects. But Śaṅkara urges that, if a single subconscious impression cannot account for a particular perception but itself depends upon a previous perception, an infinite series of subconscious impressions cannot account for the variety of perceptions. It simply multiplies the difficulties to infinity. If a single member of the infinite series cannot account for the origin of perception, an infinite number cannot do it either. The Yogācāra postulates an infinite

[1] Arthopalabdhinimittā hi pratyarthaṃ nānārūpā vāsanā bhavanti, ibid., ii, 2, 30. [2] Ratnaprabhā on S.B.S., ii, 2, 30; cf. NM

series of subconscious impressions instead of a variety of external objects to account for a variety of perceptions. But he utterly fails in his attempt to do so. His denial of the external world leads to a total collapse of practical life.

The Yogācāra proves his position by the following positive and negative judgments. Whenever there is a variety of subconscious impressions there is a variety of perceptions although there is no variety of external objects, and wherever there is no variety of subconscious impressions there is no variety of perceptions. But Śaṅkara urges that both these judgments are false, since subconscious impressions can never be explained without previous perceptions of external objects. On the contrary, the existence of external objects can be proved by the following positive and negative judgments. We have perceptions of external objects without previous subconscious impressions when external objects are present. But we cannot have subconscious impressions unless we had previous perceptions of external objects. Thus these judgments clearly establish the existence of external objects.

Further, subconscious impressions are nothing but latent dispositions, and they cannot possibly exist without a substratum. But the Yogacara does not believe in any permanent substratum of subconscious impressions, viz. the self. He believes, indeed, in ālayavijñāna or the series of self-cognitions in addition to pravṛttivijñāna or the series of object-cognitions within the stream of consciousness. But his ālayavijñāna is as momentary as pravṛttivijñāna, and consequently, it cannot be the substratum of subconscious impressions any more than the latter. If he regards his ālayavijñāna as permanent, he abandons his doctrine of momentariness. Thus the Yogācāra makes a vain attempt to explain the variety of perceptions by the variety of subconscious impressions, since they are not possible without previous perceptions of external objects, and without a permanent substratum, viz. the self, both of which are denied by him.[1]

§ 4. *Vācaspatimiśra and Sadānanda Yati's Exposition of the Yogācāra Idealism*

Vācaspati and Sadānanda Yati give many arguments of the Yogācāra against the existence of external objects of which some are given here.

(1) It cannot be argued that an external object exists because we are conscious of it, since its existence is impossible. Is a cognition different from its object, or non-different from it? If it is different from its object, it cannot apprehend it. Does the cognition manifest its object by producing another cognition even as a sense-organ manifests its object by producing a cognition of it? Since the cognition already exists, there is no need of its producing another cognition. If the cognition produces another cognition to manifest its object, the second cognition will produce a third cognition, and so on *ad infinitum.* Thus a cognition, which is different from its object, cannot manifest it by producing another cognition. Nor does a cognition manifest its object by producing manifestness (prākaṭya) or cognizedness (jñātatā) in the object as Kumārila holds. Not only present objects are cognized, but also past and future ones. A cognition cannot manifest past and future objects by producing manifestness in them, since they do not exist at the time. Thus a cognition, which is different from its object, cannot manifest it by producing manifestness in it. Hence a cognition must be different from, or identical with, its object. The perception of an object is nothing but the perception of a mere cognition endowed with that form; since this cognition is the cause of a particular reaction.[2]

(2) It may be argued that the internal form of a

[1] S.B.S., ii, 2, 30. [2] Advaitabrah masiddhi (Bib. Ind.), p. 97

cognition is similar to the form of an external object. For instance, when a jar is perceived, the form of the cognition is similar to the form of the jar existing independently of the cognition. Therefore, an object cannot be said to be only the internal form of its cognition. The Yogācāra urges that we are not conscious of two forms, viz. the form of a cognition and the form of an external object separately. We are conscious only of a single form. And this single form cognized cannot be said to be the form of an external object, for there is no need for assuming its existence.[1] It cannot be said that external objects are necessary to bring about the variety of cognitions which are essentially alike and of the nature of consciousness. The Yogācāra holds that the forms of the so-called external objects are forms or modes of consciousness itself. The variety of cognitions is due to the variety of vāsanās or subconscious impressions. Even those who believe in the existence of external objects must admit that different objects produce different forms in their cognitions ; otherwise every cognition would apprehend all objects, since all cognitions are alike. And if they admit the existence of different forms of cognitions which are sufficient to fulfil the practical needs of our life, it is needless to assume the existence of external objects. But it may be argued that the internal forms of cognitions are imprinted on the cognitions by external objects. But this argument is groundless. There is no necessary connection between the internal forms of cognitions and external objects. The internal forms of cognitions can arise independently of external objects as we find in dream-cognitions.[2]

(3) When there is a difference between two objects they are not always perceived at the same time ; they may be perceived apart from each other. The two stars

[1] Cf. Nyāya and Mīmāṁsā.
[2] Advaitabrahmasiddhi, pp. 97–8. Bhāmatī, ii, 2, 28 ; cf. Berkeley.

called *aśvinī* are different from each other ; they are not, therefore, always perceived together ; they are sometimes perceived apart from each other ; when one is hidden by the sky the other is perceived. Invariably simultaneous perception of two objects proves their identity. The identity of the blue and its cognition is proved by their invariably simultaneous perception. They appear to be different owing to an illusion.[1]

(4) If an external object exists, it must be perceived either as a number of simple atoms or as an aggregate of atoms. But it can be perceived as neither. Hence an external object does not exist.

An external object is either a number of simple atoms or a composite aggregate of atoms. If it is simply a number of atoms, either atoms only are perceived or atoms are perceived along with extension. Atoms only cannot be perceived, since a single cognition of an extended object cannot apprehend many unextended atoms. A cognition in which one object is manifested cannot apprehend another object. A cognition of blue cannot apprehend red. If it did, every cognition would apprehend all objects, and thus everyone would become omniscient. If atoms are perceived along with extension, we should regard extension either as an attribute of the apprehending cognition or as an attribute of the apprehended object. If extension is an attribute of the cognition, it apprehends its own form corresponding to which there is no real object,[2] and this is the position of the Yogācāra. If extension is an attribute of the object, it cannot be an attribute of atoms which are subtle, but it is a phenomenal appearance of many atoms which are simultaneously presented to consciousness. Extension is not an attribute of atoms, since

[1] Advaitabrahmasiddhi (Bib. Ind.), p. 98 ; Bhāmatī, ii, 2, 28.

[2] Svākārālambanameva vijñānam. Advaitabrahmasiddhi (Bib. Ind)., p. 95

they are atomic and indivisible. But when they are presented to consciousness together they appear to have extension. Extension is not perceived in a single atom. If it were perceived, it would be the real quality of atoms. But it is not possible for atoms to have extension. If extension is perceived not in a single atom but in a number of atoms, it is not the real quality of atoms but their phenomenal appearance. Hence the cognition of extension is illusory.

It may be said that when atoms without an interval of space are apprehended by a single cognition they appear to consciousness as extended. These atoms are real since the cognition of atoms is not illusory. Thus blue atoms without an interval of space being simultaneously presented to consciousness appear to be a blue object. This argument is wrong. The blue atoms are not without an interval of space. They are interspersed with atoms of smell, taste, and touch which co-exist with them in a blue object. Hence unextended atoms with an interval of space are illusorily perceived to be extended even as scattered trees are perceived from a distance as a dense forest. Thus the idea of extension is illusory.

If an external object is a composite aggregate of atoms, it is either different from atoms, or non-different from them, or both different and non-different from them. If there is difference between them, there must be some relation between them ; otherwise atoms would not constitute a composite whole and thus would not be its cause. If there is a relation between them, it is either identity or inherence. There cannot be identity between the composite whole and its constituent atoms, since they are radically opposed to each other. Nor can the whole inhere in atoms, since there is no relation of inherence. The composite whole cannot be non-different from, or identical with, the constituent atoms as found already. It cannot be both different and non-different from atoms, since it is self-contradictory. So there cannot be an external object which is a composite aggregate of atoms, there being no relation between the whole and its parts.

It cannot be said that an external object exists as a particular individual belonging to a genus or universal. What is the relation between the universal and the particular? If they are different from each other, they are independent of each other. If they are non-different from each other, they are identical with, and indistinguishable from, each other. They cannot be both different and non-different from each other, since it involves self-contradiction. An external object cannot, therefore, exist as a universal or a particular or the like. An external object does not possess a single feature which is manifested to consciousness. There is no evidence of the existence of anything that is not manifested in consciousness. Hence the Yogācāra concludes that cognitions do not depend upon external objects.[1]

The Yogācāra denies the reality of external objects, and recognizes the reality of cognitions only. But how does he account for the process of knowledge? Four factors are necessary for knowledge: (1) the agent of knowledge (pramātṛ); (2) the instrument of knowledge (pramāṇa); (3) the object of knowledge (prameya); and (4) the result of knowledge (pramiti). Take away any of these factors, and knowledge becomes impossible. So the Yogācāra who believes only in cognitions must provide for all these factors of knowledge. According to him discrete and momentary cognitions alone are real; so all these factors of knowledge must exist within the series of cognitions. Though the perceptible object (anubhāvya), the percipient agent (anubhabitṛ), and the act of perception (anubhavana) are not different from perception (anubhava) itself, yet an imaginary distinction among them is set up by intelligence within

[1] Advaitabrahmasiddhi (Bib. Ind.), pp. 95–7; Bhāmatī, ii, 2, 28.

consciousness with the help of its internal forms to serve the practical purposes of our life. They are nothing but cognitions pure and simple. They are not distinct from cognitions. A cognition specialized by a content (e.g. the idea of blue colour) is prameya or the object of knowledge ; this special content of consciousness which gives a particular form to indeterminate consciousness does not depend on an external object because it does not exist ; it is the internal form of cognition itself though it appears to be the form of an external object. The cognition in so far as it is the manifestation or consciousness of a special content is pramiti or the result of knowledge. The cognition in so far as it is the power of manifesting a special content is pramāṇa or the instrument of knowledge. And the cognition in so far as it is the abode of this power is pramātṛ or the agent of knowledge. Thus the abode of the power of cognizing is the cognizer (pramātṛ) ; the power of cognizing is the instrument of cognition (pramāṇa) ; the consciousness of a content is the result of cognition (pramiti) ; and the special content of consciousness which gives a distinct form to it is the object of cognition (prameya). Hence all the elements involved in knowledge are within consciousness.[1]

§ 5. *Vācaspatimiśra and Sadānanda Yati's Criticism of the Yogācāra Idealism*

(1) The non-existence of an external object cannot be proved. Is it non-existent because it is not perceived? Or though there is perception it does not apprehend an external object? Or though there is perception of an external object there is proof against its existence? The first alternative is not true. Everyone distinctly perceives external objects such as " this is a post " and the like.

[1] Bhāmatī, ii, 2, 28 ; Advaitabrahmasiddhi, pp. 92–3, cf. Ratnaprabhā, ii, 2, 28 ; see also Kalpataru and Parimala.

So external objects cannot be said to be non-existent because they are not perceived. The second alternative also is not true. The self not only apprehends its own cognitions but also their external objects. No one perceives a post or a wall as a mere cognition, but as an object of a cognition.[1] The Yogācāra holds that the internal form of a cognition appears like an external object, though really there is none. Here he tacitly admits the existence of an external object and undermines his own position. Nothing can appear to us as external if there is no external object at all. The third alternative also is not true. The existence of an object can be established only by right means of knowledge. An external object is distinctly perceived as " this " (or given) different from cognition. So it must exist. Its existence can never be denied. The existence of an external object which is distinctly perceived can never be disproved by abstract speculations.[2] External objects are directly perceived. The Yogācāra may hold that the direct perceptibility (āparokṣya) of objects is a mere cognition. This is wrong. Objects are directly perceived as not of the nature of cognitions, but as external to and independent of cognitions. This externality cannot be of the nature of a mere cognition, because it is not contradicted by any other empirical experience.[3] So all the arguments which have been advanced by the Yogācāra against the existence of external objects may with equal force be employed against his own position. Idle dilemmas are without any force against valid perception of external objects. Possibility or impossibility is determined by actual experience.[4]

[1] Upalabdhigrāhiṇā hi sākṣiṇopalabdhirgṛhyamāṇā bāhyaviṣayatvenaiva gṛhyate, nopalabdhimātram, Bhāmatī, ii, 2, 28, p. 548.

[2] Idantāspadamaśakyaṃ jñānādbhinnaṃ bāhyamapahnotum, Bhāmatī ii, 2, 28, p. 549.

[3] Vivaraṇaprameyasaṃgraha, pp. 54–5.

[4] Bhāmatī, ii, 2, 28; Advaitabrahmasiddhi (Bib. Ind.), pp. 99–100.

(2) The Yogācāra argues that our waking perceptions are not produced by external objects like dream-cognitions. In a dream-cognition nobody perceives an object which is other than the cognition itself; a dream-cognition apprehends itself as its object.[1] So a waking perception also apprehends itself as its object; there is no object distinct from the cognition.

Sadānanda Yati urges that this argument is wrong. Waking perceptions cannot be explained without reference to external objects which have an empirical reality. But the Yogācāra does not recognize the existence of external empirical objects. He cannot argue that in dream-cognitions the objects existing in some other time and place and perceived in the past appear to consciousness as present here and now, for he does not believe in the doctrine of anyathākhyāti.[2] The objects of dream-cognitions do not really exist at that time and in that place, since dream-cognitions of these objects are contradicted by waking perceptions. Nor are they absolutely non-existent, for in that case they would not be cognized at all like the horns of hares.[3] Nor are they both existent and non-existent, since they cannot possess two contradictory qualities. Nor are they undefinable objects with an empirical reality like the objects of waking perceptions, since they are contradicted by waking perceptions. They are only illusory (prātibhāsika) objects of dream-cognitions.[4] So the objects of waking perceptions cannot be said to have only an illusory existence (prātibhāsikasattā) like those of dream-cognitions. They have not a merely subjective existence; they are perceived as having an objective

[1] Cf. Berkeley, "In a dream we do oft perceive things as existing at a great distance off, and yet those things are acknowledged to have their existence only in the mind." (*Principles of Human Knowledge*, p. 62.)

[2] *Indian Psychology: Perception*, pp. 301–2.

[3] This is a stock example of an absolutely non-existent object.

[4] *Indian Psychology: Perception*, p. 312.

existence distinct from cognitions, and this is the reason why they fulfil the practical needs of our empirical life. The Yogācāra urges that the different forms inherent in cognitions themselves are sufficient to serve all practical purposes. Sadānanda contends that we cannot lead our empirical life unless we admit the existence of external objects. So long as our empirical life is not annulled by the realization of Brahman we must admit the empirical existence of external objects which are distinctly perceived and not contradicted by any other empirical cognition. We cannot deny the existence of external objects until we transcend our empirical life completely and realize our identity with Brahman.[1] Thus there are external objects distinct from their cognitions, which have only an empirical reality.[2]

(3) The Yogācāra argues that an object is identical with its cognition because they are always perceived together. Vācaspatimiśra urges that this proves just the contrary. Two things can be perceived together if they are different from each other. If they are identical with each other they cannot be perceived together. That they are perceived together does not mean that they are perceived as one. In fact, a cognition is perceived as internal and an object is perceived as external. So they are not perceived as one. If their being perceived together means that they are perceived by a single cognition, this does not prove their identity. This is due to the fact that the cognition and its object are related to each other as the means of knowledge (upāya) and the object of knowledge (upeya). A cognition manifests the object which it apprehends. If there is no object there cannot be a cognition. Therefore they are always perceived together.[3]

[1] Tasmāt brahmajñānāt prāk yāvadvyavahāraṃ na bāhyārthāpalāpa ucitaḥ. Advaitabrahmasiddhi, p. 101.

[2] Advaitabrahmasiddhi (Bib. Ind.), p. 101.

[3] Bhāmatī, ii, 2, 28; cf. NM., p. 541.

(4) The Yogācāra holds that the variety of perceptions can be explained by the variety of subconscious impressions (vāsanā) which exist in the ālayavijñāna or the series of self-cognitions. But Sadānanda Yati points out that a series of momentary self-cognitions (ālaya-vijñāna) cannot be the substratum of subconscious impressions. If momentary self-cognitions be the abode of subconscious impressions, there can be no recollection of objects perceived at some other time, since there is no permanent self. Moreover, subconscious impressions are either permanent or momentary. They cannot be permanent, since it is against the Buddhist doctrine of universal momentariness. Nor can they be momentary, since it makes memory impossible. Memory requires retention of subconscious impressions of past experience and their resuscitation in future. So they must continue to exist for some time. But they cannot exist in ālaya-vijñāna or the series of momentary self-cognitions. They can exist only in the permanent self which is not admitted by the Yogācāra. Then, again, if momentary self-cognitions be regarded as the substratum of subconscious impressions, either they arise simultaneously with the subconscious impressions or they arise before them. The self-cognitions and the subconscious impressions cannot arise simultaneously, for, in that case, they cannot be related to each other as the container and the contained like the right and the left horns of a cow springing up simultaneously. Nor can the self-cognitions arise before subconscious impressions, since they are momentary and do not continue to exist when subconscious impressions are produced, and cannot be the abode of these impressions. If they are supposed to continue for some time to receive the subconscious impressions subsequently produced, it will contradict the doctrine of universal momentariness. Therefore, if we do not admit the existence of one, continuous,

unchanging, all-cognizing self, there can be no substratum of subconscious impressions produced by perceptions of objects at some other time and place, and thus recollection and recognition of these objects cannot be explained. Thus the Yogācāra cannot account for the world-order.[1]

§ 6. *The Empirical Reality of the External World*

Śaṅkara and his followers recognize the empirical reality of external objects independent of cognitions of individual souls. They posit the ontological reality of the Absolute alone. The Absolute (Brahman) is pure identity. It is one, eternal, universal consciousness beyond all difference and change. It is subject-object-less transcendental consciousness. It is not immanent in the world and finite souls. "These are," Dr. S. N. Das Gupta rightly observes, "mutable and have therefore a different kind of indescribable existence from Brahman; but still they are somehow essentially of a positive nature. Śaṅkara's idealism does not allow him to deny the existence of external objects as apart from perceiving minds, and he does not adhere to the doctrine of *esse est percipi*. Thus he severely criticizes the views of the Buddhist idealists, who refuse to believe in the existence of external objects as apart from the thoughts which seem to represent them."[2] But it is absolutely wrong to brand Śaṅkara as a realist. He believes in three degrees of reality: (1) ontological reality (pāramārthika sattā), (2) empirical reality (vyāvahārika sattā), and (3) illusory reality (prātibhāsika sattā). The Absolute alone has ontological reality. The world and individual souls have

[1] Advaitabrahmasiddhi (Bib. Ind.), p. 102; see also Bhāmatī, Kalpataru and Parīmala on S.B.S., ii, 2, 28–31.

[2] *A History of Indian Philosophy*, vol. ii, pp. 268–9; see also vol. i, pp. 443 ff.

an empirical reality. Illusions have an illusory reality. Empirical reality is an appearance. Illusory reality is an illusory appearance. The former is comparably more durable than the latter, though both are devoid of ontological reality. Illusory appearances appear to consciousness and are real so long as their consciousness lasts. External objects are real so long as the senses and the intellect function. They have pragmatic value. They fulfil all our practical needs. But they are mere appearance rooted in avidyā. They vanish at the dawn of transcendental consciousness. "Śaṅkara accepts," says Dr. M. N. Sircar, "the positiveness of appearance, for it is a fact of knowledge and cannot be ignored. . . . But its positiveness and definiteness in spatial or temporal localization are no mark of its truth. Śaṅkara's test of truth is purely metaphysical. A thing may appear or may not, but this does not constitute its truth. A positive appearance which subsequently dies out is no truth. The epistemological or psychological test of truth as appearance to or object of consciousness has been set aside in favour of a transcendent test, for the epistemological dualism has no room in the transcendent identity of being."[1] Thus Śaṅkara's doctrine may be characterized as Absolute Idealism as contrasted with objective idealism, on the one hand, and subjective idealism, on the other. It is ridiculous to characterize it either as realism or as mentalism.

The Śaṅkarite holds that empirical objects are directly perceived. It is wrong to hold that they are inferred from their reflections in cognitions as their archetypes, even as a face is inferred from its reflection in a mirror as the Sautrāntika supposes. There is no scope for inference here because an object is never directly apprehended as the archetype of its reflection in a cognition which only is held to be directly apprehended by the Sautrāntika.

[1] *Comparative Studies in Vedantism*, pp. 68–9.

The direct perceptibility (āparokṣya) of the object is apprehended. Therefore it cannot be denied.[1]

§ 7. *Rāmānuja's Exposition of the Yogācāra Idealism*

The Yogācāra denies the existence of external objects. He holds that the variety of perceptions is not due to external objects, but to the variety of subconscious impressions. Variety is inherent in cognitions themselves. Even the so-called external objects cannot be used unless they are apprehended by cognitions. They can lead to reactions only when they are apprehended. If objects could be used by different persons without being apprehended by them, there would be no difference between the objects known by one person and those known by another. Therefore, objects must be known through their cognitions, and the cognitions must be admitted to have forms, since formless cognitions cannot be apprehended. We are conscious only of one form, and it must belong to cognitions. The form of a cognition appears to be the form of an external object owing to an illusion. The object is not distinct from the act of cognition because they are never apprehended apart from each other. Even the realist admits that cognitions of different objects have forms similar to those of their objects. Otherwise different cognitions cannot represent different objects. The forms of cognitions are sufficient to serve all our practical purposes. Hence it is needless to assume the existence of external objects. Cognitions alone are real. There are no external objects.[2]

§ 8. *Rāmānuja's Criticism of the Yogācāra Idealism*

Rāmānuja's exposition of the Yogācāra doctrine of subjective idealism is extremely meagre. He closely

[1] Vivaraṇaprameyasaṃgraha, p. 54.
[2] R.B.S., ii, 2, 27, p. 101 (Ananda Press, 1910).

follows Saṅkara in his criticism of it. His arguments against subjectivism are substantially the same as those of Saṅkara. But there is a difference between them, which is due to their different attitudes towards the world. Saṅkara recognizes only the empirical reality of the external world. But Rāmānuja accords it an ontological reality. He holds that both the self and the not-self are equally real, and both are revealed in an act of perception. This point has been emphasized by Rāmānuja in his arguments against the Yogācāra idealism.

(1) Rāmānuja recognizes the practical function of knowledge. It is subservient to action. The self apprehends cognitions in order to react to their objects. It does not apprehend them for their own sake. Thus cognitions enable the knowing self to react to their objects.[1] An act of cognition such as " I know the jar " is experienced by all as belonging to a knowing self and apprehending an object or not-self. Both the self and the not-self are revealed by an act of cognition.[2] The distinction between the self and the not-self is the very condition of consciousness. Any attempt to annul the distinction by reducing the object or not-self to an idea of the self must be futile. It contradicts the clear testimony of consciousness. We are distinctly conscious of external objects independent of our cognitions. So we can never deny their existence.[3] Rāmānuja holds that "consciousness is not possible without the knowing self and the known object, both of which are real. There is no objectless consciousness (nirviṣayā saṃvit). Consciousness and its object are perceived as different from each other ; one apprehends and the other is apprehended ; they are correlative to

[1] Jñāturātmano' arthaviśeṣavyavahārayogyatāpādānarūpeṇa jñānasyopalabdheḥ, R.B.S., ii, 2, 27, p. 101 ; cf. also ii, 2, 29. (Ananda Press, 1910.)

[2] Sakarmakeṇa sakartṛkeṇa jñā-dhātvarthena sarvalokasākṣikam aparokṣam, ibid., ii, 2, 27, p. 101.

[3] R.B.S., ii, 2, 27.

each other. So to annul the object altogether contradicts the clear testimony of consciousness ".[1]

Hamilton says : " In perception we have an intuitive knowledge of the ego and the non-ego, equally and at once." " We are immediately conscious in perception of an ego and a non-ego, known together and known in contrast with each other. I am conscious of both existences in the same indivisible moment of intuition." " The present-day realist asserts that idealism is not compatible with the distinction implied in all knowledge, of knowing subject from known object. . . . If the object were itself mental, as idealism requires, this distinction between subject and object would vanish. The realistic conception of the object as extra-mental is then, for epistemology, a bare necessity."[2] The modern realist looks upon the relation between subject and object as external. But Rāmānuja, like Hegel, holds to the doctrine of organic unity of the self (cit) and the not-self (acit) which are moments (prakāra) of the Absolute. Hegel also recognizes the independent existence of the self and the not-self, which are real and distinct, but yet correlative to each other. " I relate myself," he says, " to an object and then contemplate it as it is. The object, which I at once distinguish from myself, is independent. I have not made it, it did not wait for me in order to exist, and it remains although I go away from it. I and the object are therefore independent things."[3]

(2) Rāmānuja urges that it is self-contradictory to assert that an object of cognition and an act of cognition are identical with each other because they are invariably apprehended together. They can always be apprehended

[1] *Indian Psychology : Perception*, p. 220 ; R.B.S., i, 1, 1.

[2] Calkins, *The Persistent Problems of Philosophy*, p. 411.

[3] *Philosophy of Religion*, vol. i, p. 107 ; see *A Theory of Direct Realism*, p. 257.

together only if there is a real difference between them. Two really existing things can be apprehended together. But if an external object is non-existent, it cannot be perceived together with its cognition. A non-existent object cannot be apprehended along with an existent cognition. The Yogācāra contradicts himself when he argues that an object and its cognition are apprehended together, and therefore they are identical with each other. Simultaneous apprehension of the two presupposes their real existence and difference from each other.[1] Rāmānuja does not object to the simultaneous apprehension of an object and its cognition. But Kumārila and Jayanta Bhaṭṭa object to the fact itself and thus knock the bottom out of the argument. Rāmānuja points out that the specific character of a cognition is determined by its relation to a particular object, which leads to a reaction to it. Cognition is subservient to action. It reveals an object to the self, to which it reacts. Therefore, a cognition and its object which determines its specific character are, by their very nature, apprehended together.[2] From this simultaneous apprehension of an object and its cognition it is ridiculous to infer their identity.

(3) Rāmānuja holds that we are directly conscious of cognitions as referring to external objects which enable us to react to them in different ways. The specific character of each cognition is determined by its relation to a particular object.[3] The relation of a cognition to its

[1] R.B.S., ii, 2, 27, pp. 101–2.

[2] Tadarthavyavahārayogyataikasvarūpasya jñānasya tena sahopalambhaniyamaḥ, ibid., p. 102.

[3] Tattadarthavyavahārayogyatāpādānarūpatayā sākṣātpratīyamānasya jñānasya tattadarthasambandhāyattaṃ tattadasādhāraṇyam, ibid., ii, 2, 27, p. 102. Dawes Hicks holds that "the relationship between a physical object and a knowing mind is two-fold, the object forming at once the stimulus of the act of knowing, and determining its character or content." (Joad, *Introduction to Modern Philosophy*, pp. 14–15.)

object is of the nature of conjunction.[1] Cognition may be regarded as a substance, though it is a quality of the self, even as a ray of light is a substance, though it is a quality of a burning lamp.[2] Cognition implies an object. Cognition without an object is not possible. We are never conscious of it. We are never conscious of a cognition which does not refer to a knowing subject and a known object. Cognition without an object is as inconceivable as cognition without a subject.[3]

(4) Rāmānuja further contends that waking perceptions cannot be said to be without real counterparts in external objects, like dream-cognitions, since they are essentially different in character. Dream-cognitions are illusory ; they are produced by the mind overcome by drowsiness, and are contradicted by waking perceptions. But waking perceptions are not illusory, and are not contradicted. Further, if all cognitions are devoid of real counterparts, even the inference that an external object is non-existent is without a real counterpart and therefore invalid. If this inference is said to have a real counterpart, an act of perception also should be said to have a real counterpart. If an act of inference is valid, an act of perception also should be regarded as valid. An act of perception apprehends an object. Therefore

[1] " If cognition is not the universal condition of being, then cognition must take its place within being, on the same plane as space, or number, or physical nature." (*The New Realism*, p. 33.) " Let A be a mind and B another finite, distinct from that mind and lower in order. Then A's compresence with B means that A is conscious of B. Cognition, then, instead of being a unique relation, is nothing but an instance of the simplest and most universal of all relations." (*Space, Time, and Deity*, vol. ii, p. 82.)

[2] R.B.S., ii, 2, 27, p. 102 ; see *Indian Psychology : Perception*, p. 256.

[3] R.B.S., ii, 2, 29, p. 102. Professor Baillie says : " Experience always implies a relation between two distinct elements : the one is that for which something is, and the other the something which is presented. These are the so-called subject and object." (*Idealistic Construction of Experience*, p. 108.)

the object must exist. The Yogācāra indirectly denies the validity of his own inference when he denies the existence of external objects.[1] He falsifies experience when he explains away valid perceptions as dreams. Even dreams are not without a foundation in reality.[2]

A. C. Ewing puts forward an argument against epistemological idealism similar to that of Rāmānuja. " If he (the idealist) holds that the object cognized must be dependent on or inseparable from the cognition of it so that it cannot have being . . . except as and when cognized, he must apply this not only to the physical world but to other human minds, to past events, to universal laws, to the very principles which he has himself asserted. If these characteristics are implied in the nature of cognition, they must be asserted of all cases of cognition (including the idealists' inference)."[3] " He cannot even assert the validity of the idealist arguments themselves unless he assumes that they are valid independently of his thinking them and not merely because he thinks them. If their validity is inseparable from his thinking them, they only hold at the moment he thinks them and do not hold at all when he is not thinking them. If this reasoning is correct it follows that the epistemological arguments lead directly either to a complete scepticism as to everything beyond the individual's momentary experience or to a positive denial of its existence."[4]

§ 9. *Rāmānuja's Criticism of the Sautrāntika Realism*

Rāmānuja believes in the direct perceptibility of external objects. He advocates the presentative theory

[1] R.B.S., ii, 2, 28, p. 102.

[2] See also Vedāntadīpa (Ananda Press), 1910, pp. 103–4; Śrutaprakāśikā, pp. 439–442, Sarvārthasiddhi on Tattvamuktākalāpa, pp. 432 ff., and Nyāyasāra on Nyāyapariśuddhi, pp. 43–6.

[3] *Idealism*, p. 17.

[4] Ibid., p. 18.

of perception. He argues that, on the Buddhist theory of universal momentariness, nothing can be an object of cognition, because the object, which enters into connection with the sense-organ and is said to be an object of cognition, does not exist when the cognition is produced. The object must continue to exist till the cognition is produced by it so that it may be apprehended by the cognition.

The Sautrantika opposes this argument. It is wrong to argue that an object cannot be apprehended by a cognition because it does not exist when the cognition is produced. An object is apprehended by a cognition if it produces the cognition. It is apprehended by a cognition not because it continues to exist till the cognition is produced. If an object gives rise to a cognition though it does not exist at the time when the cognition is produced, it is apprehended by the cognition. The object and its cognition should not necessarily be co-existent at the same time. But this does not imply that the sense-organs are apprehended by cognitions because they give rise to cognitions. In order to preclude the perceptibility of the sense-organs, the Sautrāntika adds another condition. An object must not only be the cause of a cognition, but also impart its form to the cognition. That cause of a cognition is apprehended by it which imparts its form to the cognition. The sense-organs are not apprehended by cognitions because they do not impart their forms to the cognitions, though they are their causes. An object, on the other hand, can be apprehended by a cognition, because it is a cause of the cognition and imparts its form to it, though it does not exist at the time when the cognition is produced.

The Yogācāra wrongly holds that the forms of succeeding cognitions are due to the forms of the preceding cognitions and not to the forms of external objects. If it were true, we could not account for the sudden appearance of the cognition of yellow in the midst of a series of cognitions of blue. A cognition of blue can give rise to another cognition of blue, but it cannot give rise to a cognition of yellow. Hence the variety of cognitions must be due to the variety of external objects.

Rāmānuja contends that an object passing out of existence can never give rise to a cognition inasmuch as non-entity is never found to have causal efficiency. So the various forms of cognitions can never arise out of non-existent objects. Further, it is never found that, when a substrate has perished its attribute persists and passes over into another object. An object passing out of existence can never communicate its form to its cognition, since the object is the substrate of the form which is its attribute. Nor can the object be said to leave its form in the cognition in the shape of its reflection, since only persisting things can have reflections, and not their attributes. Hence the variety of cognitions can be produced by the variety of external objects provided the objects continue to exist till the cognitions are produced.[1] External objects are directly perceived by their cognitions. They are not momentary.

§ 10. *Nimbārka's Criticism of the Yogācara Idealism*

Nimbārka does not offer a single original criticism. He urges that to deny the existence of external objects is to contradict our experience. They are actually perceived. Waking perceptions cannot be said to be without a real foundation in external objects like dream-cognitions, since even dream-cognitions are not without a real foundation in external objects (sāvalambana). The contents of dreams are always reproductions of past experience. Only their combination is a construction of the mind. The variety of perceptions cannot be due to the variety of subconscious impressions (saṃskāra), which

[1] R.B.S., ii, 2, 25.

are the effects of previous perceptions of external objects. But the existence of external objects is denied by the Yogācāra. Subconscious impressions cannot account for perceptions. But perceptions of external objects account for these impressions. Besides, the Yogācāra does not believe in the reality of the permanent self in which the impressions may exist. So he cannot admit their existence.[1] Thus Nimbārka borrows his arguments from Śaṅkara and others.

§ 11. *Śrīnivāsa and Keśava Kāśmirin's Criticism of the Yogācāra Idealism*

Śrīnivāsa gives a succinct accounct of the Yogācāra arguments and criticizes them briefly in *Vedāntakaustubha*. Keśava Kāśmirin elaborates some of these arguments in *Vedāntakaustubhaprabhā*.

(1) The Yogācāra denies the existence of external objects distinct from cognitions. The notion of a variety of external objects is illusory. What is real is a variety of momentary cognitions which are perceived.[2] What are manifested to consciousness are determinate cognitions of blue, yellow, and the like.

Like Śaṅkara and Rāmānuja, Śrīnivasa urges that the non-existence of external objects cannot be maintained, since they are actually perceived. External objects are apprehended by direct perception as distinct from cognitions.[3] The external objects such as the sun, the moon, the earth, mountains, fire, water, etc., are established by perception as different from cognitions.

Keśava urges that these objects are perceived as existing

[1] Vedāntaparijātakaustubha on B.S., ii, 2, 28–31.

[2] Kṣaṇikaṃ vicitraṃ vijñānaṃ sākāraṃ pratyakṣaṃ cāsti, VK. on B.S., ii, 2, 28.

[3] Vijñānavyatiriktasya bāhyārthasya pratyakṣatā upalabdheḥ, ibid., ii, 2, 28.

in space with determinate forms. But cognitions of these objects are perceived as internal qualities of the self devoid of forms. The objects of cognitions are external while the apprehending cognitions are internal. The objects of cognitions have definite forms while the apprehending cognitions are formless. Hence they can never be regarded as identical with each other.[1] Keśava, like the Naiyāyika and the Mīmāṃsaka, takes cognitions to be formless.

(2) The Yogācāra argues that even the realist who recognizes the reality of external objects, admits that cognitions produced by the intercourse of various external objects with the appropriate sense-organs are endowed with forms which correspond to the forms of their objects. Thus the realist admits the forms of cognitions which serve all our practical purposes. Hence his hypothesis of external objects is needless.

Śrīnivāsa urges that if there are no external objects, the cognitions apprehending them cannot be similar to them, and cannot be endowed with their forms. Similarity of cognitions with their objects, or of their forms with those of their objects presupposes the existence of the external objects.[2] Thus external objects distinct from cognitions exist; and cognitions distinct from objects also exist.

(3) The Yogācāra argues that cognitions with determinate forms are self-luminous like light; they are perceived by themselves. Cognitions are perceived no sooner than they are produced. If cognitions themselves are not perceived, they cannot perceive external objects. If cognitions are held to apprehend objects without being perceived, there can be no distinction between my own cognitions and those of others. But, in fact, there is a

[1] VKP. on B.S., ii, 2, 28.

[2] Viṣayaṃ vinā viṣayinastatsārūpyātmakatadākāratvāsiddheḥ, VK. on B.S., ii, 2, 28.

difference between my own cognitions and those of others. I act on my own cognitions. They only lead to my actions. Hence it is conclusively proved that cognitions are perceived by themselves.

If cognitions perceive themselves with determinate forms, there is absolutely no need of assuming the existence of external objects. In fact, the distinctions among the object of cognition (prameya), the act of cognition (pramāṇa), and the resultant cognition (phala) fall within the momentary cognition itself. The form of the cognized object within the cognition is the object of cognition. The form of the apprehending cognition is the instrument of cognition. Self-conscious awareness is the resultant cognition. All these exist in the self-same cognition.[1] Hence no external object exists.

Keśava admits that cognitions are perceived, but they are not perceived before apprehending their objects. The self directly perceives cognitions after they apprehend their objects with definite forms.[2] It perceives cognitions not as mere cognitions but as cognitions of objects such as the cognition of a jar, the cognition of a cloth, and the like. Thus cognitions are not perceived by themselves as soon as they are produced before they apprehend their objects. They are perceived by the self as cognitions of external objects. The self is the cognizer. External objects are the cognized. Cognitions are the instruments by which the self cognizes external objects. Thus the distinctions among the cognized object (prameya), the act of cognition (pramāṇa), and the resultant cognition (pramiti) are not within momentary cognitions.

(4) The Yogācāra argues that whenever there arises

[1] Tatra grāhyākāraḥ prameyaṃ, grāhakākārohi pramāṇaṃ, svasaṃvittiḥ phalamiti trayamekasmin vijñāne'vakalpate, ibid., ii, 2, 28.

[2] Grāhyākārapuraḥsarameva hi saṃvedanaṃ saṃvedayituraparokṣībhavati, VKP. on B.S., ii, 2, 28.

the cognition of blue, blue is perceived[1] ; hence they are identical with each other.

Śrīnivasa urges that being perceived together (sahopalambhana) presupposes difference (bheda) between the two things that are perceived together. Keśava also urges that togetherness (sahatva) means co-existence in the same space or co-existence at the same time, both of which imply difference.[2]

(5) The Yogācāra argues that waking cognitions are without a foundation in external objects like dream-cognitions or creations of fancy because they are of the nature of cognitions.

Śrīnivāsa urges that waking cognitions are not similar to dream-cognitions, since the former are produced by sense-organs not perverted by any defects while the latter are produced by the mind perverted by drowsiness. Further, even dream-cognitions are not without any foundation in external objects. The contents of dreams are objects perceived in the past.

Keśava urges that dreams are dissimilar to waking cognitions, because dreams are sublated by waking cognitions while waking cognitions are not so sublated. It cannot be proved by inference that there are no external objects corresponding to waking cognitions which are apprehended by them. Waking cognitions are directly perceived as apprehending external objects. So they cannot be inferred to be without a foundation in external objects. Perception is superior to inference as an instrument of valid knowledge. Inference cannot override the authority of perception.[3]

(6) The Yogācāra argues that the variety of perceptions arises from the variety of subconscious

[1] Yadaiva nīlajñānaṃ tadaiva nīlamupalabhyate, ibid., ii, 2, 28.
[2] Ibid., ii, 2, 28.

impressions. Subconscious impressions and perceptions are related to each other as causes and effects of each other. There is mutual causality between them as between seeds and sprouts. Subconscious impressions are the causes of perceptions, and perceptions are the causes of subconscious impressions.[1]

Śrīnivāsa urges that subconscious impressions cannot be the causes of perceptions, because their causes are not apprehended. In fact, perceptions of external objects are the causes of subconscious impressions which, in their turn, are the causes of recollection. But, for the Yogācāra, it is not possible, because he does not admit the reality of external objects. If external objects do not exist, there cannot be perceptions ; if there are no perceptions, there cannot be subconscious impressions. Thus subconscious impressions cannot account for perceptions ; they themselves are explained by perceptions.

Keśava points out that cognitions, according to the Yogācāra, are momentary ; they do not continue to exist till succeeding cognitions arise. Therefore preceding cognitions cannot " perfume " or modalize the succeeding cognitions. Thus subconscious impressions (vāsanā) left by preceding cognitions cannot perform any function.[2]

Further, the Yogācāra cannot possibly recognize the existence of subconscious impressions, because he does not believe in any permanent substratum or the self in which they may exist. He believes, indeed, in the series of self-cognitions (ālayavijñāna), but even these self-cognitions are as momentary as object-cognitions (pravṛttivijñāna). Hence the variety of perceptions is not due to the variety of subconscious impressions, but to the variety of external objects.[3]

[1] VK and VKP on B.S., ii, 2, 28.
[2] Ibid., ii, 2, 30.
[3] Ibid., ii, 2, 31.

§ 12. *Mādhva's Criticism of the Yogācāra Idealism*

Mādhva, like Rāmānuja, holds that knowledge implies a knowing subject or self and a known object or not-self. Knowledge without a knower and a known is inconceivable.[1] Therefore both knowing subjects and known objects must exist. They cannot be reduced to each other. Known objects are as real as knowing subjects. Rāmānuja seems to recognize the not-self as the other of the self, both of which are moments in the life of the Absolute. Mādhva stands for unqualified dualism. According to him, the distinction between the self and the not-self is absolute.

Mādhva is a realist. He regards the object as absolutely different from the subject. It cannot be reduced to a mere mode of consciousness. Nobody perceives it as such. Sense-perception clearly testifies to the existence of the external reality. It apprehends it as it is. Besides, cognitions are momentary, but external objects are permanent. Therefore, objects cannot be said to be identical with cognitions.[2] So the external reality is not a mental construction.

Mādhva attaches great importance to sense-perception. As a mode of proof it is superior to inference. The senses bring the subject into contact with the object so that the subject may know the object as it really is. "The distinction between knowledge and its object is ultimate. Knowledge is real. Its object is real. The relation known as the knower-known-relation is real."[3]

Waking perceptions cannot be regarded as without a foundation in external objects like dreams and illusions. "Dream-phenomena are real."[4] They are not without

[1] Na ca jñatṛ-jñeya-rahitaṃ jñānaṃ kvāpi dṛṣṭam, Tattvanirṇaya, p. 17.

[2] Mādhvabhāṣya on B.S., ii, 2, 30–1.

[3] R. N. Sarma, *Reign of Realism in Indian Philosophy*, p. 42.

[4] Ibid., p. 45.

foundation in reality. Illusions also have a basis in reality. They are " due to a misinterpretation of sensory data. No one could question the reality of sensory data themselves. They are as real as the Absolute of the Absolutists. Only they are erroneously interpreted. . . . An analysis of perceptual illusions is bound to demonstrate the existence of a realistic residuum in all of them, and the analogy, at any rate, is hardly adequate to deprive the universe of its inalienable birth-right of reality."[1] " By no amount of ratiocination will it be possible to alienate the reality of the Cosmos guaranteed by sense-awareness."[2]

These arguments of Mādhva against the absolutism of Śaṅkara hold equally against the subjectivism of the Yogācāra. The external world is as real as the finite self and God ; there is an ultimate distinction among them.

§ 13. *Vallabha's Criticism of the Yogācāra Idealism*

Vallabha does not give any new arguments in criticizing the Yogācāra idealism. He simply repeats the arguments of Śaṅkara in brief.

The Yogācāra doctrine of the unreality of external objects contradicts the testimony of perception. External objects are not non-existent because they are perceived. Those who deny the existence of external objects, though they perceive them, are not to be trusted.[3] The Yogācāra puts waking cognitions on the same footing with dreams, and regards them both as false and without any foundation in external objects. But this is evidently untenable. Dreams are contradicted by waking perceptions. But valid waking perceptions are not liable to contradiction. A post perceived even after a year will be perceived as

[1] Ibid., p. 45.
[2] Ibid., p. 33 ; Tattvanirṇaya, p. 6.
[3] Aṇubhāṣya, ii, 2, 28.

nothing but a post.[1] This clearly shows that the object exists and its existence does not depend upon knowledge.

The Yogācāra argues that the variety of waking perceptions is due to the variety of subconscious impressions ; it is not due to the variety of external objects since they do not exist. Vallabha urges that this is putting the cart before the horse. Subconscious impressions are produced by perceptions of external objects. But the Yogācāra denies the existence of external objects. There can be no subconscious impressions, according to him, since there are no perceptions of external objects. If a single subconscious impression cannot produce a perception, an infinite series of subconscious impressions cannot help us in the matter. There are no subconscious impressions without perceptions of external objects. But there are perceptions of external objects without subconscious impressions. Hence the existence of external objects is established by positive and negative judgments.[2] Further, there is no permanent substratum of subconscious impressions. The series of self-cognitions (ālayavijñāna), which is said to be the substratum of subconscious impressions, is momentary, like the series of object-cognitions.[3]

Puruṣottamajī Mahārāja elaborates the arguments of Vallabha in *Prakāśa*, a commentary of *Aṇubhāṣya*.

(1) The Yogācāra holds that there are no external objects, but cognitions themselves assume different forms. Cognitions endowed with forms (sākara) apprehend themselves as their objects. They do not apprehend external objects, since they do not exist. But this view is wrong. Is a cognition endowed with all forms ? Or is it endowed with a particular form ? If the former, it

[1] Ibid., ii, 2, 29.
[2] Ibid., ii, 2, 30.
[3] Ibid., ii, 2, 31.

would manifest all forms cognized at the same time, since they do not depend upon external objects. If the latter, a cognition would manifest only one form at all times, and it would never manifest any other form. Both of these are absurd. Hence cognitions cannot be endowed with forms. The occasional appearance of cognitions with particular forms cannot be due to the forms of immediately preceding cognitions, since the forms of these cognitions also have to be accounted for. This is only pushing back the difficulty one step further. Hence we must admit the existence of external objects in order to account for the occasional appearance of cognitions with particular forms.[1]

(2) The Yogācāra argues that an object and its cognition are invariably perceived together (saha). Hence there is identity or non-difference (abheda) between the object and the cognition. Puruṣottamajī Mahārāja says that togetherness (sahatva) means co-existence of two different objects in the same space or at the same time. Therefore we cannot speak of the object and the cognition being perceived together, unless they are different from each other.

Then, what is the meaning of abheda? Does it mean identity (ekatva) or non-difference (bhedābhāva)? If it means identity, it means either identity in number or in some other property. If it means identity in number, then the blue and the cognition of blue, though different from each other, may possess identity in number, viz. oneness, even as a jar and a cloth possess identity in number, viz. oneness, though they are different from each other. This shows that the object is not necessarily reduced to the cognition. An external object and an internal cognition may have identity in number. This does not take away from the reality of the external object. If identity means identity in some other quality, this

[1] Aṇubhāṣyaprakāśa (B.S.S.), Benares, 1907, ii, 2, 28, pp. 654–5.

also is possible between two different objects. Evidently, the Yogācāra means by identity nothing but identity in nature (tādātmya). Puruṣottamajī's argument seems to be a verbal quibble. Then he argues that if abheda means non-difference, the Yogācāra cannot know that an object is non-different from its cognition, unless he knows already the difference between the two. The knowledge of non-difference implies the previous knowledge of difference. If the difference between blue and the cognition of blue is absolutely unknown, the Yogacara can never assert that blue is non-different from its cognition. And if he knows the difference between them, he cannot hold them to be non-different from each other. Those who actually perceive external objects as distinct from their cognitions and yet deny their existence are not be trusted.[1]

(3) It is absurd to liken waking cognitions to dream-cognitions. Dream-cognitions are different from waking cognitions. The former are confined only to the time of the dream-state, while the latter are not confined to a particular time during the waking state. The former are wrong cognitions, while the latter are valid cognitions. Others say that dream-cognitions are contradicted, but waking cognitions are not contradicted. Dream-cognitions are produced by the mind vitiated by drowsiness. But waking cognitions are produced by the sense-organs not vitiated by any defects. So it cannot be held that waking cognitions are as objectless as dream-cognitions.[2]

(4) The Yogācāra holds that the variety of sub-conscious impressions (vāsanā) is the cause of the variety of perceptions. But vāsanā is the effect of perception and the cause of recollection. It is not perceived, but

[1] Ibid., ii, 2, 28, p. 655.
[2] Ibid., ii, 2, 29; p. 656.

inferred from its effect, viz. recollection. Vāsanā cannot be produced without previous perception. And perception is not possible without an external object. But the Yogācāra does not recognize an external object. If there is no external object, there can be no perception ; and if there is no perception, there can be no vāsanā. It cannot be said that vāsanās and perceptions are related to each other as cause and effect because vāsanās can never produce perceptions, though vāsanās are produced by perceptions of external objects. If they were produced without perceptions of external objects, then a person waking from a dream would continue to perceive cognitions similar to dream-cognitions arising from their subconscious impressions, and would not perceive waking cognitions, since there are no external objects, according to the Yogācāra, which may give rise to them. But, as a matter of fact, waking cognitions do break in upon dream-cognitions, and they are brought about by external objects. We find that subconscious impressions (vāsanā) are not possible without perceptions of external objects ; but external objects are perceived without subconscious impressions. Hence external objects exist ; the external world is real.[1]

§ 14. *Baladeva Vidyābhuṣaṇa's Criticism of the Yogācāra Idealism*

Baladeva closely follows Rāmānuja in refuting the subjective idealism of the Yogācāra. He gives practically the same arguments. Every one is conscious of the existence of an external object. The Yogācāra contradicts the clear testimony of consciousness when he denies its existence. The Yogācāra may urge that he does not deny the consciousness of an external object but he regards it as an illusory appearance. He holds that what we are immediately conscious of are nothing

[1] Ibid., ii, 2, 30 ; p. 657.

but our own ideas, and hence the so-called appearance of external objects is the result of our own ideas.[1] To this Baladeva replies that the very fact of our consciousness proves that there is an external object giving rise to the idea of externality.[2] Moreover, there are three factors in the cognition " I know the jar " : the knowing subject or self, the known object, e.g. the jar, and the knowledge. An act of knowledge requires an agent as well as an object.[3] The whole world believes in it and acts upon it. The consensus of opinion proves that the object is as real as the knowing subject.[4] Therefore, to say that there is only knowledge, but no object of knowledge, is to court ridicule. Hence it is established that an object is real and distinct from knowledge.

It may be asked if an object is distinct from its knowledge, how this distinction can be known. If the knowledge of the distinction is said to shine forth in consciousness, then by knowing one object we ought to know all objects, since all objects have the common attribute of being distinct and separate from knowledge. If one thing which is distinct from knowledge is known, everything distinct from knowledge must be known. Baladeva urges that this argument is absurd. All external objects have, no doubt, this quality in common that they are different from the knowing self. They all come under the category of the not-self. Certainly, we know everything as not-self by knowing one not-self. By knowing one not-self we know the general relation of the not-self to the self, but we do not know the special relations of

[1] Berkeley also says : " What are the objects but the things we perceive by sense ? and what do we perceive besides our own ideas or sensations ? and is it not plainly repugnant that any one of *these*, or any combination of them, should exist unperceived ? " (*Principles of Human Knowledge*, p. 35.)

[2] Cf. Śaṅkara.

[3] Cf. Rāmānuja and Mādhva.

[4] Cf. Reid.

different not-selves to the self. There are many not-selves, and their special relations to the self are different. One object is yellow, another is red, and so on, and the knowledge of the yellow object cannot be said to be the same as that of the red object. The idea of yellow is quite different from the idea of red. Therefore there must be two different external objects to give rise to two different cognitions.

The object and its cognition are certainly perceived together always. But this invariable concomitance, instead of proving that objects are unreal and cognitions are real, proves just the contrary. The very fact that they are always perceived together shows that they are different and not one.

Waking perceptions are not similar to dream-cognitions. The former are of the nature of perception ; the latter are of the nature of memory. The former are invalid. They are sublated by waking cognitions. The latter are valid. They are not contradicted. Therefore, waking perceptions cannot be regarded as objectless like dream-cognitions.

The variety of perceptions cannot be due to the variety of subconscious impressions, since the impressions themselves presuppose previous perceptions of external objects, and the existence of the permanent self as their abode, both of which are denied by the Yogācāra.[1]

[1] Govindabhāṣya on B.S., ii, 2, 28–31 ; see also E.T. (S.B.H., vol. v), pp. 308–312.

INDEX

Absolute, 226, 251, 255, 266, 267
Ahaṃbuddhi (self-consciousness) apprehends the self (Kumārila), 132
Ālayavijñāna (self-cognition), 33, 34, 39, 40, 41, 207, 240, 265; cannot be the abode of subconscious impressions (*vāsanā*), 192, 250, 268
Alexander, 112 n., 130, 131, 142, 144, 210 n., 218, 234; his *Basis of Realism*, 131 n.; his *Space, Time and Deity*, vol. I, 112 n., 130 n., 142 n., 234 n.; vol. II, 120 n., 132 n., 144 n., 257 n.
Aliotta's *The Idealistic Reaction against Science*, 9 n.
Amalānanda's *Kalpataru*, 246 n., 251 n.
Analysis: by reason, cannot reveal real character of external objects which are, therefore, unreal (yogācāra), 170–1; cannot disprove the reality of the external world (Nyāya), 172; adequate to comprehension of reality, 171–2
Aniruddha, 77, 79; his *Sāṅkhyasūtravṛtti*, 79 n.
Anirvacanīya (indefinable), 226
Anyathākhyāti, 120, 248
Apekṣābuddhi, 26
Apperception, 73
Āptamīmāṃsā, 71 n.
Apyayadīkṣita's *Parimala*, 246 n., 251 n.
Arthakriyā, 163, 227
Arthasaṃvitti, 14
Association, 10, 119
Ātmasaṃvedana, 17
Ātmasaṃvitti, 13
Atoms, 3, 4, 32, 53, 61, 62, 63 64, 66, 78, 115, 170, 199, 201 227, 243; aggregates of, 61 62, 78, 168, 199, 227, 228, 243; aggregates of, different or non-different from atoms, 4, 244–5; cannot combine with one another, 4; cannot impart their form of atomicity to cognitions, 32; eternal or non-eternal, 61–3; perceived by Yogins, 61
Aversion, 187, 188

Baillie's *Idealistic Construction of Experience*, 257 n.
Baladeva Vidyābhūṣaṇa, 271, 272; his criticism of Yogācāra idealism, 271–3; his *Govindabhāṣya*, 273 n.
Bergson, 137
Berkeley, 2, 8, 9, 12, 36, 37 n., 52, 54 n., 59, 64, 64 n., 71 n., 74 n., 80, 82, 83, 103 n., 104 n., 110 n., 117, 138, 145 n., 147, 151 n., 152 n., 176, 177, 179, 196, 197, 202, 203, 214, 215, 220, 221, 226, 231, 241, 248 n., 272; his *Principles of Human Knowledge*, 5 n., 9 n., 12 n., 39 n., 41 n., 45 n., 59 n., 65 n., 71 n., 74 n., 81 n., 83 n., 104 n., 117 n., 122 n., 145 n., 151 n., 152 n., 179 n., 203 n., 214 n., 220 n., 231 n., 248 n., 272 n.; his *Dialogue between Hylas and Philonous*, 117 n., 151 n., 176, 177 n.

Bhāktavedana, 19, 20
Bhojadeva, 92, 102 n.; his *Vṛtti* on *Yogasūtra*, 93 n., 94 n., 96 n.
Brahman, 226, 251
Broad, C. D., 147; his *Perception, Physics, and Reality*, 102 n., 147 n.
Buddhist, 3; doctrine that being consists in becoming, 3; doctrine of momentariness or momentary existence, 3, 210, 236, 240, 250, 259; idealist, 170, 173, 175; doctrine of momentary cognitions, 8, 72, 73, 99, 127, 134, 159, 160

Calkins's *The Persistent Problems of Philosophy*, 255 n.
Causal theory: of knowledge, 102, 212: of perception, 3, 25; cannot account for the uniform relation between cognition and object, 5–6
Cognitive relation, 50, 51; identity (Yogācāra), 4–5 n., 5–6; conjunction (Rāmānuja), 218, 256–7; causality and similarity (Sautrāntika), 35–42; different from spatial, temporal, or any other objective relation—unique subject-object-relation (Kumārila), 137; *svarūpasambandha* (Nyāya), 217–18; not identity, 137; not causality, 6, 50, 218; not causality and similarity, 50–1, 218
Cognizability (*vedyatva*), 50, 51, 53, 54, 136, 158
Coherence of ideas, 7, 9
Complex body or object, 3, 61, 63, 66, 228
Correspondence, 22, 23, 24
Critical Realism, 21 n., 23n., 24 n.
Croce, 110 n.
Das Gupta, S. N., 86, 95, 251, his *A History of Indian Philosophy*, vol. I, 11 n.; vol. II, 10 n., 251 n.; his *Indian Idealism*, 11 n., 14 n., 15 n., 19 n., 24 n., 41 n.; his *Yoga as Philosophy and Religion*, 87 n., 95 n., 97 n.
Datum, 20, 21; sense datum, 223
Dawes Hicks, 256 n.
Delusion, 90, 92, 93
Demerit, 90, 92, 93, 179, 181
Descartes, 20, 35, 82
Desire, 174, 187, 188
Deussen, 226; his *System of the Vedanta*, 226 n.
Dharmakīrti, 1; his *Pramāṇaviniścaya*, 4 n.
Dhruva, A. B., 70 n., 71 n.
Disembodied spirits, cognitions of, 180
Dreams, 49, 52, 79, 104, 119, 120, 124, 173, 174, 192, 193, 219, 221, 258, 266, 267; their contents, objects of previous perception, 176, 260, 264; connections among their contents, creation of imagination, 176, 260; their diversity due to diversity of real external objects, 174; not objectless, 65, 178, 193, 258, 264, 266–67
Dream-cognitions, 52, 98, 99, 103, 117, 118, 121, 122, 123, 153, 160, 161, 163, 164, 166, 167, 173, 174, 176, 177, 178, 179, 207, 214, 215, 221, 229, 238, 242, 248, 257, 260, 264, 270, 271
Dream-objects, 174

Ego-centric predicament pointed out by Perry, 87 n.; anticipated by Vācaspatimiśra, 86–7, 87 n.
Esse is percipi, 14, 80, 81, 152 n., 231

Ewing, A. C., 258; his *Idealism*, 59 n., 91 n., 258 n.
Experience, basis of reasoning, 232; common, 138; self-conscious, 73; universal, 118, 167
Extension (*sthūlatva*), 88, 89, 90 208, 243, 244
Externality (*bāhyatva*), 88, 89, 90, 208

Feelings, 42, 90, 92, 93, 176; different from cognitions, 177; different feelings excited by the same object, 90, 91
Field of consciousness, 10, 41, 239
Formless cognition, 15, 17, 25, 46, 47, 49, 51, 73, 76, 99, 101, 109, 114, 115, 139, 149, 153, 166, 168, 169, 189, 222, 253, 262; never apprehended, 115
Formless consciousness diversified by different objects, 141, 222, 228, 236
Formless objects never apprehended, 115
Fraser, 145 n.
Future, 97, 126, 151, 152, 153, 212, 241; reality of, 97

Gāgābhaṭṭa's *Bhāṭṭacintāmaṇi*, 161 n.
Gaṅgānātha Jhā, 103 n., 124 n., 221 n.
Gautama, 171, 172, 173, 174, 175; his *Nyāyasūtra*, 171 n., 172 n., 173 n., 174 n., 175 n.
Gentile, 110 n.; his *Theory of Mind as Pure Act*, 110 n.
God, 9, 10, 215, 267
Govindānanda, 235, 239; his *Ratnaprabhā*, 228 n., 236 n., 239 n., 246 n.
Grāhaka (cognitive act), 4, 107, 133–4, 136, 191, 193, 194, 212, 213, 229, 235, 237
Grahaṇa (apprehension), 91, 177
Grāhya (cognized object), 4, 91, 105, 107, 133, 134, 136, 177, 191, 193, 194, 212, 213, 229, 235, 237
Green, 238 n.

Haldar, H., *Neo-Hegelianism*, 101 n.
Hallucination, 49, 192, 193 different from illusion, 192–3; due to disorder of mind, 193; not without a foundation in external objects, 193
Hamilton, 255
Haridāsa, 217
Harmony (saṁvāda), 30, 31, 164
Hasan, S. Z., 132, 138; his *Realism*, 132 n., 138 n., 211 n.
Hegel, 67 n., 226, 255; his *Philosophy of Religion*, vol. I, 255 n.
Hoernlé's *Idealism as a Philosophical Doctrine*, 10 n.
Hume. David, 7, 10, 104 n., 225

Idealism, absolute, 225–7, 252; objective, 252; subjective, 43, 105, 106, 109, 220, 225–7, 253, 271
Identity (*tādātmya*) (Yogācāra) 136, 269–270; condition of knowability, 5–6, 81–2, 213; of cognized object with apprehending cognition, 5–6, 81, 82, 83, 109; explains the relation between cognition and object, 109; of cognition with object makes knowledge impossible (realist), 137–8, 257
Illumination (prakāśa), 14, 184, 185, 186, 188
Illusion, 6, 19, 22, 32, 49, 64, 67, 103, 104 n., 118, 119, 120, 121, 133, 149, 160, 162,

165, 175, 192, 193, 208, 209, 213, 225, 230, 244, 252, 253, 266, 267; different from hallucination, 192–3; due to disorders of objects and sense-organs, 192–3; not objectless, 65, 174–5, 266–7; of *alātacakra*, 119, 120; of *gandharvanagara*, 120; of *śaśaśṛṅga*, 120, 248
Imaginary things, 8, 9, 66
Immediately preceding cognition (*samanantarapratyaya*), 50, 51, 52, 57, 58, 72, 108, 111, 162, 163, 164, 214, 269
Indifference, 91, 92, 216
Inference, 29, 55, 59, 61, 66, 69, 97, 139, 154, 155, 156, 159, 161, 165, 208; not superior to perception, 165, 208, 264
Infinite regress, 15, 48, 184, 238
Intersubjective intercourse, 9

Jaina, 18, 60, 66, 71, 72, 76, 77 n., 220, 224, 235 n.; criticism of Sautrāntika realism, 72–6; criticism of Yogācāra idealism, 65–71; realism, 65–76; contrasted with Sautrāntika realism, 71–2; relativism, 66
Jainatarkavārtika, 71 n.
James, William, 40, 157
Jayanta Bhaṭṭa, 12, 43, 77 n., 94, 181, 183, 185, 186, 187, 189, 194, 203, 205, 227, 256; his criticism of the Yogācāra idealism, 181–205; his *Nyāyamañjarī*, 1 n., 4 n., 8 n., 39 n., 44 n., 45 n., 46 n., 47 n., 48 n., 49 n., 67 n., 106 n., 107 n., 112 n., 116 n., 118 n., 131 n., 135 n., 136 n., 138 n., 139 n., 141 n., 143 n., 182 n., 183 n., 184 n., 185 n., 186 n., 187 n., 188 n., 189 n., 190 n., 192 n., 193 n., 194 n., 198 n., 199 n., 200 n., 201 n., 202 n., 204 n., 205 n., 219 n., 227 n., 235 n., 239 n.
Jñātatā (cognizedness), 13, 136, 137, 140, 149, 151, 158, 217, 241
Joachim's *The Nature of Truth*, 23 n.
Joad, C. E. M., 21; his *Introduction to Modern Philosophy*, 21 n., 223 n., 256 n.
Johnston, G. A., 2, 196, 197, 220; his *The Development of Berkeley's Philosophy*, 2 n., 37 n., 197 n., 221 n.

Kalpanā (mental construct), 33
Kamalaśīla, 15, 19, 29; his exposition of subjective idealism, 11–34; his doctrine that cognitions are self-revealing, 15–16; his *Tattvasaṃgrahapañjikā*, 12 n., 13 n., 14 n., 16 n., 17 n., 18 n., 19 n., 22 n., 24 n., 28 n., 29 n., 30 n., 31 n., 32 n., 34 n.
Kant, 66 n., 73 n.
Kapila, 77; his *Sāṅkhyasūtra*, 77 n.
Kaveeshwara's *The Metaphysics of Berkeley*, 177 n.
Keith, A. B., 11 n., 218; his *Buddhist Philosophy*, 11 n.; his *Indian Logic and Atomism*, 218 n.; his *Karma Mīmāṃsā*, 148 n.
Keśava Kāśmirin, 261, 262, 263, 264, 265; his criticism of Yogācāra idealism, 261–7; his *Vedāntakaustubhaprabhā*, 262 n., 263 n., 264 n., 265 n.
Keśavamiśra's *Tarkabhāṣā*, 190 n.
Knowability (*vedyatva*), 81, 85, 86, 88
Kṛṣṇamācārya, 17 n., 34 n.

Kumārila, 13, 15, 94, 101, 102, 103, 117, 118, 119, 121, 122, 123, 124, 126, 127, 129, 131, 132, 134, 136, 137, 138, 140, 141, 143, 144, 145, 147, 148, 160, 183, 194, 203, 205, 256; his exposition of the Yogācāra idealism, 102–117; his criticism of the Yogācāra idealism, 117–148; his *Ślokavārtika*, 1 n., 8 n., 13 n., 14 n., 65 n., 103 n., 104 n., 105 n., 106 n., 107 n., 108 n., 109 n., 112 n., 113 n., 114 n., 115 n., 116 n., 117 n., 118 n., 120 n., 121 n., 122 n., 123 n., 124 n., 125 n., 126 n., 127 n., 128 n., 129 n., 130 n., 131 n., 132 n., 133 n., 135 n., 136 n., 137 n., 139 n., 140 n., 141 n., 142 n., 143 n., 145 n., 146 n., 147 n., 148 n., 158 n., 159 n., 160 n., 161 n., 201 n., 221 n.

Laird, 130, 137, 139; his *A Study in Realism*, 59 n., 82 n., 83 n., 84 n., 86 n., 88 n., 123 n., 130 n., 132 n., 140 n.

Laṅkāvatārasūtra, 34 n.

Law of Nature (*vastusvabhāva*), 187, 189, 211, 216, 217; (*svabhāvaniyama*), 58, 223, 224

Law of Parsimony, 43, 44, 149, 183, 228, 234

Leibnitz, 23 n.

Lloyd Morgan, 133

Localization, 70

Locke, 147, 202, 203; on relativity of sensations, 117; on representative theory of perception, 20, 35, 82

Mach, 9 n.

Mādhavācārya, 1, 2, 11, 36, 59, 72, 73; his account of Yogācāra idealism, 1–9; his account of the Sautrāntika's criticism of the Yogācāra, 36–42; his account of the Jaina's criticism of the Sautrāntika realism, 72–5; his account of the Vaibhāṣika criticism of the Sautrāntika, 59–60; his *Ṣaḍdarśanasaṃgraha*, 1 n., 3 n., 4 n., 5 n., 6 n., 7 n., 8 n., 9 n., 35 n., 36 n., 37 n., 38 n., 39 n., 41 n., 42 n., 60 n., 66 n., 73 n., 74 n., 75 n., 112 n., 139 n., 171 n., 213 n., 219 n., 220 n.

Mādhva, 266, 267, 272 n.; his criticism of the Yogācāra idealism, 266–7; his *Bhāṣya* on *Brahmasūtra*, 266 n.

Mādhavācārya Vidyāraṇya's *Vivaraṇaprameyasaṃgraha*, 11 n., 247 n., 253 n.

Mādhyamika, 102, 103

Mahāyānasūtrālaṅkāra, 34 n.

Mallisena, 12, 61, 65, 67, 68, 70, 75, 220; his exposition of the Yogācāra idealism, 61–5; his criticism of the Yogācāra idealism, 65–71; his *Syādvādamañjarī*, 4 n., 7 n., 8 n., 64 n., 65 n., 66 n., 67 n., 68 n., 69 n., 70 n., 71 n., 72 n., 76 n., 118 n., 131 n., 133 n., 135 n., 139 n., 151 n., 163 n., 219 n., 220 n.

Meinong, 132, 223

Memory, 190, 193, 250, 273; indefinite, 135–6; obscuration of memory (*smṛtipramoṣa*), 166

Mentalism, 42, 252

Merit, 90, 92, 93, 179, 181

Method of difference, 58, 86, 87, 88, 104, 182, 187

Method of agreement, 58, 86, 87, 88, 104, 182, 187

Mill, J. S., 7, 225

Mīmāṃsaka, 18, 100, 124, 134, 141, 150, 189, 224, 242 n., 262; criticism of Yogācāra idealism, 98–102, 117–148, 154–161, 164–9; realism (Śavara), 98–102; (Kumārila), 117–148; (Pārthasārathimiśra), 154–161; (Prabhākara), 164–9
Mitra, Rajendra Lal, 94
Moore, G. E., 101, 105 n., 141, 195, 196, 236; his *Philosophical Studies*, 105 n., 142 n., 196 n., 236 n.
Mutual dependence (*anyonyāśraya*), 54, 108, 115, 124, 219, 220
Mukherjee, A. C., *Self, Thought and Reality*, 218 n.
Mukhyasaṃvedana, 19

Naiyāyika, 106, 171, 188, 200, 204, 262; a rationalist, 171–2
Nescience (*avidyā*), 6, 8, 19, 41, 48, 90, 92, 202, 206; cognition of nescience (*ajñāna*) proves difference between cognition and object, 156
New Realist, 2, 20
Nimbārka, 260, 261; his criticism of the Yogācāra idealism, 260–1; his *Vedāntapārijatakaustubha*, 261 n.
Not-self, 67, 68, 77, 182, 219, 254, 255, 266, 272, 273
Nyāya, 187, 247 n.; criticism of Yogācāra idealism, 170–221; criticism of Sautrāntika realism, 222–4; realism, 170–210
Nyāya-Vaiśeṣika, 5, 18, 58, 79 n., 99, 189, 224; realism, 170–224; criticism of the Sautrāntika, 222–4

Object: independent of cognition, 94, 157; independent of all minds, 90, 91, 96; common to all persons, 95, 96, 182; independent of feelings, 94; self-existent, 90, 91; different from cognition, 155–6, 177, 182

Pain, 42, 92, 93, 95, 176, 177, 182
Pārthasārathimiśra, 50, 148, 149, 154, 155, 156, 157, 158, 160, 161; his exposition of the Yogācāra idealism, 148–154; his criticism of the Yogācāra idealism, 154–161; his *Nyāyaratnākara*, 1 n., 65 n., 105 n., 106 n., 107 n., 108 n., 109 n., 111 n., 113 n., 116 n., 118 n., 119 n., 124 n., 125 n., 126 n., 128 n., 129 n., 130 n., 131 n., 132 n., 133 n., 136 n., 137 n., 139 n., 141 n., 143 n., 146 n., 148 n.; his *Śāstradīpikā*, 8 n., 39 n., 51 n., 52 n., 54 n., 55 n., 64 n., 103 n., 104 n., 111 n., 113 n., 118 n., 119 n., 122 n., 149 n., 150 n., 151 n., 152 n., 153 n., 154 n., 155 n., 156 n., 157 n., 158 n., 159 n., 160 n., 161 n., 221 n.
Past, 97, 126, 130, 135, 146, 151, 152, 159, 160, 161, 210, 221, 241; reality of, 97
Patañjali, 90, 96; his *Yogasūtra*, 79 n., 80 n., 81 n., 82 n., 83 n., 90 n., 93 n., 94 n., 96 n., 118 n., 201 n.
Perception, 29, 55, 61, 66, 69, 70, 89, 97, 105, 139, 165; determinate, 200; indeterminate, 199–200; direct or immediate, 59; indirect or mediate, 20–4; four causes of, 72–3; of an army, 198, 200–1; of a forest, 198, 200–201; of whole and part, 3–4, 63–4, 78, 79, 172–3, 197–8, 200–1; reduced to ideation by subjective idealism, 98; sense

perception, 118, 195, 214, 266; superior to imagination, 84, 88; superior to inference, 165, 208, 264
Perry, 87 n., 90 n., 142, 144, 195; his *Present Philosophical Tendencies*, 142 n., 144 n., 195 n.
Phenomenalism, 20
Physical, elements, 81; objects, 9, 21, 89, 223
Pleasure, 42, 53, 92, 93, 95, 176, 177, 182, 231
Possibility determined by actuality, 233, 247
Prabhācandra's *Prameyakamalamārtaṇḍa*, 73 n., 74 n., 75 n., 76 n.
Prabhākara, 161, 164, 165, 167, 169; his exposition of the Yogācāra idealism, 161–4; his criticism of the Yogācāra idealism, 164–67; his criticism of the Sautrāntika, 167–9; his *Bṛhatī*, 167 n.
Pragmatic, use, 53; utility, 9; value of ideas, 7, 66
Prākaṭya, 26, 241
Pramāṇanayatattvālokālaṅkāra, 71 n.
Pravṛttivijñāna (object-cognition), 33, 34, 39, 40, 41, 42, 207, 240, 265
Present, 97, 126, 160, 161, 210, 211, 212, 241
Presentative theory of perception, 60, 138, 258–9; Berkeley on, 2; Yogācāra on, 1–2, 59; new realist on, 2
Projection, 70
Proximity, 73, 74, 122, 136
Psychical dispositions, 33, 34, 107, 108, 116, 144, 203, 204, 205, 240
Psychosis, simple, 23; composite, 23
Puruṣottamajī Mahārāja, 268, 269, 270; his criticism of the Yogācāra idealism, 268–271; his *Aṇubhāṣyaprakāśa*, 269 n., 270 n., 271 n.

Radhakrishnan's *Indian Philosophy*, vol. I, 11 n.
Rajas, 92, 93
Rāmakṛṣṇa Bhaṭṭa's *Yuktisnehaprapūraṇī*, 149 n., 150 n., 152 n.
Rāmānuja, 65 n., 67, 218, 235, 253, 254, 255, 256, 257, 258, 260, 261, 266, 272 n.; his exposition of Yogācāra idealism, 253; his criticism of Yogācāra idealism, 253–58; his criticism of Sautrāntika representationism, 258–260; his *Śrībhāṣya* on *Brahmasūtra*, 253 n., 254 n., 256 n., 257 n., 260 n.
Ratnākarāvatārikā, 71 n.
Realism, 43, 105, 106; direct, 72; indirect, 72; Jaina, 61–76; Mīmāṃsā, 98–169; Nyāya, 170–210; Śaṅkara's empirical realism, 225–241, 251–3; Sāṅkhya, 77–9; Sautrāntika's indirect realism or representationism, 35–42; Vaibhāṣika's direct realism, 59–60; Vaiśeṣika, 215–221; Yoga, 83–96
Realist, 107, 108, 109, 111, 112, 127, 128, 139, 149, 162, 163, 171, 188, 230, 253; modern, 234
Reality, degrees of, 251–2; empirical, 226, 251, 252; illusory, 248, 251, 252; ontological, 225, 251
Real things, 8, 66
Recollection, 49, 97, 104, 112, 113, 120, 125, 127, 129, 130, 131, 136, 146, 159, 166, 174, 190, 191, 206, 236, 238, 251, 265, 270; direct cognition of past *things*, not of past cognitions, 130, 131

Reflective consciousness, 46, 69, 100
Reid, 71 n., 101 n., 130, 234, 272 n.
Reid, L. A., *Knowledge and Truth*, 21 n.
Relativity of sensations, 117, 147
Remoteness, 73, 74, 109, 122
Representationism, 1, 20–4, 43; of Descartes, 35–6; of the Sautrāntika, 35–42; Sautrāntika, criticized by the Yogācāra, 43–60; by the Jaina, 72–6, by the Nyāya-Vaiśeṣika, 222–4; by Rāmānuja, 258–260
Representative theory of perception, 20, 35–42, 60, 82, 138, 139, 222; of the Sautrāntika, 35–42
Right knowledge, 91, 93, 140, 163, 167
Russell, Bertrand, 121, 204 n.; his *The Problems of Philosophy*, 204 n.; his *Mysticism and Logic*, 121 n., 193 n.; his *Our Knowledge of the External World*, 121 n., 178 n.

Sadānanda Yati, 224, 241, 246, 248, 249, 250, 252; his exposition of Yogācāra idealism, 241–6; his criticism of Yogācāra idealism, 246–251; his *Advaitabrahmasiddhi*, 227 n., 229 n., 241 n., 242 n., 243 n., 245 n., 246 n., 247 n., 249 n., 251 n.
Sahopalambhaniyama (invariably simultaneous perception of cognition and object), proves their identity (Yogācāra), 6, 27–8, 36, 68, 81, 86, 152, 155, 161–2, 193, 215, 228–9, 234, 242–3; denied by Jayanta, 194; denied by Vācaspati, 194–5; criticized by Mallisena, 68–9; criticized by Śrīdhara, 218–19; criticized by Yoga, 86–8; criticized by Pārthasārathimiśra, 155–6; criticized by Prabhākara, 164–5; criticized by Śaṅkara, 235; criticized by Vācaspati, 249–250; criticized by Rāmānuja, 255–6; criticized by Śrīnivāsa, 264; criticized by a Vallabhite, 269–270; criticized by Baladeva, 273
Śālikanātha's *Prakaraṇapañcikā*, 162 n., 163 n., 164 n., 165 n., 166 n., 167 n., 168 n., 169 n.; his *Ṛjuvimalā* on *Bṛhatī*, 167 n.
Saṃvṛtisatya (false reality), 129
Śaṅkara, 199 n., 225, 226, 227, 230, 231, 233, 234, 235, 236, 237, 238, 239, 240, 251, 254, 261, 267, 272 n.; his exposition of Yogācāra idealism, 227–230; his criticism of Yogācāra idealism, 230–241; his absolute idealism, 225–7; on degrees of reality, 251–2; his *Bhāṣya* on *Brahmasūtra*, 39 n., 118 n., 122 n., 138 n., 141 n., 228 n., 229 n., 230 n., 231 n., 232 n., 233 n., 234 n., 235 n., 237 n., 238 n., 239 n., 241 n.; his empirical realism, 251–2; not a realist, 252; not a mentalist, 252; direct realism, 252–3
Sāṅkhya, 92, 93; criticism of Yogācāra idealism, 77; realism, 77
Śāntarakṣita, 11, 12, 13, 14, 16, 17, 18, 19, 21, 24, 27, 28, 29, 30, 32; his arguments for the non-existence of external objects and defence of subjective idealism, 11–34; his refutation of Kumārila's doctrine, 13–15; his criticism of the Sautrāntika doctrine of representationism, 20–4; his *Tattvasaṃgrha*, 1 n., 5 n.,

6 n., 9 n., 13 n., 14 n., 15 n. 16 n., 17 n., 18 n., 19 n., 20 n., 21 n., 22 n., 24 n., 28 n., 29 n., 31 n., 32 n., 34 n., 41 n., 181 n.
Sārūpya (similarity of cognition with object), 22, 55, 57, 168, 228; complete similarity, 22, 26; partial similarity, 22, 26; criticism of, 111
Sattva, 92, 93
Sautrāntika, 21, 22, 23, 35, 36, 37, 38, 39, 42, 51, 54, 55, 57, 59, 60, 71, 72, 75, 110, 111, 113, 139, 167, 168, 169, 185, 190, 218, 222, 252, 259; his representative theory of perception, 21, 22, 23, 35–42; his theory of correspondence, 22; his criticism of Yogācāra idealism, 36–42; his representative theory of perception criticized by the Yogācāra, 43–60
Śavara, 98, 99, 100, 102, 103, 161; his criticism of Yogācāra idealism, 98–102; his *Bhāṣya* on *Mīmāṃsāsūtra*, 99 n., 101 n., 102 n.
Seal, B. N., 30, 97; his *The Positive Sciences of the Ancient Hindus*, 31 n., 97 n.
Self, 7, 67, 68, 72, 73, 77, 158, 182, 204, 219, 225, 241, 247, 250, 251, 254, 255, 261, 262, 263, 265, 266, 267, 273; both cognizer and cognized (Kumārila), 132; object of self-consciousness (*ahampratyaya*), 158
Sense-organs, 25, 28, 29, 47, 56, 57, 72, 84, 102, 146, 159, 161, 200, 210, 211, 222, 223, 241, 259, 262, 270
Serial cognition (*dhārāvāhika-jñāna*), 51, 57, 58, 111, 169
Sharma, R. R., article on *The Yogācāra Theory of the External World*, 11 n., 16 n.
Simple apprehension, 46, 100
Sinclair, May, 85, 130; her *The New Idealism*, 85 n., 86 n., 107 n., 130 n.
Sinha, J. N., *Indian Psychology: Perception*, 5 n., 13 n., 22 n., 68 n., 123 n., 132 n., 133 n., 134 n., 135 n., 158 n., 161 n., 184 n., 193 n., 199 n., 217 n., 248 n., 255 n.
Sircar, M. N., 252; his *Comparative Studies in Vedantism*, 252 n.
Solipsism, 24
Spinoza, 226
Śrīdhara, 56, 210, 215, 218, 219, 220, 221, 223; his *Nyāya-kandalī*, 5 n., 7 n., 22 n., 39 n., 58 n., 65 n., 190 n., 211 n., 213 n., 214 n., 215 n., 216 n., 219 n., 220 n., 221 n., 222 n., 224 n.
Śrīnivāsa, 261, 262, 264, 265; his criticism of Yogācāra idealism, 261–7; his *Vedāntakaustubha*, 261 n., 262 n., 263 n., 264 n., 265 n.
Stcherbatsky, Th., *Buddhist Logic*, Vol. I, 11 n., 24 n., 41 n.
Stream of consciousness, 9, 12, 40, 51, 164, 168, 181, 191, 202, 215, 225, 227
Subconscious impressions (*vāsanā*), 6, 8, 9, 10, 11, 33, 41, 42, 48, 49, 52, 56, 64, 69, 70, 72, 77, 125, 126, 127, 128, 129, 160, 162, 164, 166, 177, 178, 190, 191, 202, 206, 207, 215, 221, 230, 238, 239, 240, 242, 250, 251, 261, 264, 265, 268, 270, 271, 273; related to perceptions as cause and effect (Yogācāra), 48–9, 190, 230, 239, 265; their variety accounts for variety of perceptions, 6–7, 7–8, 9, 10, 77, 124, 177, 191,

202, 206, 230, 238–9, 242, 250, 253, 264–5, 268, 270 (Yogācāra); cannot account for perceptions (Jaina), 69–70, (Śaṅkara) 239–240, (Vallabha) 268, 270–1, (Nyāya) 191–2, 206, (Śrīnivāsa) 265, (Baladeva) 273; cannot subsist in *ālayavijñāna* but in the permanent self, 192, 250, 268
Śubhagupta, Bhadanta, 18, 18 n., 30
Subjective: idea, 7; idealism, 43, 105, 106, 109, 220, 227, 253, 271; idealist, 44, 80, 107, 108, 109, 142, 180, 230
Subjectivism, 11, 24, 42, 211, 254, 267
Sudarśanācārya's *Śastradīpikāprakāśa*, 149 n., 150 n., 152 n., 156 n.
Sudarśana Bhaṭṭa's *Śrutaprakāśikā*, 258 n.
Svarūpasambandha, 217, 218
Svasaṃvedana, 1, 12, 13
Svayaṃvedana, 1

Tamas, 92, 93
Tarkavāgiśa, Phaṇi Bhūṣaṇa, 205; his criticism of Yogācāra idealism, 205–210; his *Nyāya Darśana* (Bengali), 18 n., 170 n., 205, 210
Tattvanirṇaya, 266 n., 267 n.
The New Realism, 234 n., 257 n.
Turner, J. E., his criticism of Critical Realism, 21; his *A Theory of Direct Realism*, 21 n., 23 n.

Udayana, 205 n., 217; his *Nyāyakusumāñjali*, 217 n., 218 n.
Udyotakara, 31, 171, 176, 177, 178, 180, 181; his critical exposition of the Yogācāra idealism, 176–181; his *Nyāyavārtika*, 31 n., 171 n., 173 n., 174 n., 176 n., 177 n., 178 n., 180 n., 181 n.
Universal and particular, 200, 245

Vācaspatimiśra, 12, 25, 80, 81, 83, 84, 85, 86, 91, 95, 96, 170 n., 181, 194, 216, 241, 246, 249; his exposition of Yogācāra idealism, 241–6; his criticism of Yogācāra idealism, 246–251; his *Bhāmatī*, 226 n., 229 n., 231 n., 242 n., 243 n., 245 n., 246 n., 247 n., 249 n.; his *Nyāyavārtikatātparyaṭīkā*, 22 n., 27 n., 170 n., 171 n., 177 n., 178 n., 181, 193 n., 195 n., 201 n., 216 n., 217 n.; his *Tattvavaiśāradī*, 5 n., 80 n., 81 n., 82 n., 83 n., 84 n., 85 n., 86 n., 87 n., 88 n., 89 n., 90 n., 91 n., 92 n., 95 n., 96 n., 97 n., 118 n., 181, 201 n., 213 n.; his *Nyāyakaṇikā* on *Vidhiviveka*, 181
Vaibhāṣika, 59, 60, 208; his criticism of the Sautrāntika theory of representationism, 59–60; direct realism, 59–60
Vaiśeṣika, 215, 222; criticism of Yogācāra idealism, 215–221; realism, 215–221
Vallabha, 268; his criticism of Yogācāra idealism, 267–8; his *Aṇubhāṣya*, 267 n., 268 n.
Value: subjective (Yogācāra), 142–3; objective (Kumārila), 144; appreciated by a person with an appropriate psychical disposition or desire (Kumārila), 144
Variety of perceptions, due to variety of *vāsanās* or subconscious impressions due to nescience (*avidyā*), 6–7, 7–8, 9, 10, 77, 124, 177, 191, 202, 206, 230, 238–9, 242, 250, 253, 264–5,

268, 270 (Yogācāra); due to variety of external objects, 191–2, 206, 229–230, 259–261, 265, 271, 273 (realist)

Various appearances of the same object prove its unreality (Yogācāra), 116, 142, 201–2, 203; do not disprove the reality of the object, 145, 147 (Kumārila), 203–5 (Jayanta); prove relativity but not unreality of the object, 147

Vāsaka (impresser), 125, 191, (*bhāvaka*) 177–8

Vasubandhu, 33 n., his *Viṃśatikārikā*, 33 n.

Vāsya (impressed), 125, 191, (*bhāvya*) 178, 191

Vātsyāyana, 170, 172, 173, 175; his critical exposition of the Yogācāra idealism, 170–6; his *Nyāyabhāṣya*, 65 n., 119 n., 170 n., 171 n., 172 n., 173 n., 174 n., 175 n., 176 n., 221 n.

Vedāntadīpa, 258 n.

Vedāntist, 19, 224, 238

Veṅkaṭanātha's *Nyāyapariśuddhi* (with *Nyāyasāra*), 258 n.; his *Tattvamuktākalāpa* and *Sarvārthasiddhi* on it, 258 n.

Vice, 124, 179

Vidyābhūṣaṇa, S. C., *History of Indian Logic*, 18 n.; his *Medieval School of Indian Logic*, 4 n.

Vijñānabhikṣu, 79, 83, 84, 90 n.; his *Sāṅkhyapravacanabhāṣya*, 79 n.; his *Yogavārtika*, 84 n., 90 n., 91 n., 95 n., 96 n.; his criticism of Yogācāra idealism, 79, 84, 90 n.; object neither a mental construct of one mind, nor of many minds but independent of all minds, 90 n.

Vijñaptimātratā, 24

Vijñaptimātratāsiddhi, 34 n.

Viparītakhyāti, 161

Virtue, 124, 179

Viṣaya-viṣayibhāva (subject-object-relationship), 29, 136, 137, 212

Viṣayatā (objectivity), 136, 217

Viśvanātha's *Nyāyasūtravṛtti*, 176 n.

Vyāsa, 79, 83, 84, 90, 95, 96, 97; his *Yogabhāṣya*, 49 n., 79 n., 84 n., 90 n., 91 n., 93 n., 95 n., 97 n., 116 n., 118 n., 143 n., 201 n.

Waking cognitions, 52, 98, 99, 104 n., 117, 118, 122, 123, 129, 153, 160, 161, 167, 177, 178, 179, 192, 207, 229, 264, 267, 270

Waking perceptions, 49, 117, 120, 122, 161, 192, 215, 221, 229, 238, 248, 257, 266, 268; essentially different from dream-cognitions, 117–18, 121–2, 161, 238

Wildon Car's *Philosophy of Benedetto Croce*, 110 n.

Whole and part perceived 3–4, 63–4, 78–9, 172–3, 197–8, 200–1; whole exists in parts, 200

Wrong cognitions, 104 n., 170, 207; have a core of truth, 174, 175; their objects, not absolutely non-existent, 175

Yoga, 76, 79, 83, 94; criticism of Yogācāra idealism, 83–96; realism, 83–96; criticism of the doctrine that the momentary present alone is real, 97; criticism of the doctrine that objects come into existence along with cognitions, 94–6

Yogācāra, 1, 2, 3, 7, 9, 10, 11, 12, 18, 24, 25, 36, 37, 43, 44, 47, 50, 51, 52, 53, 54, 55, 56, 58, 59, 61, 65, 67, 68, 70, 77, 78,

79, 80, 81, 82, 83, 84, 86, 89, 92, 98, 99, 100, 102, 103, 105, 106, 107, 108, 109, 113, 114, 117, 118, 121, 122, 123, 124, 125, 126, 127, 128, 129, 131, 132, 134, 135, 136, 138, 139, 140, 142, 145, 148, 149, 150, 151, 154, 155, 156, 157, 158, 159, 160, 161, 162, 163, 164, 165, 166, 167, 177, 178, 179, 180, 181, 182, 183, 185, 186, 187, 188, 190, 191, 192, 193, 194, 197, 199, 200, 201, 202, 203, 204, 205, 206, 207, 208, 209, 210, 211, 212, 213, 215, 216, 218, 219, 220, 221, 224, 225, 226, 227, 230, 231, 232, 233, 234, 236, 237, 238, 239, 240, 241, 242, 243, 245, 247, 248, 249, 250, 251, 254, 258, 259, 261, 262, 263, 264, 265, 267, 268, 269, 270, 271, 273; his subjective idealism (*vijñānavāda*), 1–34, 61–5, 79–83, 102-117, 148–154, 161–7, 210–15, 227–230, 241–6; his subjective idealism contrasted with Śaṅkara's absolute idealism, 225–7; his criticism of Sautrāntika representationism, 43–59; his agreement with Berkeley in denial of external objects, 7–9; his difference from Berkeley in denial of the soul and God, 9–10; his agreement with Hume in denying the existence of matter, soul, and God, 7, 9–10, 225; his agreement with Hume in recognizing the reality of discrete momentary cognitions or ideas, 10, 225; his agreement with Berkeley in recognizing the distinction between the real and the imaginary within mental contents, 7–9; in holding the presentative theory of perception, 2; his thesis: cognition alone is real, 4, 33, 64, 68, 107, 202; cognition is self-luminous, 1, 4, 12–13, 15–16, 19, 45, 48, 80, 89, 106, 112, 131, 153, 154, 165, 213, 262; cognition is self aware, 1, 12–13, 14, 15, 16, 17, 19, 111; cognition is self-subsistent, 4, 7; cognition is devoid of subject and object, 4, 12; cognitions are discrete and momentary, 10, 89, 225; cognition of an external object is not possible, 14–16; and involves self-contradiction, 17; cognition cannot be produced by an object, 3, 17; cognition cannot create its object, 17; cognition not related to object by causality, 17; cognition cannot have real knowledge of an external object, 19; cognition cannot have phenomenal knowledge of an external object, 19; formless cognition cannot apprehend an external object, 17–19, 25; cognition with a similar form cannot apprehend an external object, 20–4, 26–7; cognition with a different form cannot apprehend an external object, 24; cognition apprehends unreal forms superimposed on them owing to illusion, 18, 19; cognition cannot be completely or partially similar to object, 22; cognized object is identical with cognition, 4–5, 107, 110; cognition not distinct from apprehension of an object, 14–15; cognition reveals object-forms (illusory) without any other cognitive act, 14; cognition is objectless (*nirālambana*), 64;

external objects unreal appearances, 33; object-cognitions are transformations of self-cognitions, 33–4; distinction between subject and object is an illusory appearance due to nescience (*avidyā*), 107, 213, 219; within consciousness, 154, 162, 183, 219; distinction of object of knowledge (*prameya*), instrument of knowledge (*pramāṇa*), result of knowledge (*pramiti*), and agent of knowledge (*pramātā*) falls within consciousness, 202, 229, 245, 246, 263; an external object is a mental construct, 79; or construction of imagination, 7, 83, 84; identifies consciousness with self-consciousness, 100

Yogavāśiṣṭha, 6–7 n., 7 n., 103 n.

Yogic intuition, 97, 122, 123